The DIET Rebel's Cookbook

Eating CLEAN and GREEN

The DIET Rebel's Cookbook

Eating CLEAN and GREEN

JILLAYNE CLEMENTS and
MICHELLE STEWART

CFI
Springville, Utah

ISBN 13: 978-1-59955-361-0

Published by CFI, an imprint of Cedar Fort, Inc., 2373 W. 700 S., Springville, UT 84663
Distributed by Cedar Fort, Inc., www.cedarfort.com

LIBRARY OF CONGRESS CATALOGING-IN-PUBLICATION DATA

Library of Congress Cataloging-in-Publication Data

Clements, Jillayne.
The diet rebel's cookbook : eating clean and green / Jillayne Clements and Michelle Stewart.
    p. cm.
ISBN 978-1-59955-361-0 (acid-free paper)
1. Cookery (Natural foods) I. Stewart, Michelle, 1978– II. Title.

TX741.C59 2010
641.5'636—dc22

2009046107

Cover design by Angela D. Olsen
Cover design © 2010 by Lyle Mortimer
Edited and typeset by Katherine Carter

Printed in the United States of America

10 9 8 7 6 5 4 3 2

Printed on acid-free paper

Contents

❖ ❖ ❖ ❖ ❖ ❖ ❖ ❖ ❖ ❖ ❖ ❖ ❖ ❖ ❖

Foreword

❖ ❖ ❖ ❖ ❖ ❖ ❖ ❖ ❖ ❖ ❖ ❖ ❖ ❖ ❖

I AM SO PLEASED TO DISCOVER what Michelle and Jillayne have prepared for us in *The Diet Rebel's Cookbook: Eating Clean and Green*! These enlightened authors have hit a bull's eye when it comes to the correct methods of using foods to prevent and reverse chronic illness.

They were once students of my 90 Days to True Health program. Now they have become my teachers of whole-food recipes! Their principles are correct. Their logic is wise. Their presentation is practical and useful, and their recipes really do taste great while still avoiding processed, refined, dead foods.

These recipes go hand in hand with scientific and clinical evidence that a whole-food lifestyle is the first key to physical healing. They cleverly implement what I have promoted in my medical practice. I no longer practice the typical modern model of chronic disease care using prescription drugs. Instead, I have found that by using workshops, foods classes, and personal coaching to enforce accountability with my patients, all sorts of dramatic health improvements take place: type 2 diabetes is reversed; high blood pressure is normalized; allergies dissipate; acid reflux resolves; obesity is overcome; depression lifts; aging slows; headaches are reduced and eliminated; arthritis pains minimize; insomnia resolves; and—most importantly—relationships improve and self-love is restored.

The foundation of true health is to implement nutrient-rich, mostly raw whole foods—making meals from "scratch" and using ingredients from mother earth! I am one of very few physicians privileged to witness the health effects of this type of healthcare insurance.

Who are the true physicians today? Well, they can be anyone who will lay the foundation of true health by letting food be his or her medicine. Michelle and Jillayne teach these principles with unique clarity and provide you with whole- and raw-food recipes. So to Michelle and Jillayne, I say thank you for inspiring us as to what we can do in our own kitchens with our own families to establish the foundation of real health.

Michael Cutler, MD
Author of *90 Days to True Health*

Dr. Cutler is a Board-Certified Family Physician who specializes in a wide range of chronic degenerative diseases, anti-aging methods, general family ailments, and nutrition. With an understanding and respect for the natural harmony of the human body, he has devoted his career to learning how to optimize health through simple changes in diet and lifestyle. His goal is to educate others so they can heal and teach those around them the principles of sustainable health, thereby shifting the paradigm of health care to one of personal empowerment.

Introduction

❖ ❖ ❖ ❖ ❖ ❖ ❖ ❖ ❖ ❖ ❖ ❖ ❖ ❖ ❖

A GROWING NUMBER OF PEOPLE in this world suffer from illness in one way or another. We could go into great length describing these diseases one by one, but we won't. The list is far too long and depressing, and chances are you're already well acquainted with the items on it. Maybe you or a loved one suffers from one of them.

We too have struggled with our own personal health challenges. But instead of becoming sour with the lemons of life, we made lemonade. It turned out really good too (since we used organic lemons; natural sweeteners; and pure, mineral-rich water to quench your thirst on a hot summer day), so we put it in the recipe section.

We started by looking for nutritional truths because we felt there was an ideal diet for humans and that eating it would create health. It was harder to find truth than we thought. Everywhere we turned, we were confronted with conflicting information from various low-carb, low-fat, low-calorie, no-grain, all-raw, or vegan diets. Who was right? We felt first and foremost that what we would eat and drink should supply all needed nutrients to our bodies. Why else was food and drink created? But we also felt that food should be completely satisfying and taste good.

We devoted a lot of time to studying and pondering the correlation between diet and health. We did not gain this nutritional education from a formal institution where we would earn the right to display initials next to our names, because—in all honesty—what we discovered was not formally taught. Still, the education we received changed our lives. We developed a deeper understanding of nature's nutritional guidelines and learned the forgotten food traditions of the world's healthiest civilizations. What people have eaten and how they have prepared it has helped humans in many ages of time be free of diseases such as diabetes, tuberculosis, cancer, hypothyroidism, heart disease, autoimmune diseases, obesity, and many other problems. Their diets not only influenced their health but—to a large extent—determined it.

After applying the principles we learned to our own lives, we began feeling better, and our families got sick much less often. In fact, anything more than an occasional illness is virtually nonexistent in our homes. But what we didn't expect was that applying these lost cooking techniques to our own meals would make them taste so wonderful. We love the way they smell, the way they make us feel, and—most importantly—we love eating the meals we prepare this way because they're so scrumptious!

We have compiled this recipe book in order to share the deliciousness of these priceless cooking techniques and to pass along what we have discovered about true nutrition. Plus, we thought it would be nice to have a recipe book on hand for every time we hear, "Ooh, this is so good. I *have* to get the recipe."

The unique recipes in this cookbook are not only healthy, they actually taste better than most food available today. Compare your basic store-bought loaf and tub of margarine to the possibility of a hearty, steaming slice of sprouted, whole grain bread topped with a melting mound of freshly churned butter from pasture-fed cows. Or consider the pure pleasure of being able to enjoy ice cream made with fresh cream, real vanilla, and natural sugars that nourish the body and are gentler on blood sugar levels. When you eat fresh, wholesome food, prepared using the forgotten and tasty traditions of our ancient ancestors, your body *and* your taste buds will thank you. You really *can* have your cake and eat it too.

What *are* the forgotten and tasty traditions of our ancestors? It's no secret that a good diet was essential to their health and longevity. What did they eat, how did they prepare it, and how does this information affect the nutrition and flavor of the food we prepare today? How can applying this information help prevent disease and potentially reverse it?

We'd love to answer these questions right here in the introduction, but then it would be entirely too long, the whole organizational flow of the book would be hindered, and there would be no enticing incentive for you to read on. But rest assured, these questions will be answered in the remaining pages of this book.

So make a bowl of air-popped popcorn tossed with melted butter, coconut oil, and unrefined sea salt (the recipe for this is also in the recipe section), and sit back and discover why you can enjoy popcorn like this without feeling guilty.

❖ ❖ ❖

Special Note: There are many sick or diseased people who have been healed by eating a certain way. We make no claim that preparing food in a traditional manner as outlined in this book will guarantee healing. We also understand that everyone is different and that every body reacts differently to certain foods. The ideas in this book have worked well for our bodies, but modifications may be made to suit what works best for you.

The information in this book is not intended to diagnose, treat, or cure illness or disease and is not intended to be used as a replacement for proper medical attention. Consult your health care professional before changing your diet.

Warning: Although the sprouting process decreases the amount of gluten in grains, sprouted grain products do still contain gluten. Special care must be taken if you are celiac or gluten intolerant. Please consult your healthcare professional before trying any recipes containing gluten.

❖ ❖ ❖

Jillayne's Story

I sprouted my first tooth when I was seven months old. Unfortunately, it was a sweet tooth. From my earliest recollections, I had an unnatural craving for anything sweet. Like the jungle bars for the Christmas party that I snuck into, the Halloween candy I ate all in one day every year, and all the no-bake cookies I made as a teen (even though they turned out crumbly and crystallized because I didn't know what I was doing).

Growing up, I heard the phrase, "You are what you eat." This made sense to me since people referred to me as being sweet, but I never gave it much thought beyond that. Even if I had thought about it a little more, though, I probably would have just avoided Dum Dums, Ding Dongs, and suckers, and stuck to Smarties and Angel Food cakes instead, all while hoping to meet a Big Hunk someday. (I did, by the way. I even married him.)

Even as an adult, I had unnatural cravings for sugar. Like the time I was vacuuming when eight months pregnant with my fourth kid and I found a peanut M&M hiding under the couch. I picked it up, blew off the dust, and was actually tempted to eat it. I stared at it and twirled it in my fingers, salivating and everything. But before I did something I'd regret, my common sense kicked in, and I tossed it in the trash.

You may be thinking that I was insane for even considering eating that M&M, or you may be thinking that I had a good excuse because I was pregnant and my blood sugar must've been abnormally low. You're right about both.

Still, I wonder just how long I had issues with low blood sugar, even before I experienced pregnancy. Like the time when I was newly married and my husband promised he'd buy me a really cool computer program if I could go a whole week without sugar. "Sure, I can do that. No problem," I said. But four days into the no-sugar thing, I wasn't feeling too happy about life. My husband must've run the numbers and decided our starving student income wasn't enough to buy the program after all, so he scooped up a big bowl of caramel cashew ice cream and started eating it in front of me! How could I resist such temptation? I lost out on the computer program.

Slowly, I started becoming more concerned about good nutrition. I started eating mostly whole grains. I had fruits and veggies, animal products, and I was big into the low-fat thing. Plus, I started making my own chocolate chip cookies using whole wheat flour, and I made sure to buy Halloween candy for trick-or-treaters no sooner than twenty-four hours before they arrived so I wouldn't have time to eat it all. I even tried the one-week-without-sugar challenge again, but I failed every time. I rationalized that because sugar made me feel happy and energetic and had no affect on my weight unless I was pregnant, it had no ill affect on my health. I still felt fairly healthy.

All that changed about a year and a half after my fourth child was born. We had just moved (so I was feeling plenty of stress), I was worried about a job I was doing, I wasn't exercising like normal, and it was the holidays, which meant lots of goodies. And then it happened. I completely, totally crashed.

I was tired and grouchy all the time, and I had a lot of the symptoms of diabetes. I think I snarled at my kids a few times, showing my teeth and everything, and I even had a yellow-orange hue to my skin that made me look like I'd had a run-in with some tanning lotion gone wrong.

Eventually I found that I had hypothyroidism because of autoimmunity to my thyroid hormone, anemia, blood sugar stabilization problems (surprise), hormone imbalances, and gluten, starch, lactose, and fat intolerances (though it took several months to get these diagnosed).

At first I felt sorry for myself and cried a lot. In fact, I cried so much I thought I was pregnant. I even cried at the end of *Mulan* when her dad said she had honored him by saving China. (Sorry to spoil it for those of you who haven't seen the end of *Mulan*.) But I wasn't pregnant, and there would be no joy of holding a new little one in my arms after months of pregnancylike symptoms.

I prayed a lot, but my prayers were more like begging for my health back and promising to treat my body better. Well, God knows me better than even I do. He knew I would only revert back to my old ways and that I had the opportunity to learn a great deal from this experience. But still, it wasn't fun to be stuck in a body that suddenly wasn't me anymore. I felt like I had fallen into a deep, dark, cold pit, and I was so tired of being there day after day after day. I wasn't sweet or energetic, just chronically tired, depressed, and achy. It felt like I had arthritis in every joint in my body.

But I realized I had a choice to make. I could either wallow in self-pity and misery for the rest of my life, growling at people, or I could fight to regain my health. I chose the latter because somewhere deep down I believed that the human body could heal itself from diseases, even chronic ones, if given the right tools. I decided to learn what those tools were and use them to become healthy again.

I resolved to treat my body better. I started by eating only whole grains, abstaining completely from sugar (even at social gatherings, which was really hard), and eating plenty of fruits, vegetables, and good animal products like yogurt with live active cultures.

Then I found out I was gluten intolerant, and what a blow that was! No wheat for the rest of my life? I was only in my thirties. How was I supposed to live without wheat? That's when I started my quest for truth. Why would wheat, a staple in most people's lives, contain something that so many people are allergic or intolerant to? It didn't make any sense. I was determined to find some answers—some nutritional truths.

Before long, I discovered a little miracle—a little piece of evidence that my quest was not in vain. Soaking and sprouting wheat (and other grains with gluten) before using them for food digests the gluten to a point that my body can handle. Two weeks after I started doing this, my achy joints completely disappeared.

But the quest for nutritional truth and knowledge was not over. I delved into the history of how people have eaten for generations in order to understand what human diets were like before food was refined and processed and back when civilizations lived completely off the land—back before hypothyroidism, cancer, diabetes, heart disease, autoimmune diseases, and obesity even existed. It's no surprise that our ancient ancestors were remarkably healthy, living for years longer than we do now. Their lives were and still are an example to me in how to eat and prepare food using methods that have been long forgotten.

A while later, I learned about natural sweeteners, the nutrients they contain, and their milder effect on blood sugar. So I started experimenting, and since I was feeling better, I decided to try some. To my surprise, my blood sugar didn't go haywire as long as I watched myself (which is a lot easier to do with natural sugars than refined, believe me) and I didn't feel like I *had* to have it. Plus I was able to make some remarkably delicious desserts. So instead of feeling left out at social gatherings, I was suddenly getting compliments from people that were used to eating the typical, refined, ooey-gooey desserts. I'd hear, "This is *healthy*?" and, "This is *so* good, and I don't mean it's good for being healthy, it's just plain good."

I also started experimenting around with sprouted grain, making different breads and things, and just cooking with good, whole, fresh food. The result was that it tasted better than what I was used to making and eating before. Not only that, I felt so much better. I could almost hear my body saying, "Thank you. We, your organs and cells, really enjoyed that meal." My family even started saying the same thing, but they left out the part about the organs and cells.

From there, things just snowballed. We moved (again) to a small town where the chef for the Young Family Living Farm's restaurant tasted some of my cooking and liked it, especially the berry pie with a nut crust. The next thing I knew, I was invited to teach a healthy cooking class at the restaurant.

After that I was invited to teach at the farm's annual celebration, Lavender Days. To help promote it, by a weird twist of fate, I ended up creating Lavender Berry Cream Pie and demonstrating how to make it on live TV. I taught even more classes at the restaurant, and then I was asked to cater for a convention where I received the most heartfelt, sincere compliments and even a standing ovation for my cooking.

So where am I after all this? I'd love to say that all my health problems completely vanished from diet alone, but that wouldn't be true. What is true is that a diet based on whole, traditionally prepared foods was an essential part of the equation, along with the right professional help and lots of prayers. Most of all, I've learned that you really are what you eat, and now I'm naturally sweet and a little nuts.

Michelle's Story

I've been told that I was a very happy and healthy child. My family drank raw milk from a local dairy until I was about five years old, and I ate whole wheat bread and didn't have to be bribed to eat my fruits and vegetables. My older sisters used to giggle at me because anything they didn't want to eat they would give to me and I always drank or ate it happily, like the brewer's yeast smoothie my mom used to make for us. I think that even my parents would laugh when they saw how much I always enjoyed that drink. I grew into a strong, sturdy, healthy and happy teen too. Although my carefree and nourishing childhood would take me far in my life, I was only fourteen when my world got a little rocky.

Like so many couples now, my parents divorced, and my home life changed significantly. My dad was living somewhere else, and my mom was working graveyard shifts and going to college. I didn't feel happy about all of this change, but I didn't want to let it show. I knew that a happy face would be easier for others to accept than a sad one, so being the clever little gal that I was, I made the naïve decision to keep my feelings inside of me. I didn't want to show them to others because there was enough drama going on already, and I didn't want to add to it. I carried on with an ever-so-slightly painted smile. I think I even convinced myself everything was still perfectly fine. I was in a bit of denial, I suppose. I was still happy enough—well, kind of. Whenever someone asked how I was doing, I not-so-authentically replied, "I'm good, how are you?" (I'm fine; family's fine; school's fine; cat's fine; we're all fine.)

When I was about sixteen, I began living according to my own food pyramid with the basic food groups of fast food, candy bars, and soda pop. I didn't like fast food at all. I'll admit it was pretty fast, but I refused to call it food. However, my whole family was in survival mode and, much to my disapproval, the luxury of delicious, homemade meals that I had always enjoyed with my family were just not happening anymore. I became more independent and self-reliant.

So, based on this background, you'll be surprised to know that as a young adult I began experiencing anxiety, panic attacks, and having unexplainable fears. Okay, maybe you're not surprised at all, but I was. I was totally mystified about all these new and crazy feelings and physical ailments. I was worried and stressed about everything, and I didn't feel like I could even fake a smile anymore. I would even fall asleep anywhere without any warning. I felt like I was falling apart little by little.

After being tested for everything under the sun, I finally found out that I had a virus called mononucleosis. While I had "mono" for over a year, I got many other illnesses that were floating around. My immune system was worn down to nothing. I felt totally depleted. I had blood sugar dips, light-headedness, dizziness, hypoglycemia, hormone imbalances, fibromyalgia, headaches, insomnia, trembling and shaky hands, neck and shoulder tension, irritable bowels, nausea, systemic candida overgrowth, and chronic fatigue. Sounds pretty fun, huh?

I felt sorry for myself for a while. I thought that I was picked on and that life was a little unfair. I was thinking about complaining for the rest of my life, but then I realized that that would make me really annoying. So I made the choice to reach out and admit that I deserved some assistance to climb out of the pit I had fallen into, humbling as that was.

After a year on prescription medication, I realized that the side effects were worse than facing the root of my problem head-on, even though I didn't know what that root was yet. I no longer accepted the only thing the doctor offered me—prescription drugs to cover my symptoms. I politely refused the medications and explained that

I wanted to know what was causing my symptoms. I felt that discovering what the root of my physical problems was would make it possible to correct them. I had a strong desire to heal and feel happy—not just *appear* to be healthy and happy. I took the opportunity to look at my diet, thoughts, and my overall responsibility for my current health and happiness. I had taken my health for granted, and I was determined to earn it back, for real.

Thus began my awesome journey of awakening! I ventured out of my little comfort zone into the big old world of self-help. I read life-mastery books, researched alternative health professionals, learned about herbal medicine and cleansing, and looked into any other positive and praiseworthy healing modalities I could find. After doing all of this, I began to grasp what it was going to take for *me* to be vibrant and healthy again.

It quickly became obvious to me that my physical symptoms had been getting all of my attention but that those symptoms had an emotional root or cause. The body, mind, and spirit are connected and incredibly responsive to each other. I knew I had to heal my suppressed feelings in order to get anywhere with my physical symptoms.

It was time for me to get to work, and I felt that the obvious first task was to begin making healthy dietary choices to support my body and mind in healing. I tackled the big one first—white sugar. I experienced firsthand how very addictive refined sugar really is. I couldn't seem to leave sweets alone! It was essential for me to eliminate all sweet foods for a period of time to allow my body to regain its natural intestinal flora balance. It was difficult for me to go without any sugar, fruit, or honey for the first couple weeks, but by the third week, all I craved was fruit! I couldn't believe how flavorful and sweet a luscious organic apple was! As I mastered my body, I overcame the physical and mental addiction to sugar completely, and it felt like freedom! My body could finally tell me what it really wanted without any mixed messages of unnatural food cravings. I noticed how some foods made me feel awful and how others made me feel wonderful. I gave up all white flour, replacing it with whole wheat first and then replacing that with sprouted whole wheat. Over the course of about five years, I eliminated all refined and processed foods from my family's diet. What a huge difference this made for me!

I read dozens of conflicting "health" books, and I questioned everything. Did God really create faulty food? Did man need to eat like a rabbit *all* of the time to be healthy? I'm a human with eyeteeth, and I figured I was meant to use them for something besides nibbling carrots. I wanted to develop a deeper understanding of real nutrition. Is it actually healthy to eat soybeans and the "foods" that are processed from them? I wanted answers about *real* food and what is *nourishing* and naturally healthy to eat. I wasn't interested in all of the fad health diets, the trendy health foods, or the new studies that have only been done over the past few decades.

I looked past all the hype and into history. Over several years of personal study, I found the answers I was seeking. I discovered how real food has existed since the beginning of our planet and how I could eat it to heal and improve my health. My food became my medicine.

I was excited to learn that some of the healthiest people that have ever lived on this planet ate animal products and natural fats, including saturated fat and cholesterol. It made sense that all of these nourishing brain-foods were good for me. I noticed my hormones balancing as I incorporated these healthy fats into my diet. The truth is, people have lived on this earth for at least six thousand years, and the way I enjoy eating was normal to all who have ever lived before me—except for the last generation or so. How long have people been buying their food rather than growing their own food? Sometimes I've felt like I'm the one eating "differently," but I know that it's actually the typical American diet today that's so different from what the human diet has been historically.

Because of the obvious taste and appearance differences between fast food and real homemade foods, I began making what I called "real-food meals" and creating my very own recipes. I stopped using all of the "add one can of condensed soup" or "one packet of such-and-such" recipes, and I was thrilled at how delicious real cream and fresh mushrooms or my own mix of herbs and spices were. I began compiling all my recipes and saving them for a homemade family cookbook to pass on to my daughter. I wanted to make sure that the hidden truths about health would be passed on to my posterity. I didn't know I would be sharing them with you too!

I have since taken many courses on holistic health and nutrition over the Internet and taught what I have learned about real nutrition in cooking classes offered to the community. These have included classes at the Young Living Family Farm's yearly Lavender Days festival and classes for Dr. Michael Cutler's *True Health* program. It is so much fun for me to teach and share my passion—"real food made real good." (I know that's not proper English, but I just like it.)

I have truly made some dramatic and positive changes to my health. I can't say that I changed my diet and was miraculously healed; that is not true for me. My food choices *have* had a dramatic impact on my health. They've always affected it for better or worse, but they're only a piece of the pie. Addressing my body, mind, *and* spirit is what it took for me to heal, feel vibrant and to smile from within.

Convincing Reasons To Use This Book

We have to be honest. It does take a little time and effort to prepare whole-food meals, but we can truthfully tell you that it's worth the effort just to have the extra energy and a healthy family. Plus, the pros outweigh the cons by so much that it isn't even funny. Let's take a look and see.

Pros:

- ❖ There's absolutely no comparison with flavor. We've been asked, "How do you do it? How come your food tastes so good?" The answer is that it's whole, fresh, and prepared using traditional cooking techniques.
- ❖ Upon implementing the concepts of this book, you may accidentally (or not so accidentally) normalize your weight.
- ❖ If you're gluten or starch intolerant (like the millions who are aware of their condition or the millions of others who aren't), sprouting, or souring, grains beforehand digests the gluten and starch so you don't have to. Or at least, this process digests most of it, so your body can handle the rest.[1]
- ❖ You won't experience all the unpleasant gas, bloating, and cramps associated with improperly prepared food.
- ❖ You'll learn sound nutritional truth based on a diet that has given people health and nutrition for thousands of years. This is especially nice since we can't always count on the incomplete information given to us by today's scientists and nutritional authorities. They're still learning.

❖ Eating a properly prepared, whole-food diet can minimize food allergies and intolerances of all kinds.

❖ You'll have an interesting topic of conversation when you invite guests over for dinner, especially if your bread accidentally ends up looking more like a brick than something edible. (But at least it will taste good.)

❖ You'll be the envy of your neighbors when you have the tastiest and healthiest food storage available, and you'll know how to turn it into wonderfully tasty and nourishing meals.

❖ Your body will be healthier, stronger, happier, and better able to fight and prevent acute and chronic illness.

❖ Your spouse might rather have you than the remote and a bag of chips. (This is because of the increase of zinc in his or her diet from sprouted/soured grains, and we all know how important zinc is for reproductive health.)

Cons:

❖ It takes extra time, practice, and planning at first. (But you'll quickly get used to it.)

❖ You may have too much energy and wonder how to spend it.

❖ You won't have the opportunity to catch up on magazine reading while sitting in the doctor's office with sick kids.

❖ Your spouse might rather have you than the remote and a bag of chips. (This is only a con if you're not keeping up with the sprouted grains like he or she is.)

If you are still hesitant to try our methods out after reading this rather convincing list of reasons to eat a whole-food diet, just remember that you have a choice in the matter. Do as much or as little as you'd like. Make your transition as gradually or as suddenly as feels right to you. We hope you'll give it a try so that you can see how wonderful it tastes and experience how good you feel.

Endorsements & Testimonials

"Jillayne and Michelle's cooking abilities and teaching talents are outstanding. I've traveled the world and haven't found food anywhere as tasty as the fantastic dishes made by these two. Michelle and Jillayne have taught viewers nationwide through cooking presentations at Young Living's Lavender Days and on the popular television show, *Good Things Utah*. Jillayne and Michelle have the ability to dazzle the taste buds of even the pickiest eater and fill lives with wellness through their recipes and tips."

Tiffany Covington, Agronomist and Farm Marketing Specialist
Young Living Lavender Farm

❖   ❖   ❖

"These desserts are absolutely divine! You wouldn't guess that you would feel nourished after eating dessert, but with these culinary masterpieces, you actually do! Jillayne and Michelle have truly made this food into a delectable art. I am grateful that they are sharing their talents for consciously creating and combining healthy, tasty, nourishing food!"

Crystal Betterton, MH
Real Foods Market

❖   ❖   ❖

"Before I was introduced to the whole-foods way of life, I was overweight and covered in eczema. Even after I finished a meal, I dug through my kitchen to find something to satisfy the empty, unsatisfied feeling that I had. When my twins were diagnosed with autism, I heard about the benefits of a gluten-free, casein-free diet, so we decided to try it. My twins improved enough on this diet that I decided to stay the course, but they still struggled with their behavior.

Then I was introduced to the whole-foods world. I discovered that we could eat wheat again as long as it was sprouted, and we could have dairy again as long as it was raw. And quite possibly the most important discovery was that, although we needed to avoid refined sugars, we could have delicious treats made with whole sugars (in moderation).

It has been almost three years since the switch to a whole-foods diet, and I have been able to maintain a healthier weight. Even after having another baby! Now my twins' behavior is wonderful.

Jillayne and Michelle's recipes have been a lifesaver. My kids love the way the whole foods taste. I am so full of gratitude that I was able to discover this natural way of eating that helped my family and me become whole. I'm especially grateful for these delicious recipes that helped me along the way."

Jennilee Gardner, mother of six

Section 1

You Really Are What You Eat

❖ ❖ ❖ ❖ ❖ ❖ ❖ ❖ ❖ ❖ ❖ ❖ ❖ ❖

WE'VE ALWAYS HEARD THE PHRASE, "You are what you eat." It does sound appealing if you want to be sweet and refined, or maybe you'd just like to have "hot buns." But what does this phrase really mean? Eating healthy, nutrient-dense food in its whole, natural state will likely create a healthy, nutrient-rich body and mind, and eating food lacking in nutrients may eventually leave a person sick and may even lead to death.

This is because nutrients, and the foods they are found in, are the foundation for building, repairing, and strengthening our bodies so that they can better withstand germs, stress, environmental and emotional issues, inherited weaknesses, and other causes of illness and disease. When our bodies are undernourished or malnourished through lack of good food, they are less able to handle these outside factors.

So if you are what you eat, can refined and processed food create a refined person? Sure, and this is how. You spend a good portion of your life delving into all sorts of goodies like cookies, pies, cakes made with white flours, junk food, white sugar, soda pop, candy, white bread, processed cereal, sugary jams, and so forth with seemingly no ill health.

Slowly, your body is worn down bit-by-bit, robbed of nutrients, and steadily made more susceptible to illness. Then one day, you find yourself chronically ill, depressed, and lacking energy. Your best friends are the couch, a pillow, and maybe the remote. The laundry is piled high, your kids are running around with a swarm of flies chasing their sagging diapers, and no matter how hard you try, you just can't pull out of the depression and lack of energy that you feel. All you know is that you can't possibly live the rest of your life like this. There's got to be a better way.

Being chronically ill is no way to live. You find yourself on a path of personal refinement in search of food that gives your body the nutrients it so desperately needs. After looking hard for a very long time, finding answers to your ill health, and making steady improvement through lifestyle changes, you can eventually claim that you've been through the refiner's fire. This is how you can become refined from refined food, and it's not fun.

Pottenger's Cats

A wonderful example of the effects diet has on health was an experiment performed by Dr. Francis M. Pottenger Jr. who ran a sanatorium back in the early 1900s. His goal was to find a way to heal patients with tuberculosis. As part of the experiment, he performed adrenalectomies on cats to test the potency of certain extracts, but the cats kept dying during the operations. Then he discovered, quite by accident, that a group of cats he was feeding raw meat scraps to was actually healthier than the group of cats he used for the operations, which he was feeding what he thought was an optimum diet: cooked meat scraps, cod-liver oil, and raw milk. As a result, he decided to conduct an additional experiment of sorts on the groups of cats. He was curious to know why the cats that were fed a raw meat scrap diet were healthier than the cats that were fed a cooked diet.[2]

In his study, he fed one group of cats raw meat, raw milk, and cod-liver oil. He did this to match a cat's natural, undomesticated diet of all raw food. (And we can safely assume that a wild cat's diet is completely raw, or we would have found some evidence to the contrary by now—like catching a feline roasting a fish over a campfire when he thought no one was looking.)

He fed the other groups of cats the same foods as the first, but either the meat was cooked or the milk was pasteurized, condensed, or sweetened and condensed. He watched these cats through the course of about ten years, studying each generation closely.

The group of cats that received the raw food diet was very healthy through all the generations. They had healthy skin and fluffy, soft fur.

(You can see the pictures for yourself in his book, *Pottenger's Cats: A Study in Nutrition*.) They were resilient to infections, fleas, and parasites, and had no problems reproducing. Their jaws and teeth were well-spaced generation after generation, and they were mild mannered. We can assume these healthy cats didn't hiss and scratch just because someone looked at them wrong.

The poor cats in the other groups were less fortunate, especially those fed the sweetened and condensed milk. In the first generation of these other groups, gum diseases began within three to six months after the diet began, and by the end, some degenerative diseases had set in. The cats in the second generation were born with smaller jaws and started getting diseases and losing coordination earlier in life. By the third generation, the cats became plagued with allergies, arthritis, infections, irritability, hypothyroidism, crowded teeth, near- and farsightedness, and heart problems earlier in life. Most of this third generation was unable to reproduce, and as a result there was virtually no fourth generation. Fortunately, many of the kittens on the deficient diets were allowed to roam on grass, catching critters, eating their natural diets, and actually improving in health.[3]

So what can we learn from this study? Certainly it isn't that humans would thrive on a diet of raw meat scraps and milk; every living thing on the earth has a different ideal diet. But, just like the cats in Pottenger's study, humans do thrive on a diet rich in nutrients from fresh, whole-food sources. And just like the cats in Pottenger's study, when we are deprived of our ideal diet, the same illnesses and degenerative conditions rampant in the cats are also found in us.

Whole Food in a Nutshell

What exactly is whole food? "Whole" food doesn't mean that you eat the whole thing of whatever food meets your fancy. It simply means food in its whole state, unrefined, as close to nature as you can get. Like grinding the entire wheat kernel (germ, bran, nutrients, and all) to make bread, rather than just the starchy, nutrient devoid center that is used in white flour products. Here are some examples and explanations of various types of whole foods and their refined counterparts.

Whole Grains

Grains, like wheat, spelt, kamut, rye, barley, rice, and oats, are best in their whole state because they contain all the nutrients they were grown with. Nutrients are found in the bran and germ, both of which are removed in the refining process. For those who may ask, "Isn't enriched flour just as good for you as whole wheat flour?" there are some interesting facts about the enriching process that we need to mention. All white bread, flours, cereals, and such use enriched flours today because several years ago, when grain refining became commonplace, people got gravely ill, and many died.[4] The cause? Vitamin deficiency. Pretty soon, people started enriching flour by adding the most important vitamins back into the product so they wouldn't get beriberi, pellagra, and anemia. But they still left out all the other vitamins, minerals, oils, and fiber that the whole grain originally contained. Adding some of the vitamins back in was somewhat beneficial, but even then, the synthetic forms of vitamins are not easily absorbed into our bodies.

In actuality, *enriching* is a misleading word. Here's an example to illustrate. Picture a wealthy man who has a rare collection of all the natural stones, minerals, and metals offered by the earth. One night, some thieves sneak into his place and steal his entire collection. But the thieves aren't all bad. They replace five stones. Only, they aren't the natural stones—they're synthetic and therefore much less valuable. However, the thieves consider themselves very generous and even make the claim that they have "enriched" the man's rare collection.

Natural Sweeteners

Natural sweeteners taste wonderful, and they contain their own nutrients.[5] Plus, they're not as addictive as refined sugars and can be gentler on blood sugar levels. Natural sugars include raw honey, raw blue/amber agave, stevia, dehydrated cane juice or unrefined whole cane sugar (Sucanat or Organic Whole Cane Sugar), unsulfered molasses, and pure maple syrup. We're not talking about the kind of syrup at the store made with high fructose corn syrup and artificial maple flavor. We're talking about the good old maple syrup that comes from mature maple trees back east at just the right time of the year, drilled and prepared the old-fashioned way, then carted off to your local health food store. It's so good!

But what about artificial sweeteners? Aspartame (or aspartyl phenylalanine-methyl ester) is the sugar substitute found abundantly in diet soft drinks, table-top sweeteners, gum, and so on. It is made of synthetic isolated amino acids (excitotoxins that get your nerves so excited that it kills them) and methanol, a poisonous alcohol.[6] It's no wonder that thousands of people have complained to the FDA with symptoms attributed to aspartame such as headaches; dizziness; nausea; abdominal pain; seizures (even grand mal); menstrual, neurological, and sleep problems; and the list goes on and on.[7]

However, there are sources (who are sponsored by the multi-million-dollar industry that makes the artificial sweetener) that claim there is no harm caused by using artificial sweeteners and think these sweeteners are a wonderful way to have sweet things without the calories. But the truth is that the first response of insulin is based on the taste of something sweet, not the actual presence of sugar in the system, so consuming something sweet that doesn't actually have sugar in it confuses the body until eventually the pancreas says, "Okay, you keep tricking me. I send out insulin for this sweet taste, and it's not needed. So now, whenever there's sweetness, I just won't send out insulin. Hah!" Then your body is in a world of hurt with a pancreas that's tired of being tricked.

We urge you to do your own research, and, please, if you have any of the symptoms listed above and use artificial sweeteners regularly in your diet, try going a couple months without it. Many other people have done this and noticed an improvement in or disappearance of their health problems as a result.

Sea Salt

Unrefined sea salt is salt that has been minimally processed. Usually, it has just been sun dried or dehydrated. It contains tons of naturally occurring minerals like iodine, which has been removed from refined salt and then added back in. Unrefined sea salt, unlike refined salt, is actually health promoting.[8] It doesn't cause water retention, gross, puffy fingers and feet, and high blood pressure like its refined counterpart either. Plus, it tastes fuller. That's the best way to describe it. Once you get used to the great taste of unrefined sea salt, you can taste the emptiness of refined. It's weird, but true.

There is also a difference between authentic, unrefined sea salt, and the refined stuff labeled "sea salt" at the local grocery stores. Redmond

Real Salt, Himalayan Crystal Salt, and Celtic Sea salt are great brands that aren't refined.

Fats & Oils

Fats and oils are needed in our diets to supply warmth, energy, healthy brains and skin, and to help in the absorption of fat-soluble vitamins like vitamins A and D.[9] Coconut oil, which is antimicrobial, antibacterial, and antifungal; butter from pasture-fed cows, which is rich in vitamin A and omega-3s; and extra-virgin olive oil are all healthy oils. Some are skeptical about coconut oil and butter because they are a source of saturated fat, but we find confidence in the fact that the healthy cultures throughout the world's history, who had the same genetic makeup that we have today, ate fresh butter, coconut oil, and olive oil regularly without clogging their arteries. In truth, it's the hydrogenated and trans fats and the high heat from frying oils and other food preparations that make oil behave dangerously and, therefore, cause harm to the body.[10] When buying coconut oil, virgin coconut oil is recommended, since expeller pressed oil has been deodorized at high heat and has lost some important benefits. Cold-pressed extra virgin coconut oil is the least refined.

Fresh Produce

Fresh produce is best when grown organically in your own garden or locally. We probably don't need to explain how important it is to eat fruits and vegetables when they are fresh and in season, but we will anyway. It is *very* important. Nutrition *and* flavor are at their greatest when fruits and vegetables are ripened on the tree or vine and eaten as soon as possible after picking. Plus, greens are awesome in the spring, melons are refreshing in the summer when you're hot, and squashes are filling in the fall and winter when our bodies need warmth and fullness.[11] Isn't it perfect?

Besides, who wants icy cold watermelon in the middle of winter, or hot, thick stew filled with meat, potatoes, and carrots, when it's a hundred degrees outside? Listen to your body, and it will tell you what it truly deserves.

You Are What You Drink

If you are what you eat, then you certainly are what you drink, whether you want to be bubbly and sparkling or just light and refreshing.

What have people used to quench their thirst since the beginning of time? We're pretty sure that colas, soda pop, punch, and bottled juices hadn't been invented yet, or we would find evidence in archeological digs, like tooth-decayed, mummified bodies clutching a tin can of diet cola in one porous-boned hand, and a bottle of prehistoric head pain reliever in the other. We would also find evidence of cavities, diabetes, and kidney problems related to carbonation, along with calcium-depleted bones and all the other health problems correlated with these drinks. This is because of the sodium, sugar, high fructose corn syrup, aspartame, caffeine, phosphorous, and other components of these drinks that contribute to ill health.[12] If it weren't for these minor problems, we would be all for these kinds of drinks. But since there are so many reasons to avoid them, we really can't, in good consciousness, recommend them.

Most people would agree that water is the best way to hydrate our bodies on a daily basis. What about municipal tap water? It is convenient, but there are a few tidbits of information about tap water that we would like to share with you. Keep in mind that we have opinions about certain things, and this is one of them. We mention this not hoping to convert you to our way of thinking, but hoping that you'll do your own research on this topic and form your own opinion.

With that, here are the cons about municipal tap water and why we don't like to use it, besides the fact that it interferes with soaking and sprouting and has a bad flavor.

❖ It contains chlorine. Chlorine does a great job of killing bacteria in water, but it also kills the friendly bacteria in your digestive system. The poor little guys just don't have a chance to work and slave in your intestinal tract to help with digestion, keep yeast in check, and make you feel happier when they've been destroyed by chlorine.

❖ Lots of culinary water is recycled sewer water that has been cleaned and disinfected. However, the disinfection process doesn't actually rid the water of the prescription medications and pesticides that find their way in.[13] Call us crazy, maybe even a little old fashioned, but if by some chance we'd ever use prescription meds, we'd prefer to get them from sources other than tap water.

❖ Unnatural fluoride is added to a lot of drinking water. This is done with the hope that it will strengthen teeth, but too much of this fluoride can cause such a long list of health problems that we would run out of paper listing them all. Healthy societies studied in the past had straight, white teeth with virtually no cavities, and they didn't even brush or have a need for dentists. This wasn't because they fluoridated their water. It was because of their excellent diet—a diet devoid of refined flours and sugars but abundant in good bone-building, nutrient-rich food.[14] Now, we are not suggesting that if your diet is excellent you don't need to brush your teeth anymore. We believe in good hygiene. We are simply suggesting that a good diet is a much better solution to cavity prevention than fluoridated water.

We believe that the human body thrives on real, clean, and pure alkaline mineral water. This is what some of the world's healthiest people used for cooking, for drinking, irrigating, bathing (we assume they bathed), and watering their animals. There are many health benefits to drinking pure, mineral rich water, such as its alkalizing effect in the body, its greater capacity to hydrate, the fact that your body is being nourished while being hydrated,[15] and the bonus of not having to worry about drinking chemicals or recycled prescription meds.

It's preferable to get water from sources that haven't been touched by the environment, but since this is next to impossible, filtered, alkaline mineral water, which is ideal for drinking and cooking, is the next best thing. The best way to achieve pure-water-living in the world today is to install a water ionizer in your home. We feel that Kangen and Life Ionizer are great companies for this. There are also a lot of other sources of water and water filtration systems that you can use instead of the more costly ones. We suggest you do some research on water purity and find what best suits your needs.

Healthy Soil Makes Healthy People

One cool habit of our wise ancestors was to nourish the soil each year before planting crops.[16] The rich soil provided the plants with everything they needed to be healthy and disease-free, and they didn't even need to travel to the nearest home improvement warehouse to pick up fertilizers, pesticides, and herbicides. These were completely unnecessary. This is organic gardening at its best and is the reason why organic produce tastes better and is richer in nutrients than synthetically raised produce.

We are all about nutrition and flavor, and since we prefer our produce to be free of harmful pesticides and not to be bred through genetic modification, especially with animals (lest in the future we find ourselves eating to*moo*toes), organic is really the best way to go. This simply means that the food hasn't been genetically modified or engineered, is pesticide/herbicide free, and has been raised in similar fashion to the way our ancestors did it—like taking good care of the soil and replenishing it by natural means. Doing so will result in soil that will give the nutrients to the plant to make healthier and tastier produce. This in turn creates healthier, tastier people. At least, we assume they would be tastier.

Plants that are nourished through prosperous soils and mineral-rich water resist disease and are healthier. Animals that eat nutrient-rich plants are fed the vitamins and minerals they need and are also disease resistant and healthy. Humans that then eat healthy plants and the products from healthy animals are also nourished, disease resistant, and healthy. This works well because then the humans can have the health and strength they need to replenish the soil so that the cycle of health may continue. This is what our ancient ancestors did, and they reaped the benefits.[17]

Today, you can practice your own organic gardening in your backyard. If this isn't possible, you can purchase fresh produce from local organic farmers or buy it at the supermarket. More and more grocers are beginning to carry organic produce, but nothing beats the flavor and nutrient value of vine-ripened produce that is eaten fresh from your own garden.

Healthy Animals Make Healthy Food

If you have done any amount of research in the health world, you have probably heard all the negative attention given to animal products like cheese, milk, eggs, and meat. There's really no good reason for this negativity unless you consider that close to 70 percent of all antibiotics sold in the United States are given to livestock not only as a way to prevent illness and make up for the fact that they live in crowded and unsanitary conditions, but also to help them gain weight.[18] Okay, so maybe there is a good reason to avoid the products from these animals, but that doesn't mean that the products that come from healthy, well-nourished animals are bad. In fact, they're actually good for you.

When partaking of animal products, it is vitally important to make sure the animal is healthy and clean because what that animal eats and is injected with finds its way into the milk, organs, flesh, skin, and fat of that animal. When you eat it, it all becomes a part of you too. Kind of like a nursing woman who takes extra care to eat healthily and doesn't take substances that could pass through her milk and harm her baby.

Because of this fact, there is a huge difference in the nutrition, quality, and flavor of animal products that come from healthy animals versus sickly animals. The natural and perfect diet for cows is fresh growing pasture grass[19] and corn.[20] They also need plenty of room to roam. Cows that live in these conditions produce rich, yellow butter; sweet, nourishing milk and yogurt; and the best tasting ice cream around. Then, when winter rolls around and Old Bessie just doesn't have it in her to make milk products anymore, at least all the pasture she's eaten will make her meat lean and bright red. Just be sure not to eat too much of her meat, because even though it comes from a good source and provides nutrients, it's still acidic and harder to digest than other protein foods.

The same principle applies to chickens. When they are fed a good diet and allowed to roam freely so they can get exercise and eat little worms and other bugs, like garden-destroying grasshoppers, their yolks end up being bright orange and loaded with vitamin A and D and omega-3s.[21]

When an animal is properly fed and nourished, you can be sure that whatever part of that animal you are using will, in turn, provide you with the sustenance you need. Rather than processing animal products in a way so their sickness can't be passed on to you, it makes far more sense to raise the animal in a healthy way so that you will be rewarded with healthy, nutritious animal products.

Another reason that people may shy away from animal products is because of cholesterol. Even healthy animal products contain it. However, the human body actually needs cholesterol, or it wouldn't create it to help rebuild and repair tissues, balance hormones and serotonin to make us happy, assist in digestion through the production of bile salts, and create a healthy digestive system.[22] The problem with cholesterol isn't that it exists, because in its natural unaltered state, it is healthy. It only becomes harmful if it is damaged through heat.

The main contributor to high cholesterol in people living today isn't only the improper processing of animal food. The over-consumption of refined flours, refined sugars, as well as hydrogenated and vegetable oils; vitamin and mineral deficiencies; and a lack of antimicrobial oils like coconut oil also contribute to the problem.[23] This is why people who have lived a whole-food diet that includes properly produced animal food and no refined products have healthy cholesterol levels. The same is possible for us. For more in-depth information on cholesterol and animal fats, see *Nourishing Traditions* by Sally Fallon.

Super Foods & Real Food "Supplements"

Eating vitamins and minerals through whole-food sources, like grains, seeds, legumes, animal products, and fruits and vegetables is far superior and much tastier than getting them in isolated form. The sugary pulp inside fruit is really tasty, but the skins and seeds in fruits and veggies are especially nutrient dense. However, we can't in good conscious recommend eating banana peels or pumpkin rind.

It's far better to get nutrients from a whole-food source rather than from isolated or synthetic options, but sometimes some sort of supplement is still needed to round out a healthy diet. Here are some whole-food supplements we use when needed. We are not suggesting that you will be healed of whatever ailment you have by using them, but they can go a long way in balancing out an imperfect diet.

Superfood Plus

Made by *American Botanical Pharmacy*, this is an excellent whole-food supplement for vitamins and minerals. It can be bought in tablets or in powder form to mix in juice or water. It's a vivid, dark green and assimilates into the bloodstream quickly. It tastes like grass-berries. It is an acquired taste, but lovely once acquired.

Udo's Oil Blend or Flax Oil

This is a good source of extra omega-3s for healthy brain, skin, hormones, and other things, if you happen to be interested in nourishing them. It does not contain Docosahexaenoic acid (DHA), though.

Cod-liver Oil

This is a great source for DHA *and* omega-3s for healthy brain development and nourishment, healthy skin, balanced hormones, and so on. It also has vitamins A and D for healthy eyes and good calcium absorption, so you don't crack a rib while reaching for your supplements.

Primal Defense Probiotics

This replenishes the friendly bacteria in your intestines. Just mix it in a little juice or water and drink it. It doesn't have much of a flavor and has a slightly gritty texture. It's a must if you are or have been on antibiotics, since antibiotics also destroy your friendly intestinal bacteria.

Capra Mineral Whey

Whole food powdered goat milk whey is a convenient mineral supplement. Mix into some hot water or milk along with a little honey or maple syrup and wow! It's a yummy, warm beverage. It tastes kind of like a graham cracker, only it's not crunchy.

Why We're Not Vegans or Raw Foodists & What We Actually Are

For some people, the logic behind Veganism (or abstinence from consuming animal products) has a lot to do with all the negative comments about animal products, which we should have debunked in the "Healthy Animals Make Healthy Products" section. If we haven't debunked those negative comments enough, then go back and read that section again or read *Nutrition and Physical Degeneration* by Weston A. Price, a dentist who studied the diets of several different healthy societies—all of which ate healthy animal products.

Many of the world's healthiest societies ate animal products such as fresh (raw) milk, cheese, yogurt, kefir, eggs, animal flesh, organ meats, fish, and fish eggs.[24] There were no local grocers and pharmacies nearby, so they couldn't run to town and pick up their vitamin B12 supplements (the vitamin supplied only through animal products). They had to eat at least some foods from animals in order to get this nutrient.

Since our bodies are the same genetically, we also need vitamin B12 from our food. Any diet program that suggests going to the store to buy a specific vitamin that isn't supplied in that diet is a cause for alarm. You may ask, "But isn't vitamin B12 found in vegetarian sources like spirulina?" While that is true, some say that this source of B12 isn't genuine, that our bodies really don't absorb it, and that it can even *cause* B12 deficiency.[25] Thus begins the feud between vegetarian and animal sources of B12.

Personally, we feel that humans need animal products to avoid numb feet, jittery nerves, weepiness, and insomnia. Not everyone needs a lot of these animal products, but everyone needs at least enough to supply this vitamin. We trust that you will do what you feel is best for you.

There's another movement going around that encourages eating only raw food. We agree that raw foods contain many beneficial enzymes, nutrients, and other properties that are destroyed through cooking and irradiation, which is the process of applying radioactive gamma rays to certain grocery store produce and spices to kill enzymes, living properties, and the ability to sprout so they'll last on trucks and in the produce section for months before decaying. We even agree that living, raw food (sprouts, freshly picked produce, and so on) is highly beneficial to the human diet and should be eaten where possible. There are even certain elements found in raw, living food that have a healing effect on the body and mind.[26]

But not *all* food needs to be eaten raw. For instance, take the squashes, grains, and other starches. Somehow, pumpkin pie made with cold, inedible chunks of pumpkin in a soggy, doughy crust is largely unappetizing. This makes sense when you consider the fact that the tightly compacted starch chains in foods like this are widened in cooking, making cooked starchy foods *easier* to digest than raw ones.[27] So unless God gave us beans, grains, corn, potatoes, and squashes *just* to decorate our homes and front porches at harvest time, they were designed to be cooked and eaten. That's not even including the variety of other vegetables, like broccoli, cauliflower, cabbage, carrots, spinach, chard, and others that—for one reason or another—are easier to digest cooked than raw, especially with a little melted butter on top for added nutrient absorption.[28] So this is our little rule of thumb: if it was made to be consumed raw, eat it raw. If it was made to be cooked, cook it. Not only will it taste better, but it will be better for you because it's actually easier to digest.

So if we are not Vegans or raw foodists, then what are we? We like to call ourselves Rejoicers-of-Excellent-and-Luxurious-Food-Obtained-Only-by-Deciphering-Important-Studies-of-Traditional-Societies-ists, or REAL FOODISTS for short. In the next section, you will learn the traditional food preparation techniques used throughout the world's history and how they make food taste wonderful and—at the same time—make us healthier.

Section 2

Treasured Traditions

❖ ❖ ❖ ❖ ❖ ❖ ❖ ❖ ❖ ❖ ❖ ❖ ❖ ❖

SOMETIMES, WHEN WE TALK ABOUT our healthy ancestors and what we have learned from them, we receive blank stares. This is mainly because people have a tendency to think we are referring to the lost souls of the Dark Ages who often died in childbirth, had a tremendous infant mortality rate, were constantly sick, were considered the old and wise one in the village if they lived to be thirty-five, and who had virtually no teeth.

Modern medicine has gone far to deter the spread of infectious disease and to treat the symptoms of others, but two important factors contributed to the ill health of those living in the Dark Ages. These people were malnourished and lived in filthy conditions. We firmly believe that proper diet and hygiene go far in preventing all manners of disease.

But these are not the ancestors we mean. We are talking about our ancient ancestors who lived longer than we do, who were properly nourished and clean, and—as a result—were very healthy. We mean people like Adam and Eve, the wide variety of cultures studied by Weston A. Price, and the Hunza.

Tips from the Garden of Eden

We have often asked ourselves, "What did Adam and Eve eat?" Our reason for asking this is to discover what yummy foods played a part in keeping them so healthy that they lived to be over nine hundred

15

years old, as mentioned in the book of Genesis in the Bible. It's not that we're seeking to live this long, but we definitely don't want to die prematurely from bad health. In fact, anything short of a terrible accident at age ninety-nine, like tripping over an overgrown squash plant while plucking fresh produce in the garden, is pure robbery of life.

When we ask ourselves what they ate, for some reason, we just can't picture Adam bringing home a hot pizza from some fast food joint or Eve whipping up a batch of chocolate-chip cookies with the white, bleached flour and refined sugar she just happened to get at the neighborhood grocer.

So what did they eat that contributed to their health and longevity? We know some basic foods mentioned in the bible. Some are mentioned specifically as Adam and Eve's diet, and others as the diets of their descendants. Some of this food was bread, unleavened bread, milk, butter, honey, fish, fruits, vegetables, meat, salt, and oils.[29]

God placed these foods on the earth in their natural state for us to enjoy and to receive nourishment for our wondrous bodies. These superb foods are still available to us now; they're just not as common as commercial food.

The Healthy & Happy Hunza

The Hunza (pronounced "Hoon-za") are one of the healthiest people ever studied. Though they didn't live to be over nine hundred years old, like Adam, a great number of them lived to be over a hundred years old. Diseases like cancer, heart disease, diabetes, tuberculosis, and many others were virtually unheard of in their society. They were generally healthy, cheerful, and active,[30] even playing games, until the day they finally passed on. Can you imagine what the retirement centers were like there? Volleyball tournaments categorized by age, with seniors (those between 110 and 120) versus the young-uns (those between 90 and 100).

Now we ask ourselves, what did they eat? Did they eat saturated fat? Did they count carbs, calories, and fat grams? Did they avoid honey because of its glycemic index? Were they concerned about clogged arteries because margarine hadn't yet been invented and they were forced to eat butter?

No, they simply ate those foods they could grow and that were available to them. They truly listened to what their bodies needed for nourishment. Their food consisted of wheat and other grains, fresh and cultured goat dairy, sprouted legumes, leafy green and root vegetables, fruits like apricots, and occasional meat.[31] It was not processed, refined, or denatured in any manner, but whole and—a lot of times—living.

You may be thinking that the Hunza were just a genetically superior race and that that's the only reason for their good health, vitality, and longevity, but there were a whole slew of healthy societies all over the world that were very similar to the Hunza in health and diet. Quite a bit of information was gathered about the diets in these societies and how they prepared their food so they could avoid cavities, tuberculosis, diabetes, cancer, heart disease, autoimmune disease, and other problems.

In the 1930s, Weston A. Price, DDS, toured the world looking for the common nutritional denominators in the world's healthiest people, even though the diets and locations of every race he studied varied. People in warmer climates ate rye bread, dairy, and vegetables; oats, fish, and in-season plant life; or abundant sea and plant life. Those that lived in winter or drought conditions ate primarily animal organs, tissues, and meat along with whatever plants were available.[32] This was because these people lived where plant life was limited due to harsh conditions. But that doesn't mean that those people living in warmer climates with plenty of grains, fruits, and veggies could eat a heavy meat diet and actually be healthy. Those in cold or harsh climates relied on heavier food because their bodies needed it for warmth and nourishment.

In every instance, Price found that the diets of healthy societies were made of the whole foods that were available to them, and they all consumed both plant and animal life. Their diets supplied all needed nutrients, and as a result he found abundantly healthy, beautiful, disease-resistant humans with straight, perfectly arched, cavity-resistant teeth.[33] He also found that those who had been introduced to refined foods like white bread, jams, and sugar, had started to suffer from all sorts of disease. There was an explosion in the number of cavities and cases of tuberculosis. The younger generations, those children born to mothers who ate these refined foods while pregnant, were more sickly and had crowded teeth—unlike their older siblings who were born to the same mother before she was introduced to refined foods.[34] Overall, his finding were very similar to what Francis M. Pottenger Jr. discovered with his cat study. It's almost eerie enough to give a person goose bumps!

So where are all of these healthy societies today? Unfortunately, most of them took a dive in health when refined and processed foods were introduced into their diets (including the Hunza, whose decline in health was reported as early as 1933[35]), and they became disease-laden like the rest of the world. Their wisdom in preparing food died along with them, but we don't let that stop us from learning the lessons they learned.

Here are some rather interesting tidbits compiled about the diets of the Hunza and the people studied by Weston A. Price:

❖ Grain was allowed to germinate or sour before consumption and was a staple in many of their diets. It was used to make porridges and different kinds of bread, something that was eaten daily.[36] (They ate bread every day and didn't have diabetes?)

❖ Beans, seeds, and nuts were sprouted before being cooked or eaten so the consumer wouldn't get gas.[37] (This was before Beano was invented, but Beano wouldn't have been invented if this tradition hadn't been forgotten.)

❖ Broths and stews were made from the bones and flesh of healthy animals, which are loaded with nutrition and rich flavor. These natural flavor-enhancers also aid digestion and taste way better than those little bullion cubes.[38]

❖ Saturated fat was eaten regularly, often in the form of fresh, nutrient-rich butter and other animal products, and nobody got clogged arteries.[39] How can we know these people didn't have clogged arteries if EKGs and angiograms weren't even invented yet? Well, clogged arteries aren't exactly conducive to living over one hundred years like those in the Hunza and other societies did.

❖ Fruits and vegetables were grown in soils exploding with nutrients, so there wasn't a need for artificial pesticides, herbicides, and fertilizers. Fruits and vegetables were eaten fresh and in season, when the nutrient content and flavor were at their peak.[40]

❖ The meat of their animals was eaten only on occasion, but the fruits of their animals—fresh milk, cheese, buttermilk, and so forth—were eaten daily.[41] They also cultured much of their dairy to give them plenty of friendly bacteria in their digestive systems so that they wouldn't have to run to the nearest store for probiotics.[42]

It must also be noted that these societies *didn't indulge in any harmful or addicting habits*, and that they were physically active, they minimized stress in their lives, and they had a cleaner environment.[43] Their diet *and* lifestyle created their excellent health, and diet and lifestyle can create *our* excellent health as well.

God's Recipe for Health

God created our miraculous bodies, so naturally he's the one to ask with questions of how to run them. Kind of like the people who design the engine, body, and other features of an exotic car—they would be the ones to ask about the proper fuel and oil needed to get the best performance. Luckily, God didn't just send us to earth without an instruction manual on how to care for our bodies. He gave us instructions because he *wants* us to be healthy, happy, joyful, and successful in life. His guide for health is this:

❖ All grain, especially wheat, was created to be the staff of life.[44]

❖ Vegetables and fruits are meant to be eaten and should be eaten in their seasons.[45]

❖ Animal flesh is ordained for the use of man, but should be eaten sparingly, in cold, winter, or famine.[46]

❖ Harmful and/or addictive substances, such as alcohol, tobacco, tea, and coffee should be avoided.[47]

Now go back and read about the diets of the Hunza and the societies studied by Weston A. Price and see how remarkably well they line up with God's recommended diet. Even the ones whose primary source of nourishment came from animals because they lived in almost continuous winter and famine followed this plan. It's beyond coincidence. It's dietary truth given to us by our loving God, and the Hunza, the healthy societies Price studied, and millions of people living now are proof that it works. We know this information to be dietary truth, both from personal belief and from personal experience.

Traditional Food Preparation

The way these people prepared their food and their amazing health and longevity was not a coincidence. Unfortunately, most of these priceless preparation techniques were completely forgotten. We would like to share these techniques now because we have been waiting for pages to do so.

Why Soak or Sprout Grains, Beans, & Nuts?

Traditionally, grain was allowed to cure and even slightly germinate before it was harvested.[48] This wasn't done because the farmer was worn out and decided to procrastinate for a couple of weeks. It was done to make the grain easier to digest and more full of nutrients. (Then the farmer and all the villagers would be full of energy so they could win the big volleyball championship for all people age ninety and up.) The step of curing is completely sidestepped today, hence, the need for sprouting. Here are some other great reasons to sprout:

❖ Sprouting and souring grains predigests some of the gluten so our bodies can tolerate it better and neutralizes enzyme inhibitors to allow better digestion and absorption of nutrients.[49]

❖ Soaking/sprouting grain neutralizes phytic acid, an enzyme inhibitor found in grains, nuts, and seeds.[50] Neutralizing this acid is a good thing because phytic acid binds with nutrients like calcium, iron, magnesium, and zinc and carries them right out of your body.[51] It also does wonders for those who have tons of wheat stored in their home or garage for a rainy day and are tired of getting bloated and gassy after they use it.

❖ Sprouting increases nutrients, especially vitamin C, the B vitamins, and Carotene.[52] This will come in handy if you're ever on a long sea voyage or if you exist entirely on the wheat stored in your pantry, and you're worried about getting scurvy. You can actually prevent this deficiency disease by implementing sprouting in your diet.

- ❖ Breads made from sprouted grains are milder on blood sugars than regular whole grains and are much gentler than white flour, which is like being on a blood sugar roller coaster.[53]
- ❖ Sprouting converts starches into vegetable sugars. Vegetable sugars are much easier for people to digest than starches.[54]
- ❖ One of the reasons some health-conscious individuals avoid grain is that it's acidic and can cause cavities. Sprouting also turns grain from an acidic food to an alkaline.[55] This, along with the fact that sprouting converts starches to vegetable sugars, is one of the reasons the healthy cultures of the past didn't suffer from cavities, even though they ate grains.

A lot of the wheat varieties we are familiar with have now actually been genetically modified. This is one reason why so many people have problems with wheat. Some wheat types that have been around since the days of Joseph in Egypt are spelt and kamut. Since spelt and kamut are not genetically modified, our bodies recognize them as a food, making them easier to digest than modern wheat. (Spelt contains a lower gluten content than most wheat—a plus for anyone with gluten intolerance.)

Fortunately, there is hope for healing if you are one of the millions of people who are gluten intolerant and have been told that you will have to live the rest of your existence on rice and potato bread. It is helpful to know that a lot of gluten-intolerant individuals are actually starch intolerant and do really well with sprouted grains. However, those that have genuine issues with gluten may benefit from abstaining from grain for a time to allow their guts to heal, and then they can introduce sprouted spelt and other grains back into the diet. Just be sure to get qualified professional help with this process, preferably from someone who deals with the reversal of food allergies and intolerances. Then, if you are truly *allergic* to gluten, not merely intolerant to it, and your gut isn't healed all the way after abstaining from grain for a time, you will have help knowing when it's safe to proceed. That way, introducing a small amount of gluten prematurely won't mow down your nutrient-grabbing villi like a weed whacker. That would be really bad.

Grains aren't the only things that benefit from the soaking and sprouting process. Beans and nuts also have phytic acid and are among some of the more challenging foods to digest. Healthy societies soaked beans. Some even sprouted them and then cooked them for a long time over low heat.[56] Sprouting and proper cooking increases nutrients and makes grains completely digestible.

In ancient times, nuts and seeds were soaked in salt water then dehydrated by the sun.[57] This neutralized phytic acid and made them taste better. We can attest to that. Almonds that have been soaked in a mixture of filtered water and sea salt until they swell, and then have been dehydrated, pop in your mouth. Yet, you get the added bonus of them being more nutritious, and they're not even roasted and covered in refined salt that will make your hands look like swelled balloons.

Unfortunately, the federal government has mandated the pasteurization of all raw almonds grown in the United States,[58] which means that if you want the extra health benefit of eating soaked, sprouted, enzyme-and-nutrient-rich raw almonds, you will have to sell your arms and legs to buy them foreign. Hmm. Maybe it would be better to grow your own almond tree.

Isn't it weird how tobacco, which kills approximately 440,000 people a year,[59] is legal, yet one almond farm having an outbreak of salmonella that sends thirty-three people to the hospital is enough to make pasteurization mandatory?[60] If the farm had used organic gardening practices in the first place, the salmonella would probably never have happened. We can just see the prisons now—there are inmates lined up for all sorts of crimes: there's a business professional who did some money laundering, a guy who robbed a bank, a man who's in for assault, and a lady who went after her husband with a pair of scrapbooking scissors because he chose the remote and a bag of chips over her. And then there's you.

"What are you in here for?" you're asked.

"Buying non-pasteurized almonds for the health and well-being of my family," you say, and then the other inmates laugh at you.

We hope it doesn't come down to this. We hope to gain our health freedoms back by reversing this mandate.

Eat Your Curds and Whey and Other Cultured Dairy

Dairy products from healthy animals are an excellent source of protein and calcium, but there are some things about them that have people shying away. These things are casein, a protein that is hard to digest for a lot of people, and lactose, a milk sugar that is also hard to digest. Since casein can cause health problems, especially in genetically susceptible people, and since lactose can cause bloating, gas, and excess mucus (so that you are embarrassed to go out in public for fear that you might vent toxic gas or drool), we look to our ancient ancestors for help. What did they do?

Largely, our ancient ancestors cultured their dairy, making yogurt, cheese, and butter from healthy, pasture-fed animals. Refrigeration hadn't been invented yet, so they mostly cultured their dairy as a means of preservation.[61] One of the reasons these people were so healthy was that their yogurt was full of friendly bacteria. Yogurt uses the same friendly bacteria that digests gluten, only in this case, it digests casein and lactose.[62]

The cheese-making process digests lactose and unfriendly bacteria, but not casein. Going off our personal experiences alone, we seem to do a lot better with raw cheeses than cheeses from pasteurized milk. Some people may fair better without cheese altogether.

Cultured butter from pasture-fed, healthy animals is quite nutritious. Weston A. Price, the same dentist who studied several healthy civilizations in the 1930s, used vitamin-rich butter to help heal people inflicted with cavities, bone fractures, and deficiency diseases.[63] But the butter Weston A. Price used in his treatment wasn't the butter you can find now at the grocery store, which is produced from improperly fed, antibiotic-laden cows. Price's butter was made fresh from cows fed on rapidly growing pasture.[64] This butter had nourishing properties because of the diet and health of the cow and because it was prepared properly.

Another interesting fact about our ancient ancestors is that they didn't go to the trouble of skimming their dairy to make low-fat and non-fat versions of their food.[65] They included milk fat in their diets because of its ability to provide warmth to the body and nutrients to their brains, skin, and various other parts of their bodies.

Even though there are a lot of healthy properties in cultured dairy, some people are still sensitive to dairy from cows and do much better with products from goats, because goat milk is more similar to human milk than cow milk is. So if you are one of those cow-intolerant people, you're not alone. Most of the world gets its dairy from animals other than cows (some people don't even have dairy available at all), and it is possible to find goat products that don't taste like an actual goat.

Don't Have a Cow About Fresh Milk

Many of the healthy cultures we've mentioned drank and used fresh and cultured dairy on a regular basis.[66] This practice contributed to their immense health. When we say fresh milk, we mean raw, non-pasteurized milk.

For thousands of years, people have been safely consuming raw dairy products because they knew how to produce healthy, safe dairy. These healthy practices were given up in the 1800s when the United States saw a population explosion. In order to keep up with demand, dairy cows were kept indoors and fed a diet of whisky production leftovers to boost milk production. Unfortunately, the cows were sick because they weren't fed or cared for properly, and they lived in an unsanitary environment, often being milked by dirty and sick humans. As a result, the milk was so watery it was useless to make cheese and butter. The milk itself was unhealthy, and starch, flour, and even chalk was added to it so it would resemble normal milk.[67]

Taking any product raw from diseased, improperly nourished animals in a dirty environment is a recipe for disaster, and many people, especially children, became ill and died because of it.[68] Pediatricians and doctors at the time knew that milk from healthy, well-nourished, and clean animals made all the difference in the world and thought it much wiser and healthier to return to the traditional ways of milk production rather than just pasteurize the chalk water from sick cows.

But pasteurization won out, perhaps because it was, and still is, easier to produce masses of milk if you don't have to take the extra time, care, and money to make sure the dairy cows and their products are healthy, clean, and safe.

Fortunately, there are certified dairy farmers who still practice the traditional techniques of safe, raw milk production. We—Jillayne and Michelle—buy fresh milk for our families and ourselves. We have done a lot of study, pondering, and prayer on this controversial issue, and the fact that people have been safely consuming raw dairy from properly nourished, *healthy*, and *clean* cows, sheep, and goats for thousands of years before Louis Pasteur was even born tells us that it's possible to enjoy the same today.

Of course, we buy only from the very best—which is a certified dairy that has cute, fluffy, healthy, and clean cows, roaming and grazing freely over acres of lush green grass. The facility is immaculate, and each batch of milk is tested for bacteria content. This milk is sold at Real Foods Market, one of the best whole-food stores in the nation.

Still you may wonder, "Why raw? Isn't pasteurized/homogenized better?" The answer is no. Pasteurization kills the best parts of the milk that are needed for proper digestion, like lactase, the heat sensitive enzyme that digests lactose so you don't get bloated. Homogenization, the process of preventing the milk fat from rising to the top of your milk so you can't make your own butter and ice cream, forces the fat molecules to become so tiny that they are directly absorbed into the blood steam. Unnatural processing of milk is what is dangerous, and it's a recipe for heart disease.[69]

No matter the circumstances, there will always be people who will prefer pasteurized milk to fresh. If you are one of these people, please consider gently pasteurized milk, preferably non-homogenized, from healthy, properly fed cows or goats. If that isn't available, there are usually dairies around that sell pasteurized, homogenized dairy from healthy, properly fed cows and goats. The nutrition and health of the animal are always a top priority in any animal product.

Traditional Cooking Techniques

One of the reasons traditionally prepared food has such great flavor is due to the actual cooking techniques. So even though we would like to claim that the reason our recipes taste so good is that we are just uniquely talented, we really have to give credit to our healthy ancestors.

How does knowing the cooking traditions of our ancestors help our food taste better? Here's a simple list:

❖ Sprouted grains are lighter in texture than regular whole grains and more flavorful than refined.

❖ Homemade broths and stocks are richer in flavor because all of the nutrients and taste have been pulled from the bones.

❖ Vegetables taste better when fresh and lightly sautéed, versus canned or even frozen. Plus, the color is a lot more vibrant, and they're more appetizing.

❖ "Slow and low" cooking creates tender, juicy meats and soft eggs and beans.

❖ Whole and real dairy products taste a lot better than skimmed, non-fat, or imitation products.

❖ Real butter tastes loads better than margarine or any other imitation butter spread.

❖ Recipes calling for produce taste so much better with garden fresh, vine or tree ripened produce, than they do with the aged, waxed, irradiated, and non-organic produce available at typical grocers.

❖ Unrefined sea salt and natural sweeteners have a fuller taste than their refined counterparts.

❖ Fresh, whole, and real food just tastes better than anything you can buy in a box, bag, or can.

More details of the unique cooking processes of these healthy societies are in the recipe section for easy reference. We call these little tips "Tasty Treasures" because the cooking techniques we have learned from our ancient ancestors are real treasures to us.

Section 3

From Our Kitchens to Yours

❖ ❖ ❖ ❖ ❖ ❖ ❖ ❖ ❖ ❖ ❖ ❖ ❖ ❖

Time Saving Tips

BECAUSE SPROUTING, SOAKING, AND MAKING your own butter, ice cream, pie, and other mouth-watering dishes can seem overwhelming, and because you can't always just dump the cooking responsibility on your spouse and kids, we have come up with some timesaving tips to help you spend as little time in the kitchen as possible. Of course, maybe the kitchen is your favorite place to be, and you have no other responsibilities that draw you elsewhere. In that case, you can ignore these tips.

❖ Sprout a big batch of wheat, and then dehydrate it and store it in a container in the fridge. This is great for making a quick chicken-pot pie, rolls, or something else that would otherwise take a few days. But if you have a sudden craving for cookies and you are trying to cut back on them, it's best to be out of it. Then you might just think, "Cookies sound good right now. If I get the spelt started now, then by Thursday I can have some."

❖ Make extra and freeze it. This works especially well with stocks and broths. Simply label and freeze, and then heat them up with vegetables for a quick chicken-vegetable soup. This also works for beans, by sprouting, cooking, and then freezing in jars.

27

❖ Make a big salad and keep it in the fridge. Tear lettuce, spinach, or whatever greens you choose. Add onions, carrots, and so forth, and keep it covered in the fridge throughout the week for a snack or as part of a meal.

❖ Use a Crock-pot. These are nice because it takes just a few minutes to chop up veggies or whatever you wish to throw in. They are great, not only because they save time, but also because they cook "slow and low" for you.

❖ Buy already prepared sprouted bread, tortillas, or even sprouted flours. This is a little less economical, but if you just don't have the time, ability, or desire to make your own sprouted breads, tortillas, and flour, they can be purchased at most health food stores or online. They keep nicely in the fridge and freezer.

❖ Make a meal chart and plan menus in advance, then plan your shopping list accordingly. Meal ideas can be divided between family members who get to decide what to have for dinner that night. Kids love this because they usually eat what they plan, even the veggies. If you're lucky, they will even help make it. If you're really lucky, they will make it for you when they get older.

❖ Make breakfast the night before. Whether it's chopped fruit and yogurt, Swiss oatmeal, or cracked wheat, it can be prepared the night before for a quick breakfast the next day. In the morning, just pull it from the fridge and eat, or heat it and eat. This is especially beneficial for feeding those brains that need energy for mental, emotional, and physical labor that the day may require.

Becoming Ingredient Savvy

We could use up a lot of paper listing all of the food brands we use, so instead, we will just tell you what standards we look for when shopping. The ingredients we look for are whole, basic ingredients. For example, we use sour cream that only contains cream and cultures; fertile eggs from free-range hens; butter from healthy, pasture-fed cows (or we make our own); and bread that's made from 100-percent whole grains or 100-percent whole sprouted grain. Actually, we do have a brand of sea salt we like the best. It's called Real Salt and is available for sale at www.realsalt.com.

We avoid buying anything with high fructose corn syrup, sugar, hydrogenated oils, soybean oils (soy suppresses the thyroid),[70] refined flour, monosodium glutamate (MSG), aspartame or other artificial sweeteners, food dyes, or artificial flavors. Because it's next to impossible to find anything on the condiment aisle without all or most of these ingredients in one item, we make a lot of our own or purchase healthier alternatives, such as Vegennaise (which is made with grape seed oil), at health food stores.

We also watch out for organic junk food. Just because it says it's organic doesn't mean it's healthy. For example, we are wary if the ingredient label says it's made with organic wheat flour enhanced with nutrients (which is another way of saying that all the nutrients have been taken out and they have sprayed five back in), organic sugar (a polite way of saying that it's still refined, addicting, and blood-sugar-altering, it was just grown without pesticides), and organic hydrogenated oils (a.k.a. organic artery cloggers). At that point, who cares if it's organic? We would still get sick from eating it.

Since we don't have our own cows or chickens, we are excited to have access to a great whole-food store, *Real Foods Market*, where we can buy meat and fresh milk from healthy, pasture-fed cows and the best eggs, with bright orange yolks from free-range chickens. They are just bursting with vitamin A and omega-3s. You can research stores in your area and see which ones sell healthy animal products.

What do you do if you are a recovering chocoholic and any amount of cocoa sends you flying off the wagon? Try using carob. It's a delicious and nourishing alternative to chocolate and has a wonderful flavor of its own. Any of our chocolate recipes can be substituted with carob, and vice versa. If you are having a chocolate craving, any of our carob recipes can be substituted with cocoa. Just make sure it's organic and raw, if possible.

Peanut butter may be used in any of our recipes as long as the only ingredient is peanuts, like Adams® brand peanut butter. Well, maybe not *any* recipe. Chili just wouldn't be the same with a big blob of peanut butter stirred in, nor would it blend in a marinated chicken wrap. Keep in mind, though, that peanuts are not as healthy as some believe, and lots of people are allergic to them. We like to use sunflower seed butter as a superior replacement because it has just as much protein and more vitamin E than peanut butter. It's delicious and tastes and smells so much like peanut butter that you and your kids won't miss peanut butter at all. Another peanut butter alternative is almond butter. It has a great flavor, especially if you buy the creamy kind and then add in your own almond bits, but it's also less economical than sunflower seed butter.

Our Favorite Kitchen Equipment

We would spend way too much time in our kitchens if it weren't for the help of a few appliances. Some things we just couldn't live without are a wheat grinder, stainless steel colander, glass bowls for soaking, Crock-Pot, food dehydrator, juicer, blender, large food processor (for making flourless breads), a small food processor (for quick, small foods), and stainless steel pots and pans. Stainless steel is the best for cooking, and it doesn't even emit parakeet-killing fumes like nonstick-coated cookware does.[71]

You may already have all or most of these things, but if you don't and you are concerned about spending money, just use the money you will save from the trips you won't have to make to the doctor's office, since you'll soon be too healthy to go.

Our Least Favorite Kitchen Equipment: Microwaves

Microwaves are a pretty nifty recent invention if you consider that they heat food quickly, but for the health conscious person, they can raise some concerns about health, not to mention what they do to the flavor and nutrient content of your food. We are not trying to preach to anyone about the dangers of microwaves, but we will give you a list of pros and cons with the hope that you will do your own research.

We like to consider ourselves fairly optimistic people. For this reason, we typically start with the pros, but since we are having a little trouble thinking of the pros right now, we will list the cons first. Then hopefully by the time we get to the pros section, we'll have some.

Cons:

- ❖ They kill all enzymes (little protein catalysts that help break down your food) and make the food much more difficult to digest.[72]
- ❖ Microwaves change the molecular structure of food so your body may not recognize it as anything nourishing or digestible.[73]
- ❖ A lot more nutrients are depleted through microwave cooking than through traditional cooking methods.[74]
- ❖ If you heat your food on plastic, it can leach into the food like an added ingredient that doesn't even taste good.[75]
- ❖ Free radicals and other carcinogens are formed in the food during microwaving.[76]
- ❖ There are a number of studies and warnings about microwave use that are alarming enough to raise doubts about their safety. Several Russian scientists and a Swiss man, Dr. Hans Hertzel, have done some interesting studies on microwave use that you can research for yourselves.[77]

Pros:

- ❖ If you like your food to look, taste, and bounce like rubber, and you don't care a stitch about the bioavailability of important nutrients decreasing in your food, then you've got yourself a winner.[78]

As a final note, we personally choose to heat and thaw our food using more traditional means than the microwave. Whether or not you choose to do the same, know that we are all about nutrition and flavor, and microwaving diminishes both.

Food for Thought

We feel it's a good idea to stock up on some essential foods in case of an emergency. This really is a good idea considering the economy and the hundreds of potential disasters that could prevent us from getting food from grocers. It's a good idea to have a supply of essentials that can keep you alive for a year, but at the minimum, three months. Foods that we feel are important to store, and that store well, are wheat, spelt, kamut, and other whole grains (whole berries that haven't been ground into flour yet, for a longer shelf life), raw honey, unrefined sea salt, dry beans or legumes, oil (extra virgin olive and coconut oils are good), and baking soda to use for leavening and for basic cleaning and tooth brushing, if needed. Brown rice can be stored as well, even though it has a tendency to have a shorter shelf life than white rice (about two years versus thirty years). Rinsing it well and airing it out can get rid of the stale flavor if rancidity is suspected, but sprouting it brings it back to life and creates more nutrients. For a complete whole-foods storage list made of wholesome, nutritious food, keep reading.

It's also a great idea, and a fun one, to have your own vegetable garden, even if it's on your back porch in little pots. This is the most economical and healthiest way to get your produce. Plus, if you have tons of extra food, and your neighbors pretend they are not home when you walk around the neighborhood with a bag of give-away zucchini, you can store or preserve some for the winter. (Not necessarily zucchini, but other storable winter produce, like winter squash, potatoes, carrots, and onions.) Canning, freezing, and dehydrating are all great ways to preserve garden produce that doesn't store well through winter.

Complete One-Year Food Storage List

This is Michelle's one-year whole-food storage list for a family of four. (She's had so many people ask for it that she decided to put it in our cookbook.) She created her own food storage list because she believes you should store what you and your family will actually eat (like an extension to your pantry). Of course, eating quality seasonal foods is the best option for regular meals, but this food list contains foods that can be stored in your home as the best choices to keep you fed, nourished, and—most importantly—self-reliant! These days, having an edible "extended pantry" that has a year's worth of food for your own family (that they will actually eat) is more valuable than its weight in gold!

You can use this list or modify it to fit your own desires. For example, you may prefer to have most of your sweeteners come from raw honey and unrefined sugar and forgo the other sweeteners listed. It is a guideline with recommended approximate amounts, but you get to choose what you purchase and eat regularly in your family to equal the amounts suggested. When adapting this list, determine how many adults and children are in your family and what whole foods they like to eat. Then slowly build your supply by purchasing a few extra items each time you shop. Before you know it, you will have the greatest supply of food around. This list also contains non-food items, like toilet paper, that may be great to have on hand in case of an emergency.

Water: 56–84 gallons

This calculation takes into account drinking, cooking, and basic hygiene purposes. This is only a two-week supply and is the suggested minimum amount needed. Store at least fourteen gallons per person, or ideally twenty-one gallons per person, in your household. You can buy one-gallon jugs of filtered spring water at your local market. A great way to stock up on your water is to buy five- to ten-gallon-sized jugs every time you go to the store until you fulfill your family's requirement. Be creative and do whatever works best for you!

Organic Grains and Seeds: 1200 lbs

- ❖ Hard white wheat: 200 lbs
- ❖ Soft "pastry" white wheat: 200 lbs
- ❖ Popcorn kernels: 125 lbs
- ❖ Tinkyáda® brown rice pasta: 70 lbs
- ❖ Hard red wheat: 50 lbs
- ❖ Rye berries: 50 lbs
- ❖ Whole-grain brown rice: 50 lbs
- ❖ Old-fashioned rolled oats: 50 lbs
- ❖ Spelt or kamut berries: 300 lbs
- ❖ Whole-grain quinoa: 25 lbs
- ❖ Raw almonds: 50 lbs
- ❖ Whole-grain millet: 10 lbs
- ❖ Raw sunflower seeds: 10 lbs
- ❖ Raw pumpkin seeds: 10 lbs

Organic Beans and Legumes: 240 lbs

- ❖ Pinto beans, dry: 75 lbs
- ❖ Red beans or kidney beans, dry: 75 lbs
- ❖ Black beans, dry: 50 lbs
- ❖ Small white beans, dry: 20 lbs
- ❖ Whole green peas, dry: 10 lbs
- ❖ Red lentils, dry: 10 lbs

Organic Healthy Sweeteners: 188 lbs

- ❖ Dehydrated cane juice (Sucanat): 75 lbs
- ❖ Honey, raw and local: 30 lbs
- ❖ Raw blue/amber agave: 6 gallons = 48 lbs
- ❖ 100 percent Fruit jam: 18 jars x 10 oz each = 11 lbs
- ❖ Molasses, unsulfered: 1 gallon = 8 lbs
- ❖ Ah!laska brand chocolate syrup: 6 x 22 oz each = 8 lbs
- ❖ Chocolate chips, naturally sweetened: 12 x 10 oz each = 8 lbs

Organic Healthy Fats and Oils: 137 lbs

- ❖ Virgin coconut oil: 4 gallons = 32 lbs
- ❖ Coconut milk, whole and unsweetened: 30 x 15 oz each = 28 lbs
- ❖ Olives (preservative free), canned: 24 x 15 oz cans = 22 lbs
- ❖ Sunbutter, or sunflower seed butter: 18 x 16 oz each = 18 lbs
- ❖ Real Butter (store in freezer): 16 lbs
- ❖ Vegenaise®, mayonnaise substitute (store in refrigerator): 6 x 32 oz each = 12 lbs
- ❖ Extra virgin olive oil: 1 gallon = 8 lbs
- ❖ Cod liver oil: 3 x 8 oz each = 1½ lbs

Organic Fruits: 185 lbs

- ❖ Applesauce, unsweetened: 12 x 47 oz each = 33 lbs

❖ Peaches, canned (in 100 percent juice): 30 x 15 oz each = 28 lbs

❖ Pears, canned (in 100 percent juice): 30 x 15 oz each = 28 lbs

❖ Pineapple, canned (in 100 percent juice): 13 x 20 oz each = 16 lbs

❖ Dr. Shultz's Superfood Plus: 12 x 14 oz each = 10½ lbs

❖ Banana Slices, dried: 12 lbs

❖ Apple Slices, dried: 12 lbs

❖ Mandarin Oranges, canned (in 100 percent juice): 18 x 11 oz each = 12 lbs

❖ Raisins: 4 x 32 oz pkgs = 8 lbs

❖ Blueberries, frozen: 12 x 10 oz each = 7½ lbs

❖ Dark sweet cherries, frozen: 12 x 10 oz each = 7½ lbs

❖ Raspberries or strawberries, frozen: 12 x 10 oz each = 7½ lbs

❖ Goji berries, dried: 3 lbs

Organic Vegetables: total = 214 lbs

❖ Tomatoes, diced/pureed in cans or frozen: 30 x 28 oz each = 52 lbs

❖ Tomato sauce, canned or frozen: 30 x 15 oz each = 28 lbs

❖ Green beans, frozen or canned: 30 x 15 oz each = 28 lbs

❖ Corn, frozen or canned: 30 x 15 oz each = 28 lbs

❖ Chopped potatoes, frozen or dried: 16 lbs

❖ Chopped Onions, dried: 15 lbs

❖ Salsa, canned: 12 x 17 oz each = 12½ lbs

❖ Pumpkin puree, canned: 10 x 15 oz each = 9 lbs

❖ Tomato paste, canned: 24 x 6 oz each = 9 lbs

❖ Sliced carrots, dried: 5 lbs

❖ Chopped green sweet peppers, dried: 4 lbs (4 #10 cans)

❖ Chopped broccoli, frozen: 6 x 10 oz each = 3½ lbs

❖ Chopped broccoli, freeze-dried: 3 lbs (6 #10 cans)

❖ Sliced celery, freeze-dried: 1½ lbs (6 #10 cans)

Grass-fed/Pastured Meats: 112 lbs

❖ Whole chickens, frozen: 6 x 6 lbs each = 36 lbs

❖ Ground beef or bison, frozen: 16 lbs

❖ Boneless chicken breasts, frozen: 12 lbs

❖ Pot roast, frozen: 3 lbs each x 4 = 12 lbs

❖ Chicken chunks (preservative free), canned: 12 x 12 oz each = 9 lbs

❖ Bacon (nitrate free), frozen: 12 pkgs x 12 oz each = 9 lbs

❖ Sausage (nitrate free), frozen: 12 pkgs x 8 oz each = 6 lbs

❖ Chicken or Wild-Caught Tuna, canned: 24 x 4.5 oz each = 6 lbs

❖ Applegate Farms® beef hot dogs (no nitrates or preservatives): 4 lbs

❖ Wild game deer or buffalo jerky, dried: 2 lbs

Organic and Grass-fed Milk Products: 65 lbs

❖ Meyenberg® goat milk, canned: 24 x 15 oz each = 22 lbs

❖ Meyenberg® goat Milk, powdered: 12 x 12 oz each = 9 lbs

❖ Alta Dena brand cheddar cheese, raw (store in freezer): 24 x 12 oz each = 18 lbs

❖ Whole whey, powdered: 10 lbs

❖ Organic Valley brand cultured cream cheese (store in freezer): 12 x 8 oz each = 6 lbs

Organic Spices: total = 43 lbs

❖ Redmond RealSalt® sea salt: 25 lbs

❖ Chili powder: 2 lbs

❖ Dried, sliced chives: 2 lbs

- Onion powder: 1 lb
- Ground cumin: 1 lb
- Ground cinnamon: 1 lb
- Garlic powder: 1 lb
- Dried thyme: 1 lb
- Dried sweet basil: 1 lb
- Dried oregano: 1 lb
- Dried dill: 1 lb
- Dried parsley flakes: 1 lb
- Dried cilantro flakes: 1 lb
- Ground paprika: 1 lb
- Dried crushed red pepper flakes: 1 lb
- Ground black pepper: 1 lb

Other Organic Cooking Essentials:

- Chicken broth: 30 x 32 oz each = 60 lbs
- Beef broth: 24 x 32 oz each = 48 lbs
- Apple cider vinegar, raw: 1 gallon = 8 lbs
- Pure vanilla extract: 4 x 16 oz each = 4 lbs
- Shredded coconut, dried and unsweetened: 4 lbs
- Cacao/Cocoa powder or carob powder: 5 lbs
- Tapioca, granulated: 2 x 30 oz each = 3½ lbs
- Bob's Red Mill® baking powder: 3 lbs
- Bob's Red Mill® baking soda: 3 lbs
- Rapunzel brand cornstarch or arrowroot Powder: 2 lbs
- Rapunzel brand or Fleischmann's™ brand baking yeast: 1 lb

Non-Food Items:

- Chest freezer: 1 (for storing all frozen foods)
- Compact camping stove with small propane tanks: 1
- Global Sun Oven, solar cooking oven: 1 (excellent solar cooker! Even in winter)

- Hand Can Opener: 2
- Redmond Clay®: 3 lbs
- Peppermint essential oil, therapeutic grade: 1 x 15 ml
- Lavender essential oil, therapeutic grade: 1 x 15 ml
- Tea tree essential oil, therapeutic grade: 1 x 15 ml
- Lemon essential oil, therapeutic grade: 1 x 15 ml
- Bandages (latex free): 2 boxes
- Witch hazel: 4 bottles
- Hydrogen peroxide: 4 bottles
- Rubbing alcohol: 2 bottles
- Distilled white vinegar: 4 gallons (for cleaning)
- Liquid laundry soap (free of perfume and dyes): 5 bottles
- Liquid laundry softener (free of perfume and dyes): 4 bottles
- Liquid dish soap (free of perfume and dyes): 4 bottles
- Dr. Bronner's brand liquid soap: 1 gallon
- Dr. Bronner's brand soap bars: 12 bars
- Kirk's Castile brand soap bars: 6 bars
- Shampoo: 6 bottles
- Conditioner: 5 bottles
- Hand and body lotion (unscented): 5 bottles, and/or Organic Palm Shortening (Tropical Traditions) for skin moisturizing.
- Burt's Bees® beeswax lip balm: 6 sticks
- Toothpaste (no fluoride or sodium lauryl sulfate (SLS)): 6 tubes
- Floss: 6 spools
- Toothbrushes, soft bristle: 16
- Shaving razors: 4 pkgs
- Maxi pads: 8 standard pkgs
- Panty liners: 3 pkgs
- Unscented wipes: 4 large boxes

- ❖ Toilet paper: 144 large rolls
- ❖ Paper towels: 64 large rolls
- ❖ Cotton balls: 2 pkgs of 200
- ❖ Notebooks/Paper: 1,200 sheets,
  or twelve 100-sheet, spiral-bound
  books
- ❖ Pens: 4 pkgs of 4
- ❖ Permanent Markers: 3 pkgs of 4 (for
  labeling)
- ❖ Transparent Tape: 6 rolls
- ❖ Crayons: 3 standard pkgs
- ❖ Coloring Books: 4
- ❖ Aluminum foil: 2 standard rolls
- ❖ Plastic wrap: 1 roll
- ❖ Parchment paper: 1 roll
- ❖ Plastic bags (sealable gallon-sized):
  2 boxes
- ❖ Plastic bags (sealable sandwich-
  sized): 2 boxes
- ❖ Paper lunch sacks: 1 pkg
- ❖ 3" x 6" beeswax candles: 10
- ❖ Beeswax taper candlesticks: 6 pairs
  (12 total)
- ❖ Handheld candlestick holders: 1
- ❖ Lantern that holds a candle: 1
- ❖ Matches: 3 big boxes
- ❖ Flashlights (and batteries): 4
- ❖ Lantern, battery operated (and
  batteries): 1
- ❖ Extra batteries: 12 of each size
  needed
- ❖ Disposable filtration masks (latex
  free): pack of 20
- ❖ Vinyl gloves (latex free), disposable:
  box of 100

Section 4

Treasured & Tasty Recipes

❖ ❖ ❖ ❖ ❖ ❖ ❖ ❖ ❖ ❖ ❖ ❖ ❖

Recipes for Success

❖ ❖ ❖ ❖ ❖ ❖ ❖ ❖ ❖ ❖ ❖ ❖ ❖ ❖ ❖

❖ ❖

Sprouting for Dummies & Smarties

❖ ❖

Sprouting Grains

We hope you will find sprouting simple and fun instead of intimidating. Through trial and lots of error, we have come up with a great way to sprout with minimal effort. We have tested three different methods and have rated them for ease, with a zero being poor and a ten being perfect.

The Mason jar method uses a Mason jar and mesh lid. It's great if you are looking to make alcohol (which we don't recommend) but not necessarily great for sprouting. Grain needs good air circulation to sprout instead of ferment, and this method leaves little air circulation and makes only small batches at a time. We give this one a 1.5, maybe a 2 if you're lucky.

Another idea is to line a shallow (a woven basket) with cheesecloth, raise it off the counter, and fill it with moist wheat. This works every time. However, if you neglect it, the sprout basket can end up looking like an upside-down Chia Pet, and you'll spend hours at a time pulling the long sprouts from the cheesecloth and basket. This one scores a little higher. Overall we give it a 5.325 as long as you keep your eye on it.

Fortunately, there's the colander method. It's the easiest and by far the most preferred way to sprout. We give it a 9.989. It would be a 10 if there wasn't the off-chance possibility of forgetting about it when you go out of town for a week and coming back to find that it's moldy. (But at least you can toss the remains into the garden, cover them with a little soil, and have wheat grass in a week.) Here's how the colander method works. You fill a glass bowl with wheat, spelt, or kamut, cover the wheat with filtered water, let it sit for eight to ten hours, then dump it into a stainless-steel colander. Put the colander in a warm place and cover it with a damp cloth or paper towels. Rinse it once a day, and in a day or two, you should see cute, little tails growing.

Now you can grind up the moist wheat with tails to make whatever you wish, or you can dehydrate it and run it through your wheat grinder to make regular wheat flour that can be used in any recipe. How simple is that?

Many of our recipes are flour-free because we use fresh, sprouted wheat, spelt, or kamut that you can run through a good food processor.

Find one that has the capacity to hold several cups of food and has a strong motor. A lot of our other recipes include dehydrated sprouted wheat, spelt, or kamut that has been run through a wheat grinder. Just be sure to actually dehydrate the wheat first, or you'll end up with a bunch of gunk stuck in the rotating device and a broken grinder.

Another way to prepare grains without sprouting that still increases nutrients, digests gluten, and knocks out phytic acid is to soak and sour. In this case, non-sprouted, freshly ground whole wheat flour can be used by mixing and soaking it overnight with a little lemon, liquid whey, or raw apple cider vinegar and water.[79] This is great for pancakes and a lot of other bread recipes, including our sourdough recipes. The cool thing about sourdough is that it doesn't taste sour if you add a little baking soda to the batter. Plus you get the bonus of conducting a scientific experiment by adding soda (a base) to the acidic soured dough and watching the two have a chemical reaction. This makes the bread or batter rise and fluff. Many of our recipes use the soured-plus-soda technique or use soda in place of yeast for yeast-free breads. When souring, just remember not to soak and sour already sprouted and dehydrated flour, because soaking and souring also digests gluten, and then you'll digest so much gluten that you'll end up flipping solitary crumbs on a griddle instead of pancakes.

❖   ❖   ❖

Sprouted Wheat or Wheat Flour

Makes: 6 cups / Sprout time: 36 hours / Dehydrate time: 12–24 hours

- ❖   6 cups organic wheat berries (hard red, hard white, soft white, spelt, or kamut)
- ❖   filtered water

Rinse wheat berries, then place in a large stainless steel or glass bowl with enough filtered water to cover them by 3 inches. Soak away from direct sunlight for at least 12 but no more than 24 hours. Drain into a large, stainless steel colander and rinse well. Leave on countertop covered with a wet cloth or dish towel. Keep a plate underneath to catch any water drips. Let the grain sprout in colander for about 12 hours, rinsing once or twice. You should see tiny white buds (sprouts) at the pointed end of the grain. Don't let them sprout any longer, or they won't contain enough gluten to hold together in baking. *(continued)*

The wheat can be used at this soft, sprouted stage, or it can be dried on dehydrator screens at 110°F or on a cookie sheet in an oven no hotter than 150°F. When thoroughly dry, it is ready to be ground using a regular flour mill. If you'd rather wait, it can be stored in an airtight container and kept in the fridge or freezer until you are ready to grind it. The ground flour can be stored in the freezer for several months.

❖ ❖ ❖

Sprouted Brown Rice

Makes: 4 cups / Sprout time 36–48 hours / Dehydrate time: 12–24 hours

- ❖ 4 cups brown rice
- ❖ 5 cups filtered water

Place the rice in a stainless steel strainer and rinse well. When rinsed, place in a glass bowl and cover with filtered water. Soak on the counter for 12 to 24 hours. Afterward, pour it back into the strainer and rinse again. Set strainer over the glass bowl to catch drips, and cover it with a warm, damp cloth. Place in a warm place (like the oven with only the light on) for 3 to 4 days until the rice sprouts. Rinse twice a day and keep the cloth damp.

Rice is a little trickier to sprout than wheat, but we have found that if you keep it warm and moist, it sprouts well. Sprouting the rice in a strainer in a bowl helps it retain some of the moisture that's lost.

When the rice has sprouted, rinse it again, then spread it on dehydrator sheets and dehydrate. Once it is dry, you can steam it and use it in rice dishes. In its moist form, you can boil it, using half as much added water as you normally would.

❖ ❖ ❖

Sprouted Rolled Wheat

Makes: 2 cups / Soak time: 36 hours / Dry time: 12–24 hours

- ❖ 2 cups organic white wheat or spelt
- ❖ filtered water

Rinse wheat berries, then place in a large stainless steel or glass bowl with enough filtered water to cover them by 3 inches. Follow the directions for sprouting in the "Sprouted Wheat or Wheat Flour" recipe found earlier in this section.

Once the wheat has sprouted, spread the soaked grain on a flat surface and roll with a rolling pin. Spread the sprouted and rolled grain on dehydrator screens and dehydrate at 135°F, or spread on a cookie sheet in an oven no hotter than 150°F. Remove when completely dry.

Rolled wheat may be used in hot cereal, granola, cookies, and as a rolled oats substitute.

❖ ❖ ❖

Sprouted Quinoa

Makes: approx. 2 Cups (1 lb) of Sprouts / Sprout time: 17–24 hours

- ❖ 1 cup quinoa seed
- ❖ filtered water

Quinoa (pronounced "keen-wa") is considered a super-grain, but it is technically a seed. It is higher in nutrition and beneficial fat than any other seed or grain[80] and can be used like rice or in place of coconut or rolled oats. It's very important to rinse it thoroughly before use or it will end up tasting kind of like soap.

Place 1 cup of quinoa seed into a medium stainless steel mesh strainer. Rinse it underwater for a minute until there are no more soaplike bubbles. Leaving the rinsed quinoa in the mesh strainer, place the strainer into a medium bowl. Fill the bowl with enough cool (60 to 70°F) water to cover it. Allow seeds to soak for 20 to 30 minutes. Rinse again, leaving soaked quinoa in strainer. Place it back in the bowl, without water this time. Place a damp cloth over the top so the seeds do not dry out during the sprouting process. Set anywhere out of direct sunlight and at room temperature (70° is optimal) for 8 to 12 hours. Rinse and drain again. Leave covered with damp cloth for another 8 to 12 hours. Rinse and drain again.

We usually stop here. Drain as thoroughly as possible; the goal during the final 8 to 12 hours is to minimize the surface moisture of your sprouts. They will store best in the refrigerator if they are dry to the touch. *(continued)*

When it is done sprouting, transfer your sprouted quinoa to a plastic bag or sealed container of choice—glass is ideal. Store them in your refrigerator. When the quinoa sprouts are very short, they can last for up to two weeks in the refrigerator.

Note: *Quinoa can be sprouted for a few days, but its texture will change from a soft, crunchy sprout to a very soft sprout. If you sprout it long you'll have to use it soon, as it won't keep well.*

❖ ❖ ❖

Basic Millet

Makes: 4 cups cooked millet / Prep time: 1 minute / Cook time: 40 minutes

- ❖ ½ cup millet, rinsed
- ❖ 1½ cups chicken or beef broth
- ❖ 1–2 Tbsps. butter or coconut oil

Rinse millet thoroughly in a mesh strainer. Melt butter over medium heat in a medium saucepan and add millet. Stir and brown for about 2 minutes. Add the broth and bring to a boil, then cover and reduce to a simmer for about 30 minutes. Remove from heat and let stand for a few minutes, then fluff with a fork. This can be used like rice.

❖ ❖

Sprouting Nuts & Seeds

Sprouting nuts and seeds is quite similar to sprouting grains, and it accomplishes the same goal, which is to increase nutrients and neutralize phytic acid. Any nut or seed can be soaked for at least seven hours to get rid of enzyme inhibitors. They are easy to sprout as well.

To soak, place nuts or seeds in a glass bowl and cover with filtered water. The water line should be about an inch above the nuts so they will have plenty of water to absorb. After 8 to 12 hours, the nuts can be placed in a stainless steel colander or strainer and covered with a damp cloth and rinsed daily until tails begin to grow.

Larger nuts, like almonds, require a longer sprout time than seeds, but since raw, sprout-able almonds are hard to find, you'll likely end up just soaking them rather than actually sprouting them.

Sprouted Sesame Seeds

Buy them hulled or shell them yourself. Place seeds in a small colander and rinse well. Wet a clean dish towel, ring it out, and place it on top. Rinse the seeds 4 times a day for 2 to 3 days.

❖ ❖ ❖

Sprouted Pumpkin Seeds

Buy them hulled or shell them yourself. Place seeds in a small colander and rinse well. Wet a clean dish towel, ring it out, and place it on top. Rinse the seeds 3 times a day for 3 days.

❖ ❖ ❖

Traditional Almonds

Makes: 2¼ cups / Soak time: 8–24 hours / Dry time: 12–24 hours

- ❖ 2 cups almonds, raw (if possible)
- ❖ 3 cups filtered water
- ❖ 1 tsp. sea salt

In a glass or stainless steel bowl, add all ingredients and let soak for 7 to 24 hours. Drain and spread soaked almonds in a single layer in a food dehydrator at 145°F or spread them on a stainless steel cookie sheet and dry in a 150°F oven (no higher) for 12 to 24 hours, until crunchy and crisp. Store in an airtight container. This recipe can be used with pecans and walnuts too and is based on the Crispy Almonds recipe found in *Nourishing Traditions* by Sally Fallon, page 515.

Sprouting Beans & Legumes

Beans that haven't been sprouted contain a difficult-to-digest starch and may cause bloating, cramps, or painful gas. So unless you actually enjoy these uncomfortable symptoms after eating beans, we suggest sprouting. The process of sprouting beans, as well as grains, converts starches into vegetable sugars,[81] making it much easier to digest and offering a rich array of vitamins and enzymes in addition.

Beans are one food that should definitely be cooked before eating, and not just because they taste so nasty raw. Raw beans, especially raw kidney beans, can be toxic. Luckily, cooking neutralizes these toxins.[82] But even though the actual bean is toxic, bean sprouts (the greens grown from the seed) are actually quite nutritious raw.

Sprouted beans can be used in any recipe that calls for regular beans. They cook twice as fast as beans that haven't been sprouted, and they can also be canned or frozen for future use.

You can use any amount of bean, legume, lentil, or pea when sprouting. (Use whole peas, not split peas.) If the beans are too old or have been sterilized, they won't sprout, and after a couple days you will end up with a colander full of smelly, slimy beans.

To sprout beans, place them in a large stainless steel or glass bowl with enough filtered water to cover them by 3 inches. Let them soak for 12 hours. Next, drain and rinse in a stainless steel colander. Place a plate underneath to catch any water drips. Cover with a damp cloth to keep them moist. They will need to be rinsed very thoroughly every morning and evening for 3 to 4 days to rinse off any bacteria, fungus, or mold that may try to form. Keep away from direct sunlight and make sure the air temperature is no lower than 70°F.

When sprouted, they will triple in size, and you will see sprout tails that are ¾ to 1 inch long. At this point, they can be refrigerated for up to a week, or they can be cooked low and slow for use in chili, tacos, soups, dips, and so forth.

❖ ❖ ❖

Sprouting Peas

Makes: approx. 2 cups / Prep time: 12 hours

- ❖ 1 cup dried whole peas
- ❖ warm, filtered water

Put the peas (seeds) into a bowl and cover them with warm water (about 80°F). The warm water temperature is the initial temperature only—it's intended to cool off as time passes. Allow the seeds to soak for a full 12 hours. Be sure to examine your peas after soaking them to make sure there are no hard seeds lurking at the bottom. If there are, throw them out. They are easy to spot, as they are smaller than those that are swollen with water.

Pour soaked pea seeds into a stainless steel colander. Rinse well in cool water. Allow to drain thoroughly. Set anywhere out of direct sunlight and at room temperature (70°F is optimal) with a damp cloth over the top. Rinse and drain at least three more times every 8 to 12 hours. Depending on the climate, the time of year you are sprouting, and your personal preference, you may rinse and drain again at 8-to-12-hour intervals for up to 6 days. However, we prefer to sprout only to the point where most of the seeds have sprouted tiny ¼ inch roots, which is typically after just three rinse and drain cycles.

❖   ❖   ❖

Cooking Sprouted Beans

Makes: 5 cups / Cook time: 1½–2 hours

- ❖ Sprouted beans
- ❖ filtered water
- ❖ sea salt

Place beans in a pot and cover with water by a couple inches. Bring them to a boil on high heat, and then turn the heat down to medium. Continue boiling uncovered for about 10 to 15 minutes. Reduce to a simmer and cover, cooking for about 1½ to 2 hours, or until tender. Drain the liquid and discard.

❖ ❖

❖ ❖

Basic Dairy Recipes

❖ ❖

It's always best to use real dairy products for best health and flavor. For example, use real sour cream instead of imitation, butter instead of margarine or shortening, heavy whipping cream instead of whipped topping, and so on. Brown Cow™ makes really yummy yogurt that has live, active cultures with the cream on the top. It can even be used as a sour cream substitute.

If you are one of the many people who can't have cow dairy or don't want to use it, try goat milk instead. Goat dairy is much more common than cow across the globe, and it is generally easier to digest than cow's milk.[83] Just look for brands that don't actually taste like a goat.

❖   ❖   ❖

Whole Plain Yogurt

Makes: 32 oz. / Prep time: 5 minutes / Cook time: 3 hours

- ❖ 1 partially used 32-oz yogurt container with about ¼ cup of leftover plain yogurt that has live, active bacteria
- ❖ 3¾ cups raw milk

Wash out yogurt container and replace remaining yogurt into the bottom. Stir in the milk and blend well. Place the lid on top and poke a meat thermometer through the center. Place the container in a pan of hot water on the stove and turn to the lowest setting. When the temperature inside yogurt container reaches 105°F, start timing for three hours. Watch closely to make sure the temperature doesn't reach above 118°F. After 3 hours, remove the container from the heat and refrigerate. Homemade yogurt has a different texture than store bought and usually has more whey, or the liquid that often separates from yogurt. Whey can be used in place of lemon water in any recipe, including smoothie recipes.

❖   ❖   ❖

Yogurt Cheese

Makes: 1–2 cups / Prep time: 12–24 hours or more

Prepare homemade yogurt using the Whole Plain Yogurt recipe. When done, place the yogurt in cheesecloth or in a strainer over a bowl and refrigerate for 12 to 24 hours, or until firm and creamy. This can be sweetened with a natural sweetener and fruit or mixed with onions, garlic, and sea salt for a veggie dip or bagel spread.

❖   ❖   ❖

Cream

- ❖ 1 gallon non-homogenized milk, preferably raw

Let the milk sit for a few hours in the fridge and allow the cream to rise to the top naturally. Hold the milk jug over a large bowl, poke a hole in the bottom of the milk jug, and allow all of the "skim" milk to drain into the bowl. When it gets close to draining the cream, stop it and pour the cream out of the top of the milk jug into a separate container.

Note: warm milk seems to yield more cream than cold milk.

❖   ❖   ❖

Fresh Butter

Makes: approx. ½ cup / Prep time: 25–30 minutes, if using jar method

- ❖ cream from 1 gallon non-homogenized milk, preferably raw
- ❖ ⅛ tsp. sea salt

Let cream sit at room temperature until it reaches between 55 and 60°F.

Jar Method: Pour cream into a mason jar with a tightly fitting lid. Sprinkle with sea salt. Tighten lid and shake for about 25 minutes until butter is yellow and separated from the buttermilk. Strain and rinse with water until water is clear. Press the butter until most of the water is out. Salt to taste. Keep refrigerated. Keeps for about 1 week in the fridge. Use buttermilk in recipes in place of lemon water.

Blender Method: Place cream in blender and blend on low speed until the butter "breaks" and separates. Strain out the buttermilk. Rinse with water. Press out the water and sprinkle with salt. Keep refrigerated.

❖ ❖

Stocks & Broths Basics

❖ ❖

What did healthy societies of the past do for enzyme-rich food when all of their raw summer food was gone for the winter? They ate soups made with rich broths and stocks, which act like raw food because they attract digestive enzymes to the meal.[84] Plus, stocks and broths have healing properties that have been used as nature's medicine for centuries. If you aren't able to make these broths yourself, there are some traditionally made broths at most health food stores. However, it is much more economical to make them yourself.

Note: When homemade broth is cold, it is gelatinous (from the healthy bones it came from), but it will liquefy again when heated.

❖   ❖   ❖

Beef Stock

Makes: 1 gallon / Prep time: 20 minutes / Cook time: 12–72 hours

- ❖   3 lbs. beef marrow and knucklebones
- ❖   2 lbs. meaty bones, pre-cooked (rib, neck, and so forth.)
- ❖   3 qts. filtered water
- ❖   2 Tbsps. apple cider vinegar
- ❖   1 large onion, coarsely chopped
- ❖   several garlic cloves, peeled

Place marrow and knucklebones in an eleven-quart stainless steel stock pot. Add the water and vinegar, and let it sit for about an hour. Add vegetables and bring to a boil over high heat. It is important to remove any scum or debris that rises to the top while bringing it to a boil. A slotted spoon works well for this. Reduce heat, cover, and simmer for at least 12 but no more than 72 hours. Pour the broth through a mesh strainer into a large bowl and let it cool in the refrigerator. Remove the congealed fat that rises to the top. Transfer to four quart-sized containers. Keep refrigerated or freeze for long-term storage.

❖   ❖   ❖

Chicken Stock

Makes: 1 gallon / Prep time: 20 minutes / Cook time: 12–24 hours

- ❖ 5 lbs. free-range, organic, whole chicken bones, precooked with meat removed
- ❖ ½ gallon–¾ gallon cold filtered water
- ❖ 1 Tbsp. raw apple cider vinegar

Place the chicken bones in an 11-quart stainless steel stockpot with cold water and vinegar. Let stand for 30 minutes to an hour to let the vinegar draw the minerals out of the bones. Bring to a boil over high heat, using a slotted spoon to remove any scum or debris that may rise to the top. Reduce heat to low, cover, and simmer for 12 to 24 hours. Pour the stock through a mesh strainer into a large bowl and refrigerate until the fat congeals at the top. Spoon the fat off the top and transfer the broth to four quart-sized containers. Keep refrigerated or freeze for long-term storage.

❖ ❖

Natural Sweeteners 101

❖ ❖

There are many different kinds of natural sweeteners and they all have different uses. There are so many that we have decided to go over which ones we use and why so you don't have to figure that out on your own—unless you really want to.

❖ Dehydrated cane juice, or unrefined cane sugar, is granulated and brown. It has a rich molasses content and contains a variety of micronutrients including chromium, which is important for sugar metabolism.[85] Since it's dry, it can be substituted for white or brown sugar on a 1 to 1 ratio. The commercial names for this sweetener are Organic Whole Cane Sugar and Sucanat (SUgar CAne NATural). They're both found in most health food stores.

❖ Pure maple syrup comes in two grades that we have seen; grade A and grade B. Grade B has been boiled down more and has more nutrients and flavor than grade A, but it's also more expensive. Since we should use sweeteners sparingly, we use both grade A and B in our cooking.

❖ Raw honey has many beneficial properties, including internal and external healing properties. It can even help with seasonal allergies.[86] Cooking destroys all of the good qualities about honey, so it's best to use it raw whenever possible. We buy raw honey that hasn't been cooked or filtered and is taken from local bees.

❖ Agave has a light flavor and a low glycemic index, but it's a controversial sweetener because it's made of fructose. Some say that nectar processed from plants other than the blue agave plant contain toxins and that the fructose content causes health problems.[87] We've looked into these allegations and have formed our own opinion. We feel that using agave, especially raw, blue or amber agave, in place of white sugar won't cause any health problems. And we definitely think it's of more value than high fructose corn syrup! Do your own research on this sweetener before deciding to use it or not.

If you are uncomfortable using it, it can easily be substituted with pure maple syrup or raw honey.

❖ Stevia is a plant that has a sweet flavor but no actual sugars. It's almost like nature's safe, blood-sugar-stabilizing version of aspartame. Stevia is several times sweeter than sugar and can be found in powdered or liquid form. Very little is needed for sweetening. We find that stevia is great for adding to warm drinks for a little sweet flavor but not as useful in baking desserts because it provides no bulk. Stevia also has an aftertaste that some people don't care for.

❖ ❖

Recipes for Taste

❖ ❖ ❖ ❖ ❖ ❖ ❖ ❖ ❖ ❖ ❖ ❖ ❖ ❖

Drinks, Smoothies, & Popsicles

Tasty Treasure #1

If you want the nutrients of fresh veggie juices but don't care for the flavor, they can be added to fruit smoothies. Any liquid sweetener can be used in the following beverage recipes, such as pure maple syrup, raw blue/amber agave or raw honey.

Tasty Treasure #2

We recommend the Blendtec® blender. See recommended equipment for where to buy one. Just be sure not to let your teenagers conduct scientific "will it blend" experiments with it, lest you find your cell phone and car keys missing one day.

Traditional Mild Grain Drink

Makes: approx. 1½ cups / Soak time: 8 hours

- ❖ 1 cup organic whole wheat or barley
- ❖ 2 cups filtered water
- ❖ a squeeze of fresh lemon juice
- ❖ 1½ tsp. raw honey or pure maple syrup

Combine the wheat or barley and water and soak overnight in a glass bowl. In the morning, strain the soaked grains, reserving the liquid in a cup. Add a squeeze of lemon juice and some honey or maple syrup to the liquid and enjoy!

❖   ❖   ❖

Almond Milk

Makes: 4 cups / Prep time: 10 minutes / Soak time: 7 hours

- ❖ 2 cups almonds, soaked for 7 hours
- ❖ 4 cups filtered water
- ❖ ½ tsp. pure vanilla extract
- ❖ 1–2 Tbsps. pure maple syrup or raw honey

Combine all ingredients and blend well. Strain the liquid (this is the almond milk) and keep it in a quart jar with a tightly fitting lid in the refrigerator. Use within one week. The remaining almond "pulp" can be used in granola or cereal or can be thrown out for compost.

❖ ❖ ❖

Chocolate Milk

Makes: approx. 4½ cups / Prep time: 5 minutes

- ❖ 3½ cups raw milk
- ❖ 1 cup filtered water
- ❖ 1–2 Tbsps. organic cacao powder or carob powder
- ❖ 2 Tbsps. maple syrup or raw blue/amber agave

Combine all ingredients and blend well. Keep chilled.

❖ ❖ ❖

Carrot Apple Juice

Makes: 1½ cups / Prep time: 9 minutes

- ❖ 4 carrots, scrubbed with the tops cut off
- ❖ ½ cup pineapple, peeled and cored or 1 orange, peeled
- ❖ 1 small handful spinach or kale leaves, rinsed well with stems cut off
- ❖ 1 sweet apple, stems and cores removed

Combine all ingredients and run them through a juicer. Skim off any foam that rises to the top. For most people, especially children, dilute juice 30 to 50 percent with filtered water, whole milk, or cream. You can also add a little lemon-flavored fish oil to it and shake it up to blend the oil. Serve immediately. What a tasty combination!

❖ ❖ ❖

Veggie-licious Juice

Makes: approx. 1 cup / Prep time: 10 minutes

- ❖ 2 carrots
- ❖ 2 stalks celery with leaves
- ❖ ⅓ of a beetroot *(continued)*

- ❖ 1 cup spinach or beet greens
- ❖ 1–2 apples
- ❖ 1 orange with peel

Combine all ingredients and put them through a juicer. When finished, dilute with an equal amount of filtered water. You can drink this juice plain or add it to smoothies.

❖ ❖ ❖

Fresh Lemonade

Makes: ½ gallon / Prep time: 10 minutes

- ❖ 10 cups cold water
- ❖ ⅔ cup maple syrup or blue/amber agave
- ❖ 12 ice cubes
- ❖ 1 cup freshly squeezed lemon juice (about 8 organic lemons)
- ❖ 1 organic lemon, sliced and seeded

Stir syrup or agave into the water to dissolve; then add then add the ice cubes. Juice the lemons and strain them. Pour the juice into the sweet water mix and add the sliced lemon to make it look appetizing and attractive. Keep refrigerated.

❖ ❖ ❖

Lavender Lemonade

Makes: ½ gallon / Prep time: 10 minutes

- ❖ 20 cups cold filtered water
- ❖ 1⅓ cups raw blue/amber agave or pure maple syrup
- ❖ 12–24 ice cubes
- ❖ 2 cups freshly squeezed lemon juice (about 8 organic lemons)
- ❖ 1 drop lavender essential oil, therapeutic grade
- ❖ 1 organic lemon, sliced and seeded

Stir the agave or syrup into the water to dissolve. Add the ice cubes. Juice the lemons and strain them. Add the juice to the sweet water mix. Add the sliced lemon for an attractive look in a clear glass pitcher. Keep refrigerated.

❖ ❖ ❖

Warm Whey Drink

Makes: 2 cups / Prep time: 4 minutes

- ❖ 1¼ cup boiled filtered water
- ❖ ¾ Tbsp. Capra Mineral Whey™ powder
- ❖ 3 Tbsps. whole milk or cream, optional
- ❖ 1 tsp. pure maple syrup or raw blue/amber agave
- ❖ frozen whipped cream for top (optional)

Divide hot water between two mugs. Stir in Capra Mineral Whey™ to dissolve. Add syrup and cream or milk. This drink is brown and has a delicious, rich graham cracker flavor. Top with frozen whipped cream.

Warm Carob

Makes: 1 serving / Prep time: 15 minutes

- ❖ ½ Tbsp. roasted carob powder
- ❖ 1 cup warmed raw milk (not over 118°F)
- ❖ 2 tsps. Capra Mineral Whey™
- ❖ 2–3 drops Stevia
- ❖ ½ tsp. vanilla

While milk is warming, place carob powder and whey in a large mug. Add warmed milk a little at a time, stirring well. Stir in vanilla and stevia.

Hot Cocoa

Makes: 4 servings / Prep time: 5 minutes / Cook time: 10 minutes

- ❖ 4 cups raw milk
- ❖ 2 Tbsps. organic cacao powder
- ❖ 1 tsp. pure vanilla extract
- ❖ 3–4 Tbsps. organic pure maple syrup or raw blue/amber agave
- ❖ a pinch of cayenne powder (optional)
- ❖ pinch of cinnamon or 1 drop peppermint extract (optional)
- ❖ whipped cream for top (optional)

Whisk all ingredients in pot until smooth. Continue to whisk over medium heat until very warm to the touch (test using pinky knuckle) *not* hot, about 5 to 10 minutes. Do not boil.

Wassail

Makes: 6 cups / Prep time: 5 minutes / Cook time: 10 minutes

- ❖ 4 cups apple juice
- ❖ 2 cups orange juice
- ❖ ½ tsp. ground cinnamon
- ❖ 2 Tbsps. honey

Combine and heat in a saucepan. Bring to a boil, cover, and reduce heat for 5 to 10 minutes until flavors are well blended. Stir in honey and serve warm. Can be kept warm for a longer time in a Crock-Pot or slow cooker.

Egg Nog

Makes: approx. 2½ cups / Prep time: 5 minutes

- ❖ 2 cups raw milk
- ❖ ½ cup cream, preferably raw, *not* ultra-pasteurized
- ❖ 2 egg yolks
- ❖ 1 tsp. pure vanilla extract
- ❖ 3 Tbsps. pure maple syrup
- ❖ ¼ tsp. ground nutmeg

Combine ingredients in a bowl and blend with a hand blender. Or, combine all ingredients but cream in a blender. Blend well. Then stir in cream.

Cream Soda

Makes: approx. 2 cups / Prep time: 3 minutes

- ❖ 2 cups naturally sparkling mineral water (use a highly effervescent type)
- ❖ 2 tsps. pure vanilla extract
- ❖ 2–4 Tbsps. pure maple syrup or raw blue/amber agave
- ❖ 1–2 Tbsps. cup heavy cream

Stir ingredients together in a large glass and serve immediately.

Fresh Orange Julius

Makes: approx. 3½ cups / Prep time: 10 minutes

- ❖ 2 cups fresh-squeezed orange juice
- ❖ 1 tsp. pure vanilla extract
- ❖ 1 cup whole milk or coconut milk
- ❖ ¼ cup whole plain yogurt or vanilla ice cream
- ❖ 3–4 Tbsps. pure maple syrup, blue/amber agave, or raw honey
- ❖ 10–12 ice cubes

Place all ingredients in a blender and blend until smooth.

Orange Julius

Makes: 4 servings / Prep time: 5 minutes

- ❖ 4–5 Tbsps. of concentrated, frozen orange juice
- ❖ 1 cup raw milk
- ❖ 10–12 ice cubes
- ❖ 1 tsp. pure vanilla extract
- ❖ 1 cup cold water
- ❖ 2–3 Tbsps. raw blue/amber agave

Combine all ingredients in a blender. Blend until ice is finely ground. Serve immediately.

Banana Yogurt Smoothie

Makes: 2 servings / Prep time: 5 minutes

- ❖ 1 cup plain whole yogurt
- ❖ 1 cup coconut milk or whole milk
- ❖ 2 small, very ripe bananas, peeled
- ❖ 2 Tbsps. pure maple syrup
- ❖ ½ tsp. pure vanilla
- ❖ ½ tsps. cinnamon
- ❖ a pinch of nutmeg

Combine all ingredients in a blender. Blend until smooth. Divide into glasses and enjoy!

Fruit Smoothie

Makes: 2 servings / Prep time: 5 minutes

- ❖ 1 cup frozen fruit
- ❖ ½ cup plain whole yogurt
- ❖ ½ cup whole milk or coconut milk
- ❖ 3–4 Tbsps. pure maple syrup

Combine ingredients in a blender and blend until smooth.

Apricot Smoothie

Makes: 6–8 servings / Prep time: 7–15 minutes

- ❖ 4 cups freshly squeezed orange juice or 6 oz. orange juice concentrate with 3 cups water
- ❖ 1 quart bottled apricots, in juice
- ❖ 1 very ripe banana
- ❖ 12 ice cubes
- ❖ 1½ cups whole milk

Combine all ingredients in a blender. Blend well.

Green Smoothie

Makes: approx. 6 cups / Prep time: 15 minutes

- ❖ 5–6 handfuls of fresh, raw dark greens (spinach, kale, beet greens, collards, or chard)
- ❖ 2 cups water
- ❖ 2 Tbsps. flax oil
- ❖ 1 ripe banana, peeled
- ❖ ½–1 small apple, cored and seeded
- ❖ 2 cups ice cubes
- ❖ 2 cups frozen blueberries or strawberries
- ❖ 2–3 Tbsps. raw blue/amber agave

Rinse the dark greens well. Fill blender with greens to the top, cover with the water. Blend and then add flax oil, banana, apple, ice, frozen berries, and agave. Blend until smooth.

Berry Pink Smoothie

Makes: approx. 6 cups / Prep time: 15 minutes

- ❖ 15 oz. unsweetened whole coconut milk
- ❖ 1 cup water
- ❖ ¼ of a medium beetroot
- ❖ 1 Tbsp. pure vanilla extract
- ❖ 10 oz. frozen strawberries or dark sweet cherries
- ❖ 3–4 Tbsps. raw blue/amber agave
- ❖ 2 cups ice cubes

Blend all ingredients until smooth. The raspberries have a seedier texture than strawberries and require a bit more sweetening. Regardless, make it for the kids and don't tell them what you put in it. Then watch them drink it down!

Chocolate Milkshake

Makes: 2 servings / Prep time: 5 minutes

- ❖ 2 Tbsps. cocoa powder or carob powder
- ❖ 3 tsps. natural liquid sweetener
- ❖ 2½ cups homemade vanilla ice cream
- ❖ ½–1 cup raw milk
- ❖ 10 ice cubes

Place all ingredients into a blender and blend until smooth. Serve immediately.

Real Strawberry Milkshake

Makes: 3 cups / Prep time: 5 minutes

- ❖ ½ cup plain whole yogurt, whole coconut milk, or raw milk
- ❖ 2 cups vanilla ice cream
- ❖ 5 oz. frozen strawberries
- ❖ ¼ cup natural liquid sweetener

Combine all ingredients in a blender and blend well. Serve immediately.

Chocolate-Yogurt Smoothie

Makes: 2 servings / Prep time: 5 minutes

- ❖ 2 cups raw milk
- ❖ 1 cup whole plain yogurt
- ❖ 2 bananas, peeled
- ❖ 1 tsp. pure vanilla
- ❖ 2 Tbsps. natural liquid sweetener
- ❖ 10 ice cubes
- ❖ 1 heaping spoonful cocoa powder or carob powder

Place all ingredients into a blender and mix until smooth.

Blueberry Milkshake

Makes: 2 servings / Prep time: 5 minutes

- ❖ ½ cup fresh or frozen blueberries
- ❖ ½–1 cup plain whole yogurt or raw milk
- ❖ 2 cups homemade vanilla ice cream
- ❖ ½ tsp. pure vanilla extract
- ❖ 2–3 Tbsps. raw honey or pure maple syrup

Combine all ingredients in a blender and blend well.

Breakfast Smoothie

Makes: 4 cups / Prep time: 15 minutes

- ❖ 1 banana
- ❖ 1½ cups frozen berry mix
- ❖ 2 Tbsps. freshly ground flaxseed
- ❖ ¼ cup yogurt
- ❖ 2 Tbsps. ground Traditional Almonds (see "Sprouting Nuts and Seeds" section)
- ❖ 1 cup fresh juice (from Veggie-licious Juice recipe)
- ❖ ½ cup filtered water

In a blender, combine banana, berries, flaxseed, yogurt, almonds, juice, and filtered water. Blend until smooth.

Banana Berry Smoothie

Makes: approx. 4 cups / Prep time: 5 minutes

- ❖ 1 ripe banana
- ❖ 1½ cups frozen berry mix
- ❖ ¼ cup plain yogurt
- ❖ 1 tsp. vanilla
- ❖ 1 Tbsp. raw blue/amber agave (optional)
- ❖ juice from 1 orange
- ❖ 1–1½ cups filtered water

Place banana, berries, yogurt, and orange juice in a blender. Add filtered water. Blend until smooth. Add vanilla and agave. Add more or less liquid for desired consistency.

❖   ❖   ❖

Tropical Smoothie

Makes: approx. 5 cups / Prep time: 15 minutes

- ❖ ½ fresh pineapple, cored and chopped
- ❖ 1 mango, sliced from the pit
- ❖ 2 kiwis, peeled
- ❖ 1 banana, peeled
- ❖ 1 small papaya
- ❖ 1 cup coconut milk
- ❖ 1 tsp. vanilla

Slice papaya in half, scoop out seeds, and then scoop pulp into the blender. Add the other fruit, coconut milk, and vanilla. Blend until smooth. Add extra vanilla and natural sweetener if desired.

❖   ❖   ❖

Watermelon Coconut Smoothie

Makes: 2–4 servings / Prep time: 15 minutes

- ❖ 3 cups watermelon, seeded and cut up
- ❖ ¾ cup whole unsweetened coconut milk
- ❖ ¼ cup dehydrated cane juice *(continued)*

- ❖ ¼ cup pure maple syrup
- ❖ 1 tsp. pure vanilla extract
- ❖ 2 cups ice cubes

Place ingredients in a blender and blend until smooth. Add more or less of any ingredient to suit personal taste.

Island Smoothie

Makes: 4 cups / Prep time: 10 minutes

- ❖ ½ of a fresh pineapple, cored and peeled
- ❖ 2 kiwis, peeled
- ❖ 1 banana, peeled
- ❖ 15 oz. whole unsweetened coconut milk
- ❖ 1 tsp. pure vanilla extract
- ❖ 2 Tbsps. raw honey or pure maple syrup
- ❖ 8–10 ice cubes

Combine all ingredients in a blender and blend until smooth.

Blueberry Banana Popsicles

Makes: 12 (3-oz.) Popsicles / Prep time: 5 minutes

- ❖ 5 oz. frozen blueberries
- ❖ 2 small, very ripe bananas, peeled
- ❖ 4–5 Tbsps. pure maple syrup
- ❖ 1 cup raw milk
- ❖ ½ tsp. pure vanilla extract
- ❖ ½ cup plain whole yogurt

Blend all ingredients in a blender. Pour into Popsicle molds or 3-ounce plastic cups (mouthwash-cup size). Put a wooden craft stick in the middle and freeze in freezer. To get the stick to stay in the center, let popsicles sit in freezer for about five minutes, and then re-adjust sticks. This is also a great creamy smoothie, of course.

Banana Cream Popsicles

Makes: 12 (3-oz.) Popsicles / Prep time: 5 minutes

- ❖ 4 very ripe bananas, peeled
- ❖ 2 Tbsps. natural liquid sweetener
- ❖ 1 tsp. pure vanilla extract
- ❖ 2 cups raw milk
- ❖ ½ cup vanilla yogurt

Combine all ingredients in a blender. Blend well and pour into 3-ounce plastic cups (mouthwash cup size). Place a wooden craft stick in each one. Place on a small cookie sheet and put in a freezer. Wait five minutes then readjust the sticks to the center of the popsicles. Leave in freezer for about 2 hours. After they are frozen, they can be stored in a labeled, gallon-size freezer bag.

Best-Ever Grape Popsicles

Makes: 12 (3-oz.) popsicles / Prep time: 3 minutes

- ❖ 1 (12-oz.) can frozen grape juice concentrate (save can)
- ❖ 2½ cans (36 oz.) filtered water (use grape juice can)

Mix grape juice concentrate and water together. Pour juice into Popsicle molds or 3-ounce plastic cups (mouthwash cup size) and place a wooden craft stick in each one. Put in freezer, wait ten minutes, readjust sticks to the middle, and leave in freezer until frozen. These grape popsicles are sweet enough on their own without any added sweeteners.

Orange Popsicles

Makes: 7 (3-oz.) Popsicles / Prep time: 5 minutes

- ❖ ¼–½ cup whole yogurt (optional)
- ❖ 5 Tbsps. natural liquid sweetener
- ❖ 4 cups freshly squeezed orange juice
- ❖ ⅓–⅔ cup fresh carrot juice
- ❖ ¼–½ tsp. natural organic orange flavor (optional) *(continued)*

Combine all ingredients in a blender and blend. Pour into a Popsicle mold or 3-ounce plastic cups. Place a wooden craft stick in each one. Place in freezer, wait five minutes, and adjust the stick to the center. Leave in freezer until frozen. The yogurt is optional. If it is not included, only a couple tablespoons of sweetener is needed.

Breads

Tasty Treasure #3

Ancient societies didn't go to the effort of souring and sprouting grains just because TV hadn't been invented yet and they were bored. Sprouting and souring grains not only digests gluten and starch, increases nutrients, and makes grain easier to digest, but it also gives it a finer, lighter consistency—almost like half-white, half-whole wheat bread.

Tasty Treasure #4

Different varieties of wheat give different flavors when sprouted. White wheat has a sweet flavor and is good for sweetbread recipes, while spelt and kamut are better for traditional bread recipes. Hard, red winter wheat is darker and more flavorful. Hard white wheat is perfect for bread because it is high in protein and gluten, like red wheat, only it's lighter in color and taste. Soft white wheat (or pastry wheat) is perfect for pastries, cakes, muffins, pancakes, and so forth, because it is lower in gluten and protein. Make sure to use the wheat that best suits your recipe and personal taste.

Tasty Treasure #5

Typically, sprouted grains need more moisture in recipes than regular flour, but we find that humidity, temperature, and dehydration-time all play factors into how moist or dry flour is. Most of these recipes were prepared using sprouted wheat or a combination of spelt and kamut. Kamut flour alone tends to be drier and requires a little more liquid. Spelt is wetter and requires less water.

✧ ✧

Traditional Basic Breads

Sprouted Whole Wheat Bread

Makes: 1 loaf / Prep time: 1 hour 20 minutes / Bake time: 30 minutes

- ❖ 1 cups warm water
- ❖ 1/4 cup butter, softened
- ❖ 2½ teaspoons yeast
- ❖ 6 tablespoons honey or agave
- ❖ 4½ cups Sprouted wheat flour (we like using half sprouted spelt flour and half sprouted kamut flour, but hard white wheat works well too.)
- ❖ 1¾ teaspoons real sea salt

Grease three bread pans with palm shortening or coconut oil. Heat the oven to 350° and then turn it off. Turn the light on to help retain the heat in the oven. In a medium bowl, mix the warm water, butter, yeast, and honey or agave. Let the mixture sit for 10 minutes. In a large bowl, whisk the flour and salt together. Add the wet mixture to the dry and mix them together with a wooden spoon or spatula. Knead dough with hands. Dough will seem a bit sticky at first, but will become less so as after kneading for about 5 to 10 minutes. Separate into dough into thirds and, with greased hands, shape each into a loaf. Place the loaves in the previously warmed oven to rise for approximately 50 minutes. Turn oven on and bake for 25 to 30 minutes.

Cream Puffs

Makes: 12 cream puffs / Prep time: 20 minutes / Bake: 30 minutes at 400°F

- ❖ 1 cup filtered water
- ❖ ¼ tsp. sea salt
- ❖ ½ cup butter or coconut oil
- ❖ 1 cup sprouted wheat flour
- ❖ 4 eggs

In a saucepan bring water, sea salt, and butter or coconut oil to boil. Add flour and stir until it forms a ball. Remove from heat and allow to cool for at least 10 minutes. After 10 minutes, stir eggs into mixture one at a time, and then drop the dough into 12 equal mounds on a well-buttered cookie sheet. Bake for 30 minutes at 400°F, then cool, slice off the top and scoop out the doughy center.

Fill with pudding or strawberries and whipped cream to make a dessert, or fill with chicken salad, tuna, or hummus for lunch or dinner.

❖ ❖ ❖

Sprouted Flour Tortillas

Makes: 20 (7-inch) tortillas / Prep time: 5 minutes / Cook time: 40 minutes (if cooked one at a time)

- ❖ 4 cups sprouted kamut flour
- ❖ 2 tsps. sea salt
- ❖ ½ cup extra virgin olive oil
- ❖ 1½ cups warm water

In a medium bowl, whisk the flour and salt together. Blend in the oil. Add the water and knead with hands a few times to make dough smooth. Dough should be quite moist, but not sticky.

Divide dough into 20 pieces and make them into balls. Roll each ball out like a pie crust. Keep hands oiled with a bit of coconut oil as needed to handle the dough and keep it soft. Start from the middle of the dough and work your way out to the edges so that the whole tortilla is the same thickness. Roll them out until they are about 7 inches across and round. They should be quite thin.

Heat a skillet over medium heat with just a drizzle of olive oil, if needed, to coat the pan. Cook each tortilla individually for about 1 minute per side. Stack them in a tortilla warmer as they finish cooking and serve immediately or store them in an airtight bag in the refrigerator or freezer for longer storage.

❖ ❖ ❖

Sprouted French Bread

Makes: 2 loaves / Prep time: 20 minutes / Bake time: 45–50 minutes

- ❖ 8 cups sprouted wheat flour
- ❖ 2½ tsps. sea salt
- ❖ 2 tsps. baking soda
- ❖ 3 Tbsps. honey
- ❖ ½ cup coconut oil
- ❖ 3 eggs
- ❖ 2–2¼ cups water
- ❖ 2 Tbsps. sesame seeds (optional)

Mix flour, sea salt, and soda in a large mixing bowl. In a separate bowl, mix together eggs, honey, oil, and water. Pour liquid into the flour mixture and stir and knead until well combined. Form into two French loaves and place on a buttered cookie sheet. With a sharp knife, make three ½-inch-deep diagonal slices along the top of each loaf. Sprinkle with sesame seeds and bake for 45 to 50 minutes at 350°F. When done, top with Garlic Spread (see recipe in "Spreads, Sauces, Dips, and Marinades").

❖   ❖   ❖

Yeast-Free Flourless Bread

Makes: 1 loaf / Prep time: 30 minutes / Bake time: 30 minutes

- ❖ 4 cups slightly sprouted spelt or kamut berries
- ❖ 1 tsp. sea salt
- ❖ 1½ tsps. baking soda
- ❖ 1 Tbsp. honey
- ❖ ¼ cup coconut oil
- ❖ 1 egg
- ❖ 1 Tbsp. sesame seeds

Blend spelt or kamut sprouts in a food processor until they form a ball of dough. Add remaining ingredients (except sesame seeds) and mix well. Form into a loaf and place on a buttered cookie sheet. With a sharp knife, make three ½-inch-deep diagonal slices along the top. Sprinkle with sesame seeds and bake at 350°F for 30 minutes.

❖   ❖   ❖

Sourdough Bread

Makes: 2 loaves / Soak time: 12–24 hours / Prep time: 15 minutes / Bake: 50–60 minutes

- ❖ 4 cups freshly ground wheat, spelt, or kamut flour
- ❖ Juice from half a lemon
- ❖ 1–1⅓ cups warm water
- ❖ 3 Tbsps. olive oil
- ❖ ⅓ cup raw honey or pure maple syrup
- ❖ 1 egg
- ❖ 1 tsp. sea salt
- ❖ 1½ tsps. yeast

Mix fresh flour with lemon, water, and oil to form a stiff ball of dough. Cover with a damp towel and put in a warm place for 12 to 24 hours. (The oven with only the light on is a good place, especially in colder weather.) After at least 12 hours, mix in the remaining ingredients and form the dough into two loaves. Let the dough rise in the oven again for 1½ to 2 hours, and then bake at 350°F for 50 to 60 minutes.

❖   ❖   ❖

Flourless Biscuits

Makes: approx. 20 biscuits / Prep time: 20 minutes / Bake time: 20 minutes

- ❖ 5 cups moist sprouted spelt or kamut berries
- ❖ 2 tsps. baking soda
- ❖ ½ tsp. sea salt
- ❖ 2 Tbsps. coconut oil

Blend moist, sprouted wheat berries in a food processor until a ball of dough forms (about 5 to 6 minutes). Add remaining ingredients and blend for another minute. Roll out on oiled surface and cut with a jar lid or a round cookie cutter. Place on a buttered cookie sheet and bake for 20 minutes at 350°F.

❖   ❖   ❖

Yeast-Free Pizza Crust

Makes: 2 (12-inch) pizza crusts / Prep time: 30 minutes / Bake time: 10 minutes

- ❖ 3 cups sprouted wheat flour
- ❖ 2 tsps. baking powder
- ❖ 1 tsp. sea salt
- ❖ ½ tsp. dried oregano
- ❖ ½ tsp. onion powder
- ❖ ¼ tsp. garlic powder
- ❖ ¼ cup coconut oil
- ❖ 2 tsps. raw honey
- ❖ 1 cup water
- ❖ cornmeal for sprinkling on pans

In a medium bowl, whisk the flour, baking powder, salt, oregano, onion powder, and garlic powder together. In a small saucepan, melt the coconut oil over low heat. Remove from heat promptly. Stir in the honey, and then the water. Pour this water mixture into the flour mixture and stir well with a fork. Knead 15 to 20 times. Separate the dough into two equal balls. Let them stand for 10 minutes. Preheat oven to 375°F.

On a silicone mat or wax paper, roll each ball of dough out with a rolling pin to an even 12 inches round. Coat each pizza pan or cookie sheet with cornmeal. Prick pizza circle with holes and bake for 10 minutes at 375°F. Add toppings and cook an additional 10 to 12 minutes.

Thin Pizza Crust

Makes: 2 (12-inch) pizzas / Prep time: 10 minutes / Cook time: 15–20 minutes

- ❖ 3½ cups sprouted white wheat flour
- ❖ 1 tsp. sea salt
- ❖ ¼ tsp. garlic powder
- ❖ ½ tsp. onion powder
- ❖ ½ tsp. dried oregano
- ❖ 1–1½ cups warm water
- ❖ ¼ cup butter or coconut oil, softened
- ❖ 1 Tbsp. honey, agave, or syrup
- ❖ cornmeal for sprinkling on the pan

Preheat oven to 350°F. In a medium bowl, whisk flour, salt, and spices. Add water, butter, and sweetener to flour mixture and blend until smooth. Dough should be moist but not sticky. Divide the dough into two balls and roll each out like a pie crust until it reaches 12 inches round. Prick holes all over. Bake for 15 to 20 minutes, or until cooked through. Remove from oven and put toppings on, or store in an airtight bag in the freezer. After the toppings are added, return it to the oven and bake for an additional ten minutes.

❖   ❖   ❖

Garlic Herb Biscuits

Makes: 12 biscuits / Prep time: 15 minutes / Cook time: 20 minutes

- ❖ 3 cups moist sprouted spelt or kamut
- ❖ ¼ cup butter or coconut oil
- ❖ 3 cloves garlic, minced
- ❖ 1½ tsp. parsley flakes
- ❖ ½ tsp. sea salt
- ❖ 1 tsp. baking soda

Blend sprouts in a food processor until they form a ball of dough. While the processor is still in motion, add butter a little at a time, and then add other ingredients. Drop by spoonfuls on a buttered cookie sheet. Bake at 350°F for 20 minutes.

❖   ❖   ❖

Sweet Corn Bread

Makes: 6–8 servings / Prep time: 20 minutes / Bake time: 17–19 minutes:

- ❖ 1 cup sprouted soft white wheat flour
- ❖ 1 cup freshly ground yellow cornmeal (from unpopped popcorn)
- ❖ 2½ tsps. baking powder
- ❖ ½ tsp. sea salt
- ❖ ¼ cup butter or coconut oil
- ❖ ¼ cup plain whole yogurt
- ❖ 1 cup water
- ❖ ½ cup raw blue/amber agave or raw honey
- ❖ 1 large egg, beaten *(continued)*

In a large bowl, whisk the flour, cornmeal, baking powder, and salt together. Melt the butter or coconut oil in a medium saucepan. Remove from heat and allow to cool. Stir the yogurt, water, and sweetener into the melted oil. Whisk in the egg. Pour the wet mixture into the flour mixture and mix just until blended. Pour into an 8-inch, square baking dish oiled with coconut oil. Bake at 375°F for about 17 to 19 minutes.

❖   ❖   ❖

Corn Bread

Makes: 1 (9x13) pan or 24 muffins / Prep time: 20 minutes / Bake time: 20–25 minutes

- ❖   1 cup freshly ground cornmeal (from unpopped popcorn)
- ❖   2 cups sprouted wheat flour
- ❖   ½ tsp. sea salt
- ❖   1 tsp. baking soda
- ❖   2 eggs
- ❖   ¼ cup olive oil or coconut oil
- ❖   2 cups raw milk, water, or almond milk

Preheat oven to 350°F. Combine dry ingredients and mix well. Combine wet ingredients in a separate bowl and mix. Add dry ingredients to wet ingredients and mix just until combined. Pour into an oiled 9x13 metal pan or fill the cups in a muffin tin three-quarters full. Bake muffins for 20 minutes and pan for about 25.

❖   ❖   ❖

Yeast-Free Breadsticks

Makes: 12 breadsticks / Prep time: 15 minutes / Bake time: 15 minutes

- ❖   4 cups moist sprouted spelt or kamut
- ❖   ½ tsp. sea salt
- ❖   1 tsp. baking soda
- ❖   2 Tbsps. butter or coconut oil

Blend sprouts in a food processor until they form a ball of dough. Add the remaining ingredients and blend well. Divide the dough into 12 portions and shape into bread sticks. Arrange on a buttered cookie sheet and bake for 15 minutes at 350°F.

Yeast-Free Bagels

Makes: 12 bagels / Prep time: 1 hour / Cook time: 25 minutes

- ❖ 4 cups moist sprouted spelt or kamut
- ❖ ¼ tsp. sea salt
- ❖ 1 tsp. baking soda
- ❖ 1 Tbsp. raw honey or pure maple syrup

Blend sprouted wheat until it forms a ball of dough. Add sea salt, baking soda, and honey or syrup. Divide the dough into 12 balls and shape into bagels. Place bagels on a cookie sheet and let them rise for about 30 minutes in a warm place.

When the bagels are almost finished rising, fill a large pot three-quarters full with water and heat to boiling. Boil a few bagels at a time in filtered water for 6 minutes, flipping halfway. When each bagel is done, drain it in a colander and place it on a cookie sheet.

After all of the bagels have been boiled, bake them at 350°F for 25 minutes, or until golden-brown. Remove to a cooling rack. When cooled, slice the bagels in half and top them with cream cheese, honey, or homemade jam, or use them for sandwiches.

Sprouted Wheat Rolls

Makes: 24–40 rolls / Prep time: 1 hour 20 minutes / Bake time: 17–25 minutes

- ❖ 7½ cups sprouted hard white wheat flour
- ❖ 1¼ tsps. sea salt
- ❖ 2 cups very warm water
- ❖ 1½ Tbsps. dry yeast
- ❖ ⅓ cup raw honey
- ❖ 2 eggs, beaten
- ❖ ¾ cup butter or coconut oil, melted and cooled

In a medium bowl, mix the warm water, honey, and yeast together. Set aside for 10 minutes. In a large bowl, mix the flour and salt together. Pour the yeast mixture into the flour mixture. Add the beaten eggs and melted oil. Blend well with a large wooden spoon. *(continued)*

Grease a 15x10 glass baking dish or a large cookie sheet with coconut oil. Knead dough and divide into about 24 balls for a 15x10 pan or about 40 balls for a cookie sheet. Butter some plastic wrap and cover the rolls. Let rise in a warm place for one hour. When large enough, place in a cold oven and then turn the oven on to bake at 375°F. Bake 17 minutes for a cookie sheet and 20 to 25 minutes for a 15x10 pan.

❖   ❖   ❖

Pumpernickel Bread

Makes: 1 loaf / Prep time: 35 minutes / Bake time: 35–40 minutes

- ❖   3 cups fresh, sprouted rye
- ❖   2½ cups fresh, sprouted spelt, kamut, or wheat
- ❖   1 egg
- ❖   2 Tbsp. roasted carob powder
- ❖   1 Tbsp. molasses
- ❖   3 tsps. caraway seeds
- ❖   2 tsps. baking soda
- ❖   ½ tsp. sea salt

Grind wheat and rye sprouts in a food processor until they form a ball of dough. Add egg, carob, molasses, baking soda, sea salt, and 2 teaspoons of the caraway seed. Blend well, then shape into a round loaf and place on a buttered cookie sheet. Sprinkle with remaining caraway seeds and let rise for about 20 minutes. Bake at 350°F for 35 to 40 minutes.

❖   ❖   ❖

English Muffins

Makes: 12 muffins / Prep time: 1 hour 20 minutes / Cook time: 30 minutes

- ❖   5 cups moist, sprouted spelt or kamut
- ❖   2 Tbsps. butter
- ❖   1 Tbsp. raw honey or pure maple syrup
- ❖   ½ tsp. sea salt
- ❖   1 tsp. yeast
- ❖   cornmeal

Blend wheat sprouts in a food processor until they form a ball of dough. Add butter, honey or syrup, sea salt, and yeast, and blend until well mixed. Place in a glass bowl, cover with a moist cloth, and let rise for about 30 minutes. Mash dough down with fist. Oil a rolling mat or other smooth surface. Roll out dough to be about ½ inch thick and cut with a cookie cutter or the lid of a jar. Sprinkle a handful of cornmeal onto a cookie sheet, and then place the muffins on top. Let rise for about 30 more minutes in a warm place.

To bake, warm oven to 325°F and bake for about 30 minutes, flipping the muffins over every 5 to 7 minutes.

Note: To use sprouted flour instead of moist sprouts in this recipe, substitute the wheat sprouts with 5 cups sprouted wheat flour and add 1¾ to 2 cups milk, almond milk, or water to the recipe.

Muffins and Sweet Breads

Blueberry Muffins

Makes: approx. 20 muffins / Prep time: 15 minutes / Bake time: 18–20 minutes

- ❖ 3½ cups sprouted white wheat flour
- ❖ ⅔ cup dehydrated cane juice
- ❖ 2 tsps. baking soda
- ❖ ⅛ tsp. real salt
- ❖ 2 eggs
- ❖ 1 cup water or milk
- ❖ ½ cup liquid sweetener
- ❖ ½ cup coconut oil, melted
- ❖ 1½ cups fresh blueberries or frozen blueberries, partially thawed

Preheat oven to 350°F. Grease stainless steel muffin pans with coconut oil. In a large bowl, whisk together the flour, salt, and baking soda and set aside. In a medium bowl, beat the eggs, then whisk in the cane juice, vanilla, melted oil or butter, honey or syrup, and water. Let the cane juice dissolve for 5 minutes. *(continued)*

Pour the wet mixture into the dry mixture and stir just until mixed. Gently fold in the fresh or frozen blueberries. Scoop the batter into greased muffin cups. Divide them equally among the muffin cups, filling them about three-quarters full. Bake at 350°F for 18 to 20 minutes. Let cool in pan for 5 minutes. Remove them from the pan and cool on rack.

❖ ❖ ❖

Basic Sweet Muffins

Makes: 24 muffins / Prep time: 20 minutes / Cook time: 25 minutes at 350°F

- ❖ 3 cups moist sprouted wheat
- ❖ 3 eggs, beaten
- ❖ ½ cup processed dates or ⅓ cup pure maple syrup or raw honey
- ❖ 3 Tbsps. melted butter or coconut oil
- ❖ 1 tsp. vanilla
- ❖ 1 tsp. sea salt
- ❖ 2 tsps. cinnamon
- ❖ 1 tsp. baking soda
- ❖ 2 cups grated zucchini, mashed banana, or fruit/veggie pulp
- ❖ ½ cup chopped Traditional Almonds (see "Sprouting Nuts and Seeds" section)
- ❖ ½ cup raisins

Process wheat sprouts in a food processor until they form a ball of dough. Add eggs, sweetener, butter or oil, vanilla, sea salt, cinnamon, and baking soda. Blend well. Pour mixture into a bowl and stir in zucchini, mashed banana, or pulp, as well as the nuts and raisins. Pour into buttered muffin tins, and bake at 350°F for 25 minutes.

❖ ❖ ❖

Apple Cinnamon Muffins

Makes: 18 muffins / Prep time: 20 minutes / Bake time: 15 minutes

- ❖ 2 eggs
- ❖ ¾ cup dehydrated cane juice
- ❖ 1 tsp. pure vanilla extract
- ❖ ¼ cup liquid sweetener of choice
- ❖ ¾ cup water

- ❖ ½ cup coconut oil or butter, melted
- ❖ 3½ cups sprouted white wheat flour
- ❖ ¼ tsp. sea salt
- ❖ 2 tsps. baking powder
- ❖ 1½ tsps. ground cinnamon
- ❖ ½ tsp. ground nutmeg
- ❖ ½ cup unsweetened shredded coconut
- ❖ 1 apple, cored and diced small (about 1½ cups)

Whisk the eggs well in a medium bowl. Mix in the cane juice, vanilla, water, and butter or oil. Set aside. In a large bowl, mix the flour, salt, baking powder, cinnamon, nutmeg, and coconut flakes together. Pour the wet mixture into the dry mixture and gently blend. Then add the diced apples. Scoop ⅓ to ½ cup batter into greased muffin tins. Bake at 350°F for 15 minutes.

Oatmeal Raisin Muffins

Makes: 24 muffins / Prep time: 12–24 hours / Cook time: 25 minutes

- ❖ Juice from ½ lemon
- ❖ 1 cup water
- ❖ 1⅓ cups freshly ground white wheat, spelt, or kamut
- ❖ ¾ cup fresh oat flour
- ❖ 1 tsp. baking soda
- ❖ ¼ tsp. sea salt
- ❖ 1 tsp. cinnamon
- ❖ 1 egg
- ❖ 2 Tbsps. melted butter/coconut oil
- ❖ 3 Tbsps. pure maple syrup or raw honey
- ❖ ¾ cup raisins
- ❖ ½ cup Traditional Almonds (see "Sprouting Nuts and Seeds" section), pecans, or walnuts (optional)

Combine lemon juice and water. Soak wheat flour and oat flour in mixture for 12 to 24 hours, covered with a damp cloth and put in a warm place. When finished, add soda, sea salt, cinnamon, egg, butter, and honey or syrup, and stir until mixed. Stir in raisins and nuts, and pour the batter into buttered muffin tins. Bake at 350°F for 25 minutes.

Banana Oatmeal Muffins

Makes: 12 muffins / Prep time: 10–20 minutes / Bake time: 25 minutes

- ❖ 1½ cups sprouted wheat flour
- ❖ 2½ tsps. baking powder
- ❖ ½ tsp. sea salt
- ❖ ¼ tsp. baking soda
- ❖ ½ cup shredded, unsweetened coconut
- ❖ 1 egg
- ❖ ½ cup water
- ❖ 3 small, very ripe bananas, peeled and mashed
- ❖ 3 Tbsps. butter or coconut oil
- ❖ 1 tsp. pure vanilla extract
- ❖ ¾ cup quinoa flakes or soaked oatmeal

Whisk flour, baking powder, salt, soda, and coconut. In a large bowl, whisk the egg. Add the banana, water, vanilla, and butter or oil. Add the quinoa or oatmeal. Mix the wet and dry mixtures together until just moistened. Grease a muffin tin with coconut oil. Fill each cup three-quarters full. Bake at 350°F for 25 minutes.

Raisin Cinnamon Bread

Makes: 1 loaf / Prep time: 20–40 minutes / Bake time: 30 minutes

- ❖ 6 cups fresh sprouted spelt, kamut, or white wheat
- ❖ ½ tsp. sea salt
- ❖ 1½ tsps. baking soda
- ❖ 2 tsps. cinnamon
- ❖ ½ cup Traditional Almonds (see "Sprouting Nuts & Seeds" section)
- ❖ ¾ cup raisins

Blend fresh sprouts in food processor until they form a ball of dough. Add salt, soda, and cinnamon, and blend well. Pour almonds in while processor is still moving (to chop). Mix raisins in by hand, or mix briefly with the processor. Shape dough into a loaf and place on a buttered cookie sheet or in a buttered bread pan. Let rise for 20 minutes (optional) and bake for 30 minutes at 350°F.

Orange Cranberry Scones

Makes: 24 scones / Prep time: 20 minutes / Bake: 15 minutes

- ❖ 4 cups sprouted wheat flour
- ❖ ½ cup dehydrated cane juice
- ❖ 2 tsps. baking soda
- ❖ ½ tsp. sea salt
- ❖ 1 tsp. cinnamon
- ❖ ⅔ cup butter or coconut oil, melted
- ❖ 2 eggs
- ❖ 1 cup water or milk
- ❖ 2 tsps. finely grated orange peel or 3–4 drops orange essential oil
- ❖ ½ cup dried cranberries (fruit juice sweetened)

Mix flour, dehydrated cane juice, soda, sea salt, and cinnamon together. Add melted butter or oil, eggs, and water or milk. Stir well, and then add orange peel and cranberries. Drop by spoonfuls on a buttered cookie sheet and bake for 15 minutes at 400°F.

Banana Bread or Muffins

Makes: 2 loafs or 24 muffins / Prep time: 20 minutes / Bake time: 25–55 minutes

- ❖ 2 cups mashed bananas (about 6 small bananas)
- ❖ ½ tsp. vanilla
- ❖ 2 eggs
- ❖ ½ cup butter or coconut oil, softened
- ❖ 2 cups sprouted soft white wheat flour
- ❖ 2 tsps. baking soda
- ❖ ½ tsp. sea salt
- ❖ ½ tsp. cinnamon
- ❖ 1 cup dehydrated cane juice
- ❖ ½ cup crushed Traditional Almonds (see "Sprouting Nuts & Seeds" section)
- ❖ ½ cup raisins *(continued)*

In a large mixing bowl, mash bananas and add remaining wet ingredients. In a separate bowl, mix together dry ingredients. Pour dry ingredients into the banana mixture and blend. Then add the nuts and raisins. Pour into two buttered loaf pans, or fill the cups of two buttered muffin tins three-quarters full, and bake at 350°F. Muffins will take about 25 minutes, and loaves will take 50 to 55 minutes.

❖   ❖   ❖

Flourless Cinnamon Rolls

Makes: 12–15 rolls / Prep time: 30 minutes / Cook time: 35–40 minutes

Rolls:
- ❖ 6 cups sprouted, moist white wheat, spelt, or kamut
- ❖ 2 Tbsps. raw honey or pure maple syrup
- ❖ ½ tsp. sea salt
- ❖ 2 tsps. baking soda

Filling:
- ❖ ¼ cup butter, melted
- ❖ 2 Tbsps. raw honey or pure maple syrup
- ❖ 2 tsps. cinnamon
- ❖ ½ cup raisins
- ❖ ½ cup Traditional Almonds (see "Sprouting Nuts and Seeds" section), chopped well

Topping:
- ❖ ¼ cup butter
- ❖ ¼ cup coconut oil
- ❖ ½ cup raw honey
- ❖ 1 tsp. cinnamon

Blend the wheat sprouts in a food processor until they form a ball of dough. Add honey or syrup, sea salt, and baking soda and mix well. Roll dough out in a rectangle on an oiled rolling mat to be about a ½-inch thick. Mix melted butter and honey or syrup and pour the mixture over rolled out dough. Sprinkle with cinnamon, raisins, and nuts. Roll dough from one side and pinch ends to seal. With a sharp knife, cut into ¾-inch-thick wedges and lay them on a buttered 9x13-inch metal pan. Bake at 350°F for 20 minutes.

While baking, mix together topping by creaming butter and coconut oil. Then mix in the honey and cinnamon. After rolls have cooled slightly, spread topping over tops and serve.

❖ ❖

Breakfasts, Brunch, & Eggs

❖ ❖

Tasty Treasure #6

Protein foods, like eggs, meat, and beans, are best cooked slowly on low heat. This makes them easier to digest, and also makes them more tender. If your eggs have the bounce of a rubber ball, chances are they were cooked too quickly and on too high a temperature.

Tasty Treasure #7

It's a great idea to get fresh, fertile eggs from healthy, free roaming chickens that are fed a natural diet. The yolks should be deep orange and will be loaded with omega-3s and vitamin A.

❖ ❖

Sprouted Flour Pancakes

Makes: 6 servings / Prep time: 10 minutes / Cook time: 5 minutes per batch

- ❖ 2¼ cups sprouted white wheat flour
- ❖ ½ tsp. sea salt
- ❖ ¾ Tbsp. baking powder
- ❖ 3 Tbsps. liquid sweetener
- ❖ 2 eggs, beaten
- ❖ 2 Tbsps. butter or coconut oil, melted
- ❖ 1–1¼ cups water
- ❖ ¼ cup whole plain yogurt

In a medium bowl, whisk flour, salt, and baking powder. In a large bowl, combine sweetener, eggs, butter, water, and yogurt. Add the dry mixture to the wet ingredients and mix well. Add more flour or water to adjust consistency, if needed. Drop batter by two tablespoonfuls onto a heated pan greased with coconut oil. Cook until bottoms are golden and bubbles have formed on top, about 2 to 3 minutes. Flip and cook other side until browned, 1 to 2 minutes. Serve topped with unsweetened applesauce and cinnamon or butter and pure maple syrup.

Apple German Pancakes

Makes: 6–8 servings / Soak time: 12–24 hours / Prep time: 15 minutes / Bake time: 35–40 minutes

- ❖ 2 cups freshly ground whole wheat flour
- ❖ juice from half a lemon
- ❖ 2 cups water
- ❖ 2 eggs, beaten
- ❖ ¼ cup honey or pure maple syrup
- ❖ ½ tsp. sea salt
- ❖ 1 tsp. ground cinnamon (optional)
- ❖ ¼ cup dehydrated cane juice
- ❖ 1 tsp. baking soda
- ❖ 2 Tbsps. butter or coconut oil
- ❖ 4 medium apples, cored and thinly sliced but not peeled

Mix flour with lemon juice and water and cover with a moist towel. Place in a warm place for 12 to 24 hours. After it has had a chance to sit, add eggs, honey, salt, cinnamon, cane juice, and soda and stir well. The mixture should be a fairly thick batter. Preheat oven to 350°F. Place butter in a 9x13 metal pan and melt in preheating oven. When the butter has melted, remove it from the oven and layer the bottom of the pan with apple slices. Pour the batter over the apples and bake at 350°F for 35 to 40 minutes or until golden and cooked through. Serve with cinnamon honey butter.

Blueberry Sourdough Pancakes

Makes: approx. 30 pancakes / Prep time: 12–24 hours / Cook time: 5 minutes per batch

- ❖ 3 cups freshly ground *non*-sprouted whole wheat flour
- ❖ juice from half a lemon
- ❖ 2¾ cups water or milk
- ❖ 2 eggs
- ❖ ¼ cup liquid sweetener
- ❖ ½ tsp. sea salt
- ❖ 1 tsp. baking soda
- ❖ 1½ cups fresh or frozen blueberries *(continued)*

In a large bowl, mix fresh flour with lemon juice and water or milk, cover, and put in a warm place for 12 to 24 hours (24 hours is best). When done, add eggs, honey or syrup, salt, and baking soda and mix well. Stir in blueberries and cook on a hot, buttered griddle. Top with homemade blueberry syrup or applesauce.

Note: whenever using a sourdough recipe, always start off with flour that hasn't been sprouted first, or the combined effect of sprouting and then souring (both of which digest gluten) will cause nothing but crumbs.

❖   ❖   ❖

Quinoa Pancakes

Makes: 3 servings / Prep time: 10 minutes / Cook time: 5 minutes per batch

- ❖ ½ cup sprouted wheat flour
- ❖ 1½ tsps. baking powder
- ❖ ½ tsp. sea salt
- ❖ 1 egg
- ❖ 2 Tbsps. butter or coconut oil
- ❖ ½ cup unsweetened applesauce
- ❖ 2 tsps. honey or maple syrup
- ❖ ¼ cup milk or water
- ❖ ½ cup quinoa flakes

In a large bowl, whisk the flour, baking powder, and salt together. In a smaller bowl, whisk together the egg, butter or oil, applesauce, honey or maple syrup, and milk or water. Stir in the quinoa flakes. Combine the flour mixture and wet mixture; stir just until moistened. Pour batter by two tablespoonfuls onto a griddle greased with coconut oil. Flip pancakes over when bubbles form on top. Cook until both sides are golden brown. Serve with butter and pure maple syrup or homemade topping.

❖   ❖   ❖

Egg-less Banana Pancakes

Makes: 6 servings / Prep time: 6 minutes / Cook time: 5 minutes per batch

- ❖ 2 cups sprouted white wheat flour
- ❖ ½ tsp. sea salt
- ❖ 1 Tbsp. baking powder
- ❖ 2 small, very ripe bananas
- ❖ ¼ cup unsweetened applesauce
- ❖ 2 Tbsps. butter or coconut oil

Whisk the flour, salt, and baking powder together. Set aside. Mash the bananas well and mix in the applesauce and butter or coconut oil. Pour the banana mixture into the flour and mix gently. Pour batter by two tablespoonfuls onto a griddle greased with coconut oil. Flip pancakes over when bubbles form on top. Cook until both sides are golden brown. Serve with butter and applesauce or pure maple syrup.

❖ ❖ ❖

Overnight French Toast Casserole

Makes: 6 servings / Prep time: 25 minutes / Soak time: 8 hours / Bake time: 40 minutes

- ❖ 8 slices sprouted wheat bread, torn into chunks
- ❖ 6 eggs
- ❖ ½ cup milk or yogurt
- ❖ 1 tsp. ground cinnamon
- ❖ ¼ tsp. ground nutmeg
- ❖ 3–4 medium apples, cored and sliced with skins on
- ❖ ½ cup raisins (optional)
- ❖ ½ cup Traditional Almonds (see "Sprouting Nuts and Seeds" section), chopped

Place bread crumbs in the bottom of a 9x13 glass pan. Mix together eggs, milk or yogurt, cinnamon, and nutmeg. Pour over the torn bread. Cover and refrigerate overnight, or about 8 hours. In the morning, slice the apples and place on top. Sprinkle the raisins and nuts over the apples. Bake for 40 minutes at 350°F or until apples are tender. Top with slightly melted honey butter or pure maple syrup.

French Toast

Makes: 5 servings / Prep time: 5 minutes / Cook: 10 minutes

- ❖ 2 eggs, beaten
- ❖ 3 Tbsps. plain whole yogurt
- ❖ ¼ cup maple syrup
- ❖ 1½ tsps. pure vanilla extract
- ❖ ¼ tsp. ground cinnamon
- ❖ ⅛ tsp. sea salt
- ❖ pinch of ground nutmeg
- ❖ ¾ cup raw whole milk
- ❖ 3 Tbsps. coconut oil for cooking
- ❖ 10 slices sprouted grain bread

Beat eggs in a small bowl. Then add yogurt, maple syrup, vanilla, cinnamon, sea salt, and nutmeg. Mix well. Stir in milk and mix again. Melt 1 tablespoon of the coconut oil in a skillet over medium heat. Dip each bread slice in the egg and milk mixture for 5 seconds. Brown for two minutes on each side. Add additional coconut oil as needed while cooking. Serve with butter and unsweetened applesauce.

Breakfast Casserole

Makes: 1 (9x13) pan / Prep time: 30 minutes / Bake time: 30–35 minutes

- ❖ 2 medium red potatoes, scrubbed and shredded with skins left on
- ❖ ½ lb or 8 oz. turkey sausage, cooked
- ❖ 10 eggs
- ❖ ¼ cup milk
- ❖ ½ medium onion, chopped
- ❖ 1 green bell pepper, chopped
- ❖ 4–6 mushrooms, diced (optional)
- ❖ 1 tsp. sea salt
- ❖ ¼ tsp. freshly ground black pepper
- ❖ ¼ tsp. garlic powder
- ❖ 2 Tbsps. butter or coconut oil
- ❖ 1 cup raw cheese, shredded (optional)

Steam potatoes, until tender (about 20 minutes). When finished, drain thoroughly. Meanwhile, cook the sausage until browned evenly. In a bowl, mix together eggs, milk, sausage, chopped onion, bell pepper, optional mushrooms, sea salt, pepper, and garlic powder. Butter the bottom of a glass 9x13 baking dish. When the potatoes have drained sufficiently, layer them on the bottom of the buttered dish. Cover them with the egg and vegetable mixture and bake for 30 to 35 minutes at 350°F, or until done. Top with shredded cheese and serve.

❖   ❖   ❖

Breakfast Casserole with Cream of Mushroom

Makes: 1 (9x13) pan / Prep time: 3–8 hours / Bake time: 1½ hours

- ❖ 6 slices sprouted wheat bread
- ❖ 1 lb homemade hot Italian turkey sausage
- ❖ 1 dozen eggs
- ❖ 1 cup milk
- ❖ 1 green bell pepper, chopped
- ❖ ½ yellow onion, chopped
- ❖ ½ cup sliced olives
- ❖ 2 cups cream of mushroom soup (see below)
- ❖ 1 cup raw cheese, shredded

Peel crusts off bread. Break remaining bread into bite-sized chunks and line the bottom of a glass 9x13 pan. In a frying pan, cook sausage until brown, and then sprinkle it over bread. In a bowl, mix eggs, milk, peppers, onions, and olives. Pour over bread mixture. Let casserole sit in the refrigerator for a couple hours, even overnight, if desired. In the morning, top the casserole with cream of mushroom soup and bake at 325°F for 1½ hours. Top with raw cheese and place back in the oven, just until melted.

Cream of Mushroom Soup for Breakfast Casserole:

- ❖ 2 cups sliced, fresh mushrooms
- ❖ ½ onion
- ❖ 1 clove garlic
- ❖ 4 cups milk
- ❖ 2–4 Tbsps. organic cornstarch
- ❖ sea salt to taste
- ❖ freshly ground pepper to taste *(continued)*

Sauté the mushrooms, onion, and garlic in a saucepan until tender. Pour in milk, season with salt and pepper, and heat to a boil. Mix the cornstarch with a little cold milk and pour it into soup. Stir until thickened.

Breakfast Steaks

Makes: 4 servings / Prep time: 10 minutes / Cook time: 20 minutes

- ❖ 3 Tbsps. coconut oil or butter
- ❖ 4 small, thin boneless breakfast steaks
- ❖ ½ a medium yellow onion, thinly sliced
- ❖ 2 cloves garlic, minced
- ❖ 3–4 large, fresh mushrooms, chopped (optional)

Heat coconut oil or butter in a skillet over medium-low heat. Add steak, onion, garlic, and mushrooms. Cook over medium to low heat until browned, about 20 minutes. Serve with eggs.

❖ ❖ ❖

Egg-Potato Stir-Fry

Makes: 6 servings / Prep time: 10 minutes / Cook time: 15 minutes

- ❖ 3 Tbsps. coconut oil
- ❖ 2–3 medium potatoes, scrubbed and diced with skins left on
- ❖ ½ of medium onion, chopped
- ❖ 4–5 eggs, lightly beaten
- ❖ 3 Tbsps. raw milk
- ❖ ⅛ tsp. cayenne powder
- ❖ ¼ tsp. paprika
- ❖ ¼ tsp. ground turmeric (optional)
- ❖ ¾ tsp. sea salt
- ❖ ½ tsp. freshly ground black pepper
- ❖ 1 green pepper, seeded and diced
- ❖ 1 medium tomato, chopped and seeded
- ❖ shredded raw cheese (optional)

Heat coconut oil in skillet over medium heat. Add the potatoes and onions. Keep covered, but stir occasionally. In a medium bowl, whisk the eggs, milk, cayenne, paprika, turmeric, salt, and pepper. When the potatoes are done cooking (about 10 to 15 minutes), add the egg mixture in with the potatoes. Then add the green pepper and tomatoes. Cook over medium-low heat, uncovered, until eggs are done. Do not overcook. Top with cheese, if desired.

❖ ❖ ❖

Breakfast Sandwich

Makes: 2 servings / Prep time: 2 minutes / Cook time: 10 minutes

- ❖ 4 eggs
- ❖ ¼ tsp. sea salt
- ❖ pinch of black pepper
- ❖ 1 Tbsp. coconut oil or butter
- ❖ 2 sprouted wheat English muffins, halved, toasted, and buttered
- ❖ 2 slices raw cheddar cheese (optional)
- ❖ 2 sausage patties or a couple of bacon slices, precooked

Blend eggs with salt and pepper. Melt butter or coconut oil in saucepan on medium heat. Add eggs and cook like crepes, about 2 to 3 minutes. Remove and cut in half. Fold up and put on slice of toasted muffin. Top egg with cheese and place on a cookie sheet. Melt cheese on broil for only a minute. Remove and add sausage or bacon to the top and close with the other toasted muffin half. Serve warm.

❖ ❖ ❖

Breakfast Burritos

Makes: 4 servings / Prep time: 10 minutes / Cook time: 20 minutes

- ❖ 4 sprouted wheat or corn tortillas
- ❖ 4 Tbsps. butter
- ❖ 6 eggs
- ❖ 3 Tbsps. milk or yogurt
- ❖ ½ tsp. ground cumin
- ❖ 1 tsp. sea salt
- ❖ 1 potato, scrubbed and diced *(continued)*

- ❖ 1 small onion, diced
- ❖ ½ tsp. chili powder
- ❖ ¼ tsp. oregano
- ❖ ¼ tsp. dried basil
- ❖ 1 green bell pepper, seeded and diced
- ❖ 1–2 tomatoes, seeded and diced

Warm tortillas at 250°F for 1 to 2 minutes. Divide the butter into two different skillets and scramble eggs, milk, cumin, and salt in one, and potato, onion, and remaining spices in the other. Add the green pepper and tomato at the end. Wrap in tortillas and top with sour cream and salsa.

Fluffy Oven Omelet

Makes: 6–8 servings / Prep time: 15 minutes / Cook time: 30–35 minutes

- ❖ 8 eggs, separated
- ❖ ¼ tsp. sea salt
- ❖ pepper to taste
- ❖ 1 cup sliced mushrooms
- ❖ 2 bell peppers, chopped
- ❖ 2 zucchini, chopped
- ❖ ½ onion, sliced
- ❖ ½ tsp. basil
- ❖ 1 tsp. oregano
- ❖ ½ cup shredded raw cheddar cheese (optional)

Beat egg whites until fluffy. Fold in egg yolks and other ingredients, except cheese. Pour into the bottom of a glass 9x13 pan and bake at 325°F for 30 to 35 minutes or until a knife inserted into the center comes out clean. Top with raw cheese if desired.

Scrambled Veggie Omelet

Makes: 4 servings / Prep time: 15 minutes / Cook time 15 minutes

- ❖ 1 green bell pepper, seeded and chopped
- ❖ 1 very small zucchini, diced
- ❖ 4–6 mushrooms, chopped (optional)

- ❖ ½ onion, diced
- ❖ 15 oz. black olives, drained and sliced
- ❖ 8 eggs
- ❖ ½ tsp. sea salt
- ❖ ¼ tsp. ground black pepper
- ❖ 1 dash hot sauce
- ❖ 1–2 tomatoes, seeded and chopped
- ❖ 1½ cups shredded raw cheddar cheese (optional)

Sauté bell pepper, zucchini, mushrooms, onion, and olives in an oiled pan just until crisp-tender. In a bowl, whisk together the eggs, salt, pepper, and hot sauce. Add the egg mixture to the veggies and scramble and it together until the egg whites are cooked through and the yolks are three-quarters done. (They will continue to cook on a plate.) Top with shredded cheese and chopped tomatoes.

Veggie Omelet Wrap

Follow recipe for scrambled veggie omelet and serve in a warmed, sprouted wheat tortilla with shredded raw cheese.

❖   ❖   ❖

Super Grain Quinoa Cereal

Makes: 4 servings / Prep time: 5 minutes / Soak time: 8 hours / Cook time: 20 minutes

- ❖ 1½ cups quinoa, rinsed very well
- ❖ 3 cups filtered water for soaking
- ❖ filtered water for cooking
- ❖ 1–2 Tbsps. butter or coconut oil
- ❖ ¼ tsp. sea salt
- ❖ raw milk or cream
- ❖ pure maple syrup or honey

Rinse the quinoa in a mesh strainer until there are no more soap-like bubbles. Rinse well, or it will taste like soap! Soak the rinsed quinoa in 3 cups water overnight, or for 8 hours. Rinse them again in the morning. Cover with new, clean water. Then add butter or oil and salt and cook over medium-low heat for about 20 minutes. Add milk or cream and maple syrup or honey.

Swiss Oatmeal

Makes: 6 servings / Prep time: 15 minutes / Soak time: 8 hours

- ❖ 2 cups rolled oats
- ❖ 2 cups water or milk
- ❖ 1 tsp. fresh lemon juice
- ❖ 2 Tbsps. raw honey or pure maple syrup
- ❖ ⅛ tsp. sea salt
- ❖ 1 banana, peeled and sliced
- ❖ 1 apple, cored and grated with skins on
- ❖ 1 orange, peeled and diced
- ❖ ½ cup fresh or partially thawed frozen berries
- ❖ ½ cup Traditional Almonds (see "Sprouting Nuts and Seeds" section), chopped
- ❖ ½ cup raisins, coarsely chopped (optional)
- ❖ ½ cup unsweetened shredded coconut flakes (optional)

The night before, mix the rolled oats, water or milk, and lemon juice together. Cover and leave on the counter overnight. In the morning, mix in the remaining ingredients and serve uncooked.

Apple-Cinnamon Breakfast Pudding

Makes: 4 servings / Prep time: 10 minutes / Cook time: 35 minutes

- ❖ ¼ cup filtered water
- ❖ 4 apples, washed and cut into chunks
- ❖ 6 slices sprouted wheat bread
- ❖ 5 eggs, slightly beaten
- ❖ 1 banana, mashed
- ❖ 1½ tsp. cinnamon
- ❖ ¾ cup raisins

Combine water and apples in a saucepan. Cover and simmer for about 20 minutes, or until apples are soft. When done, mash the apples and any remaining water lightly with a fork. Tear bread into bite-sized chunks and stir into apples. Pour eggs into bread and apples and stir well. Cook on medium-low heat for about 15 minutes, until eggs are cooked and mixture is thicker. In a bowl, mash banana thoroughly and stir in cinnamon. Pour banana into bread mixture, stir well, and then fold in raisins.

Oat Groats Cereal

Makes: 4 servings / Prep time: 5 minutes / Soak time: 8 hours / Cook time: 10–15 minutes

- ❖ lemon juice from half a lemon
- ❖ 3 cups water
- ❖ 1½ cups whole oat groats (This is the whole grain that makes rolled oats.)
- ❖ ¼ tsp. sea salt

Combine lemon juice and water. Soak oat groats for 8 hours, or overnight, in lemon water. In the morning, drain and process until finely cut. Put in pan. Cover with filtered water and the sea salt. Bring to a boil over medium heat and reduce to low. Simmer until thick, about 10 minutes. Serve with raw honey or agave and raw milk or cream.

Quinoa Blueberry Cereal

Makes: 6 servings / Prep time: 8 hours / Cook time: 7 minutes

- ❖ ½ cup rolled oats
- ❖ ⅓ cup filtered water
- ❖ 1 Tbsp. plain whole yogurt
- ❖ 2⅓ cup filtered water
- ❖ ½ tsp. sea salt
- ❖ ⅔ cup quinoa, rinsed well and sprouted
- ❖ ½ cup fresh or frozen blueberries
- ❖ 4 Tbsps. pure maple syrup or honey
- ❖ ½ tsp. pure vanilla
- ❖ ⅔ cup raw milk

Soak rolled oats for 8 hours, or overnight, in ⅓ cup water and 1 tablespoon yogurt. In the morning add water, salt, and rinsed quinoa and bring to a simmer. Then cook on medium heat for about 5 to 7 minutes. Add the blueberries and syrup. Simmer for about 2 minutes more. Stir in the vanilla and raw milk and enjoy!

Overnight Oatmeal Porridge

Makes: 4 servings / Prep time: 8 hours / Cook time: 5 minutes

- ❖ 2 cups rolled oats
- ❖ 2 cups filtered water
- ❖ 2–3 Tbsps. plain whole yogurt, whey, kefir, or buttermilk
- ❖ ½ tsp. sea salt
- ❖ 1½ cups filtered water
- ❖ 4 Tbsps. raw honey or pure maple syrup
- ❖ ½ tsp. pure vanilla extract
- ❖ 1 Tbsp. coconut oil or butter
- ❖ 1 tsp. ground cinnamon or ½ cup frozen blueberries
- ❖ raw milk

Combine the rolled oats, water, and yogurt and soak for 7 to 24 hours, or overnight. In the morning add the salt and 1½ cups of the water. Stir and heat over medium heat until thickened, about 3 to 5 minutes. Remove from heat and stir in the honey or syrup, vanilla, coconut oil or butter, and blueberries or cinnamon. Stir in raw milk before serving.

Rice Pudding Cereal

Makes: 4 servings / Prep time: 5 minutes / Cook time: 10 minutes

- ❖ 2 cups cooked brown rice, left whole or mashed
- ❖ 2 eggs or egg yolks, beaten
- ❖ ¼ tsp. sea salt
- ❖ ½ cup whole raw milk or coconut milk
- ❖ ¼ cup cream, preferably raw
- ❖ 2 Tbsps. raw honey or pure maple syrup
- ❖ 2 Tbsps. coconut oil and/or butter
- ❖ ½ tsp. pure vanilla
- ❖ ½ cup raisins
- ❖ ½ cup Traditional Almonds (see "Sprouting Nuts and Seeds" section), chopped
- ❖ 1 medium apple, cored and diced (optional)
- ❖ 1 tsp. ground cinnamon (optional)
- ❖ ¼ tsp. ground nutmeg (optional)

Combine rice and beaten egg yolks in a saucepan and heat over low heat. Mix thoroughly until heated through, but do not cook the eggs fast. The mixture should have a pudding consistency and should *not* be like scrambled eggs. Remove from heat and stir in all the other ingredients. Return to low heat and cover to warm through. Serve warm.

❖ ❖ ❖

Cream of Sprouted Wheat Cereal

Makes: 5 cups / Prep time: 5 minutes / Cook time: 5–15 minutes

- ❖ 4 cups filtered water
- ❖ ¼ tsp. sea salt

- ❖ 1 cup sprouted and dehydrated wheat, coarsely ground into a gritty flour texture
- ❖ 2 Tbsps. coconut oil or butter
- ❖ 3 Tbsps. pure maple syrup or raw honey
- ❖ raw milk or cream

Bring water and salt to a boil in a medium saucepan. Reduce heat to low and whisk in flour, stirring constantly. Add oil or butter and simmer covered for about 5 minutes until thick. Remove from heat and stir in honey or syrup. Add enough milk or cream for desired consistency. Serve warm.

❖ ❖ ❖

Sprouted Cracked Wheat Cereal

Makes: 4 servings / Prep time: 5 minutes / Cook time: 20 minutes

- ❖ 2 cups moist, freshly sprouted wheat
- ❖ 2 ½ cups filtered water
- ❖ ¼ tsp. sea salt
- ❖ raw honey or pure maple syrup
- ❖ raw milk or cream

In a food processor, process wheat sprouts for a couple minutes until chopped. Mix water, sea salt, and sprouted cracked wheat in a saucepan. For maximum nutrition, Cook on low for a few hours without boiling. Or boil on medium heat, then reduce to low and simmer for about 15 minutes or until tender. Add honey or maple syrup and raw milk or cream. Serve.

Traditional Cracked Wheat Cereal

Makes: 4 servings / Prep time: 12 hours / Cook time: 20 minutes

- ❖ 2 cups filtered water
- ❖ juice of half a lemon
- ❖ 2 cups whole wheat berries, milled very coarsely (cracked wheat)
- ❖ ¼ tsp. sea salt
- ❖ raw honey or pure maple syrup
- ❖ raw milk, cream, or butter

Combine water, lemon juice, and cracked wheat in a bowl and soak overnight for about 12 hours. In the morning, move the mixture to a pan and add salt and more water if needed. Simmer about 20 minutes until thick. Flavor with honey or syrup and raw milk, cream, or butter.

❖ ❖ ❖

Corn Grits Cereal

Makes: 4 servings / Prep time: 8 hours / Cook time: 20 minutes

- ❖ 3 cups filtered water
- ❖ the juice of half a lemon or a lime
- ❖ 1½ cups freshly ground popcorn kernel flour (popcorn kernels make fresh cornmeal or corn flour, depending on how finely ground they are)
- ❖ ½ tsp. sea salt
- ❖ raw milk
- ❖ 2–3 Tbsps. raw honey or pure maple syrup
- ❖ butter or coconut oil

Combine water, lime or lemon juice, and cornmeal, and soak for 8 hours, or overnight. In the morning, add sea salt and bring to a boil. Simmer for about 20 minutes, or until thick. Serve with raw milk, honey or maple syrup, and butter or coconut oil.

❖ ❖ ❖

Apple Breakfast Wrap

Makes: 4 servings / Prep time: 15 minutes

- ❖ 2 apples, finely chopped
- ❖ ½ cup raw almonds
- ❖ ½ cup raisins
- ❖ yogurt sauce (optional, see next recipe)
- ❖ 1 tsp. cinnamon (omit if using optional yogurt sauce)
- ❖ sprouted whole wheat tortillas

Mix apples, almonds, raisins, and cinnamon in a bowl until well coated. Spoon into a warm tortilla shell and serve. Add yogurt sauce if desired.

Yogurt Sauce

Makes: 4 servings / Prep time: 3 minutes

- ❖ ⅓ cup plain yogurt
- ❖ 1 tsp. agave
- ❖ 1 tsp. cinnamon

Mix yogurt, agave, and cinnamon together. Serve stirred into apples, or serve over the top of Apple Breakfast Wrap (see previous recipe).

Breakfast Fruit Bowl

Makes: 6 servings / Prep time: 15 minutes

- ❖ 1 apple, chopped
- ❖ 1 banana, sliced
- ❖ 1 orange, peeled and cut up
- ❖ 1 cup fresh strawberries or raspberries, chopped
- ❖ 1 cup fresh blueberries (optional)
- ❖ 2 kiwis, peeled and sliced
- ❖ ½ pineapple, chopped

Combine ingredients in a large, glass bowl. Serve with sprouted wheat toast topped with butter or coconut oil.

Morning Fruit Salad

Makes: 6 servings / Prep time 15 minutes

- ❖ 1 cup whole plain yogurt
- ❖ 1 Tbsp. honey or pure maple syrup
- ❖ 1 tsp. pure vanilla extract
- ❖ 1 cup sprouted moist wheat, cracked or partially blended and chilled
- ❖ 1 cup frozen blueberries
- ❖ 1 apple, cored and diced
- ❖ 1 banana, peeled and sliced
- ❖ ½ cup raisins (optional)
- ❖ unsweetened shredded coconut and/or chopped Traditional Almonds for top (optional)

Mix yogurt, honey or syrup, and vanilla in a medium bowl. Add all other ingredients and stir well. Make the night before for a quick breakfast in the morning.

❖ ❖ ❖

Fruit and Almond Cluster Granola

Makes: approx. 10 cups / Prep time: 35 minutes / Dehydration time: 12–14 hours

- ❖ 5½ cups almond flour (dehydrated pulp leftover from almond milk, run briefly through a food processor)
- ❖ ½–1 pineapple, thinly sliced
- ❖ 1 cup maple syrup
- ❖ 2 apples, thinly sliced
- ❖ 2 pears, thinly sliced
- ❖ 3 bananas, thinly sliced
- ❖ 2 mangos, peeled and thinly sliced
- ❖ ½ cup raisins
- ❖ ½ cup dried cranberries
- ❖ ½ cup raw sunflower seeds
- ❖ ½ cup raw pumpkin seeds
- ❖ ¼ cup raw flax seed

Slice all fruit thinly then lay slices out on dehydrator trays. Dehydrate for 12 to 14 hours at 115°F.

To make almond clusters, stir together the almond flour with the maple syrup until it is just damp and sticks together. It should still be fairly dry. Place on a food dehydrator solid sheet and dehydrate for about 12 to 14 hours at 115°F. When done, crumble into a bowl and add dehydrated fruit and seeds. Serve with raw milk and fresh fruit.

❖ ❖

Salads & Dressings

❖ ❖

Tasty Treasure #8

Fresh produce tastes so much better than the wax covered, three-month-old stuff at the grocery store. It's almost impossible to make good-tasting, fresh salsa with the mushy, orange tomatoes from the store instead of the vine-ripe tomatoes from your own garden. There's no comparison in flavor or nutrition.

Tasty Treasure #9

The edible skins of fruits and veggies are nutrient and fiber dense, so it is best to leave them on. Just wash them well before eating. Most of our recipes, even potato dishes, include the skins.

❖ ❖

Summer Fruit Salad

Makes: 15–20 servings / Prep time: 25 minutes

- ❖ ½ cup orange juice
- ❖ 1 apple, cored and chopped
- ❖ 2 cups fresh cherries, pitted and halved
- ❖ 1 cup fresh blueberries
- ❖ 1 whole fresh pineapple, peeled, cored, and diced
- ❖ 2 cups grapes, cut in half
- ❖ 2 oranges, peeled and cut into bite-sized pieces
- ❖ 4 kiwis, peeled and sliced
- ❖ 1–2 bananas, peeled and sliced

Put orange juice in a medium bowl. Add apples and let them soak for 5 minutes. In a large bowl, combine cherries, blueberries, pineapple, grapes, and oranges. Mix gently. Place kiwis on top and add apples and juice. Slice and add the bananas right before serving. Toss gently.

❖ ❖ ❖

Leafy Pineapple Salad

Makes: 15 servings / Prep time: 10 minutes

- ❖ 2–3 heads romaine lettuce, rinsed and chopped
- ❖ 2 cups chopped fresh pineapple
- ❖ 1 cup chopped apple
- ❖ 2 carrots, scrubbed and grated
- ❖ 1 cup Traditional Almonds (see "Sprouting Nuts and Seeds" section), chopped

Place all ingredients in a large, glass bowl. Toss well and serve with your dressing of choice.

Tropical Coleslaw

Makes: 8–10 servings / Prep time: 20 minutes

- ❖ 1 banana
- ❖ 1 cup plain yogurt
- ❖ ½ tsp. vanilla
- ❖ 1 tsp. raw blue/amber agave
- ❖ ½ medium pineapple, diced
- ❖ ½ head green cabbage, thinly shredded
- ❖ 2 medium carrots, grated
- ❖ ½ cup dried, unsweetened coconut
- ❖ ½ cup raisins

In a bowl, mash banana. Stir in yogurt, vanilla, agave, and pineapple chunks, squeezing a little juice out into the bowl. Add cabbage, carrots, coconut, and raisins, and stir.

Spinach Fruit Salad

Makes: 4 servings / Prep time: 15 minutes

- ❖ 1 bunch fresh spinach, washed and torn into pieces
- ❖ 1 apple, cored and diced
- ❖ 1 orange, peeled and chopped
- ❖ 2 kiwis, peeled and sliced (optional) *(continued)*

- ❖ ½ cup Traditional Almonds (see "Sprouting Nuts and Seeds" section), chopped
- ❖ ½ cup dried unsweetened cranberries or raisins
- ❖ ¼ of a medium red onion, thinly sliced

Toss all ingredients together in a medium bowl and keep tightly covered in refrigerator. Serve with Sweet Poppy Seed Dressing, Honey Dijon Dressing, or Orange Vinaigrette (see recipes later in this section).

❖ ❖ ❖

Grapefruit Salad

Makes: 4–6 servings / Prep time: 15 minutes

- ❖ 3 grapefruits, peeled and cut into bite-sized pieces
- ❖ seeds from 1 pomegranate
- ❖ 1 pineapple, cored and chopped into bite-sized pieces
- ❖ 2 Tbsps. raw blue/amber agave
- ❖ 2 drops therapeutic grade lavender essential oil (optional)

Combine all ingredients in a glass bowl and toss to coat well.

❖ ❖ ❖

Spinach Cranberry Salad

Makes: 4 servings / Prep time: 15 minutes

- ❖ 2 cups baby spinach, washed well and dried
- ❖ 2 cups baby green mix or red leaf lettuce, washed and dried
- ❖ ½ a red onion, quartered and thinly sliced
- ❖ 1 cup dried, naturally sweetened cranberries
- ❖ 1 cup Traditional Almonds (see "Sprouting Nuts and Seeds" section)

Combine ingredients in a glass bowl and toss with Strawberry Vinaigrette (see recipe later in this section).

❖ ❖ ❖

Perfect Pasta Salad

Makes: 20 servings / Prep time: 20 minutes

- ❖ 16 oz Tinkyáda® organic brown rice pasta (shells, macaroni, or spirals)
- ❖ 1 Tbsp. sea salt
- ❖ 6 slices bacon, cooked and cut in little pieces
- ❖ 1½ cups fresh green onions, sliced
- ❖ ½ cup grated carrots
- ❖ 1 cup halved cherry tomatoes
- ❖ 1 cup chopped cucumber
- ❖ ¾ cup sliced olives
- ❖ ¼ cup fresh or frozen and thawed green peas or ½ of a green pepper, chopped
- ❖ ¼ cup small raw cheddar cheese cubes
- ❖ Parmesan cheese (optional)

Boil pasta according to package instructions with 1 tablespoon sea salt. Drain and rinse under ice-cold water. Blot with a paper towel and transfer to a large bowl. Add all the other ingredients and the prepared pasta salad dressing. Toss gently and keep chilled.

Pasta Salad Dressing:

- ❖ ⅔ cup Vegenaise®
- ❖ ⅓ cup plain whole yogurt
- ❖ 3 Tbsps. fresh lemon juice or raw apple cider vinegar
- ❖ ½ tsp. garlic powder
- ❖ 1 Tbsp. dried parsley flakes
- ❖ 1 tsp. dried dill

Combine all ingredients and mix well.

❖   ❖   ❖

Caesar Salad

Makes: 6 servings / Prep time: 5 minutes

- ❖ 2 heads romaine lettuce leaves, washed and torn into bite-sized pieces
- ❖ 1½ cups chopped, cooked chicken (optional)
- ❖ 2 cups croutons (see following recipe)
- ❖ One recipe Caesar dressing (see following recipe)
- ❖ ¼ cup grated Parmesan cheese

Toss torn lettuce, chicken, and croutons. Drizzle dressing and toss to coat. Sprinkle Parmesan cheese on top.

Caesar Dressing

Makes: enough for one Caesar salad / Prep time: 2 hours, 10 minutes

- ❖ 1 egg yolk (either organic and raw from an organic free-range chicken or hard-boiled)
- ❖ ¼ cup extra virgin olive oil
- ❖ 1 Tbsp. raw apple cider vinegar
- ❖ 2 garlic cloves, minced
- ❖ 2–3 tsps. fresh lemon juice
- ❖ 1½ tsps. Dijon mustard
- ❖ 4 Tbsps. grated Parmesan cheese

Blend all ingredients well and refrigerate for at least 2 hours.

Croutons

Makes: 1½–2 cups / Prep time: 25 minutes

- ❖ ¼ cup olive oil, melted butter, or coconut oil
- ❖ 1 clove garlic, minced
- ❖ 1 tsp. parsley flakes
- ❖ 4 pieces of sprouted bread, cut into cubes

Mix oil, garlic, and parsley in a bowl. Add bread cubes and toss until well coated. Bake in the oven on a cookie sheet at 300°F for 15 to 20 minutes, or until crisp, stirring midway. Cool and serve with salad.

Fiesta Chicken Salad

Makes: 8 servings / Prep time: 20 minutes / Cook time: 45 minutes

- ❖ 2 chicken breasts
- ❖ 1–2 heads romaine lettuce, washed and torn into bite-sized pieces
- ❖ ½ cup fresh corn or thawed frozen corn
- ❖ 1 tomato, seeded and diced
- ❖ 1 handful fresh cilantro, chopped
- ❖ 1 red or green pepper, seeded and chopped
- ❖ 1 handful green onion or chives, sliced
- ❖ 1 cup black olives, sliced
- ❖ 1 cup shredded, raw cheese

Cook chicken breasts as desired and chop. Combine chicken with remaining salad ingredients in a large bowl and toss. Make the dressing and either mix and toss it into the salad, or drizzle it over the top of individual servings.

Fiesta Chicken Salad Dressing:

- ❖ ¾ cup Vegenaise®
- ❖ 6 Tbsps. extra virgin olive oil
- ❖ ¼ cup fresh lime or lemon juice (about 2 lemons or 3 limes)
- ❖ 1 tsp. ground cumin
- ❖ 1 tsp. dried oregano
- ❖ ½ tsp. garlic powder

Combine all ingredients and mix well.

Ultimate Chef Salad

Makes: 8 servings / Prep time: 30 minutes

- ❖ 1–2 heads romaine lettuce
- ❖ 1 handful fresh spinach leaves
- ❖ 1 chicken breast, cooked
- ❖ 4 bacon strips (nitrate free), cooked and crumbled
- ❖ ½ cup shredded raw cheese
- ❖ ½ cup halved cherry tomatoes
- ❖ 2 hard boiled eggs, peeled and sliced *(continued)*

- ❖ ½ small cucumber, sliced
- ❖ ½ green pepper, seeded and sliced
- ❖ 1 avocado, peeled, pitted, and sliced
- ❖ ¼ cup chopped green or red onions

Divide greens on 6 to 8 different single plates. Arrange additional ingredients of choice on top. Serve with Classic Ranch Dressing (see recipe later in this section).

❖ ❖ ❖

Coleslaw

Makes: 6 servings / Prep time: 20 minutes / Chill time: 2 hours

- ❖ 1 cup shredded red cabbage
- ❖ 1 cup shredded green cabbage
- ❖ 1 cup shredded carrots
- ❖ ¼ of a medium-sized red onion, minced
- ❖ 1 cup diced celery
- ❖ 1 Tbsp. dried parsley flakes or ¼ cup chopped, fresh flat-leaf parsley

Coleslaw Dressing:

- ❖ ⅓ cup Vegenaise®
- ❖ ⅓ cup plain whole yogurt
- ❖ 1 Tbsps. red wine vinegar or raw apple cider vinegar
- ❖ 2–4 Tbsps. liquid sweetener
- ❖ ¼ tsp. Dijon mustard
- ❖ ¼ tsp. black pepper
- ❖ ¼ tsp. sea salt

Shred and slice cabbage, carrots, and onion in a food processor. (Use the slice blade for cabbage and the shred blade for carrots and onion.) Add the celery and parsley and toss the vegetables lightly. Blend the dressing ingredients in a small bowl. Add dressing to vegetables and mix until vegetables are well coated. Cover and chill for at least 2 hours before serving.

❖ ❖ ❖

Three-Bean Salad

Makes: 6–8 servings / Prep time: 45 minutes

- ❖ 2 cups fresh green beans, cut in half, steamed until tender, and cooled
- ❖ 2 cups black beans, cooked "slow and low", and then chilled
- ❖ 2 cups kidney beans, cooked "slow and low", and then chilled
- ❖ 1 bell pepper, chopped
- ❖ ½ medium red onion, quartered and thinly sliced
- ❖ ¼ cup raw apple cider vinegar
- ❖ ¼ cup natural sweetener
- ❖ ¼ cup olive oil

Place all of the chilled beans in a large glass bowl. Add chopped pepper and onion. In another bowl, mix together vinegar, sweetener, and oil. Stir well then pour over beans. Toss to cover. Serve cold.

Traditional Potato Salad

Makes: 12 servings / Prep time: 30 minutes / Chill time: 4 hours

- ❖ 7 medium red or yukon gold potatoes, washed and scrubbed with the skins left on
- ❖ 1½–1¾ cups Vegenaise®
- ❖ 1 Tbsp. regular or Dijon prepared mustard
- ❖ ¾–1 cup seeded and diced cucumber
- ❖ 1½ cups celery, thinly sliced
- ❖ 1 small red or yellow onion, minced or ¾ cup sliced green onions
- ❖ 1 tsp. sea salt
- ❖ ½ tsp. dried dill
- ❖ ½ tsp. black pepper
- ❖ 1 tsp. paprika
- ❖ 6 hard boiled eggs, diced

Place potatoes in a large pot and cover with water. Boil until tender, about 20 to 30 minutes. Drain and let cool a bit, then chop or dice them. In a large bowl, combine the Vegenaise®, mustard, cucumber, celery, onion, salt, dill, pepper, and paprika (the paprika may be sprinkled on top of finished salad or mixed in). Add the potatoes and eggs last. Toss gently to coat. Cover and chill for at least 4 hours before serving.

Seven-Layer Salad

Makes: 8 servings / Prep time: 20 minutes

- ❖ 1 head leaf lettuce, rinsed and torn
- ❖ ½ cup rinsed and torn spinach
- ❖ 1 cup fresh peas
- ❖ 1 cucumber, quartered and sliced
- ❖ ½ a red onion or 2–4 green onions, chopped
- ❖ 2 stalks celery, thinly sliced
- ❖ 2 medium carrots, grated
- ❖ 1 bell pepper, diced
- ❖ ¾ cup Vegenaise®
- ❖ ¾ cup plain yogurt
- ❖ 2 tsp. raw vinegar
- ❖ 2 tsp. agave
- ❖ ¼ tsp. sea salt
- ❖ 2 tomatoes, chopped
- ❖ 1 can sliced olives

In a serving dish, layer lettuce, spinach, peas, cucumber, onion, celery, carrot, and bell pepper. Mix mayo, yogurt, vinegar, agave, and sea salt in a bowl, and pour over salad. Top with chopped tomatoes and olives.

Beefy Taco Salad

Makes: 8 servings / Prep: 25 minutes / Cook time: 20 minutes

Taco chili topping:

- ❖ 1 lb. ground hamburger
- ❖ 3 Tbsps. olive oil
- ❖ 1 medium onion, chopped
- ❖ 1–2 garlic cloves, minced
- ❖ 2 cups sprouted and cooked pinto and/or kidney beans
- ❖ 2 Tbsps. chili powder
- ❖ 2 tsps. ground cumin
- ❖ 1 tsp. oregano
- ❖ ½ tsp. paprika
- ❖ 2½ tsps. sea salt
- ❖ 2½ cups blended tomatoes or 15 oz. tomato sauce and ½ cup water

Salad and toppings:

- ❖ 2 heads romaine lettuce, washed and torn
- ❖ 1 bag of corn chips, crushed
- ❖ raw cheese, grated
- ❖ tomatoes, chopped
- ❖ 15 oz. olives, drained and sliced
- ❖ 1 avocado, peeled, pitted, and diced
- ❖ ¼ of an onion, thinly sliced
- ❖ sour cream
- ❖ salsa

In a large frying pan, brown hamburger and onion in olive oil until hamburger is cooked through. Add seasonings, beans, and tomatoes. Cook until warm. Set taco chili aside. On each serving plate, place torn lettuce topped with broken chips, and then add shredded cheese. When ready to eat, top with taco chili and other remaining toppings.

Taco Salad

Makes: 4 servings / Prep time: 30 minutes

- ❖ 1 cup sprouted and cooked pinto or red beans
- ❖ ½ Tbsp. chili powder
- ❖ 1 head of leaf lettuce, washed and shredded
- ❖ ½ an onion, chopped
- ❖ 1 ripe bell pepper, chopped
- ❖ 1 avocado, sliced
- ❖ 1 can olives, drained and sliced
- ❖ 1 large tomato, diced
- ❖ ¼ cup shredded raw cheese (optional)
- ❖ ½ cup fresh salsa
- ❖ 2 Tbsps. plain whole yogurt
- ❖ tortilla chips

Combine beans and chili powder and stir well. Set aside. Combine prepared vegetables together in a bowl. Add the flavored beans and toss. For sauce, stir together salsa and yogurt. Pour over salad, and add tortilla chips. Serve immediately.

Broccoli Cauliflower Salad

Makes: 6 servings / Prep time 30 minutes

- ❖ 1 crown broccoli, finely chopped
- ❖ ⅔ head cauliflower, finely chopped
- ❖ ½ a red onion, quartered and thinly sliced
- ❖ 1 cucumber, quartered and sliced
- ❖ ½ cup crushed Traditional Almonds (see "Sprouting Nuts and Seeds" section)

Sauce:

- ❖ ½ cup olive oil
- ❖ ½ cup raw apple cider vinegar
- ❖ ½ cup raw blue/amber agave
- ❖ ½ cup plain yogurt or Vegenaise®
- ❖ ½ tsp. sea salt
- ❖ 1 tsp. Dijon mustard
- ❖ 2 tsps. celery seed

Combine vegetables in a medium-sized bowl. To make the sauce, mix yogurt and mustard in a small bowl, then stir in olive oil, vinegar, agave, sea salt, and celery seed. Pour sauce over vegetables. Refrigerate overnight. Add almonds just before serving.

Creamy Vinaigrette Dressing

Makes: approx. 1 cup / Prep time: 7 minutes

- ❖ ¼ cup red wine vinegar
- ❖ 1 Tbsp. Dijon mustard
- ❖ 2 Tbsps. Vegenaise®
- ❖ 2 small cloves garlic, minced
- ❖ ⅔ cup olive or grape seed oil, or a mixture of both
- ❖ 1½ tsps. parsley flakes
- ❖ 1½ tsps. oregano

In a glass jar, mix all ingredients together and either stir or shake with a lid tightly in place. Serve immediately or refrigerate.

Classic Ranch Dressing

Makes: approx. 2 cups / Prep time: 20 minutes / Chill: 30 minutes

- ❖ 1½ tsps. dried parsley flakes
- ❖ ½ tsp. dried dill weed
- ❖ ¼ tsp. garlic powder
- ❖ 1–1½ tsps. onion powder
- ❖ ½ tsp. sea salt
- ❖ ¼ tsp. freshly ground black pepper
- ❖ 1 cup Vegenaise®
- ❖ ¼ cup milk
- ❖ ¼ cup plain whole yogurt
- ❖ ¾ tsp. raw apple cider vinegar

Combine all ingredients in a small mixing bowl. Mix well and refrigerate for at least 30 minutes before serving. Keeps for about 2 to 4 weeks.

Honey Dijon Dressing

Makes: 2 servings / Prep time: 5 minutes

- ❖ 1 Tbsp. prepared Dijon mustard (Make sure ingredients are basic, whole ingredients)
- ❖ 1 Tbsp. raw honey
- ❖ ¼ cup olive oil

Combine ingredients in a jar and stir well with a fork. Serve.

❖ ❖ ❖

Sweet Poppy Seed Dressing

Makes: approx. 2 cups / Prep time: 10 minutes

- ❖ ⅓ cup dehydrated cane juice
- ❖ ¼ tsp. sea salt
- ❖ ⅓ cup raw apple cider vinegar
- ❖ 1 tsp. mustard
- ❖ 1¼ cups extra virgin olive oil
- ❖ 2 Tbsps. poppy seeds

Combine all ingredients in glass jar or bowl. Blend well. Keep refrigerated.

Creamy Pasta Salad Dressing

Makes: approx. 1 cup / Prep time: 7 minutes

- ❖ ⅓ cup Vegenaise®
- ❖ ⅓ cup sour cream
- ❖ ¼ cup plain yogurt
- ❖ 3 Tbsps. fresh lemon juice, red wine vinegar, or brown rice vinegar
- ❖ 1–2 fresh cloves of garlic, minced
- ❖ 1 Tbsp. dried parsley flakes
- ❖ 1 tsp. dried dill

Combine all ingredients in a glass jar and mix or shake until well mixed. Serve immediately or refrigerate.

❖   ❖   ❖

Orange Vinaigrette

Makes: 4 servings / Prep time: 5 minutes

- ❖ ½ cup fresh-squeezed orange juice
- ❖ 2 Tbsps. olive oil
- ❖ 2 Tbsps. vinegar
- ❖ ½ Tbsp. honey (optional)

Combine all ingredients in a jar with a lid and shake or stir well with a fork. Serve.

❖   ❖   ❖

Strawberry Vinaigrette

Makes: 1¼ cup / Prep time: 5 minutes

- ❖ ⅓ cup raw apple cider vinegar
- ❖ ⅓ cup extra virgin olive oil
- ❖ ⅓ cup agave
- ❖ ¼ cup blended strawberry pulp (5–7 fresh or thawed frozen strawberries run through a food processor)

Combine all ingredients and mix well. Serve with Spinach Cranberry Salad (see recipe earlier in this section).

Creamy Italian Dressing

Makes: approx. 1 cup / Prep time: 5 minutes

- ❖ ⅓ cup extra virgin olive oil
- ❖ ⅓ cup raw apple cider vinegar
- ❖ ¼ cup plain yogurt
- ❖ ¼ tsp. sea salt
- ❖ 1 tsp. oregano
- ❖ 1 tsp. basil
- ❖ 1 clove garlic, minced

Combine ingredients in a jar with a tight fitting lid and shake well. Serve.

❖ ❖

❖ ❖

Sandwiches & Wraps

❖ ❖

Tasty Treasure #10

Not only are these sandwiches delicious, they digest well. Most commercial sandwiches combine a starch (white or whole wheat bread) with a protein (meat), which is a difficult combination for the body to digest properly. When you make a sandwich with sprouted grain bread, it digests like a vegetable because there is less starch. Taste, nutrition, and digestibility—now you can have it all with these delicious recipes!

❖ ❖

Almond Apple Wrap

Makes: 6 servings / Prep time: 20 minutes

- ❖ ⅓ cup Vegenaise® or plain whole yogurt
- ❖ 1 tsp. raw apple cider vinegar or fresh lemon juice
- ❖ 1 tsp. liquid sweetener
- ❖ ¼ tsp. sea salt
- ❖ 2 apples, diced
- ❖ 4 stalks celery and leaves, finely diced
- ❖ 1 can olives, drained and chopped (optional)
- ❖ 1 green bell pepper, seeded and diced
- ❖ ½ cup Traditional Almonds (see "Sprouting Nuts and Seeds" section), chopped
- ❖ ½ cup finely shredded fresh spinach
- ❖ ¼ of a medium red onion, diced
- ❖ sprouted wheat tortillas or sprouted wheat bread

Mix yogurt, vinegar, honey, and sea salt in a small bowl. Set aside. In a separate bowl, mix remaining ingredients except tortillas or bread. Add yogurt sauce and mix well. Spoon into tortillas or serve on bread.

❖ ❖ ❖

Grilled Cheese Sandwiches

Makes: 4 sandwiches / Prep time: 5 minutes / Cook time: 15 minutes

- ❖ 8 slices sprouted wheat bread
- ❖ 4 slices of raw sharp cheddar cheese
- ❖ butter

Butter a pan and heat over medium heat. When butter has melted, place four of the slices of bread onto the skillet or grill, in a single layer. Cover each piece of bread with a slice of cheese, and then place the other slice of bread on top. When brown, flip over, and repeat until cheese has just melted. This goes great with Cream of Tomato Soup (see recipe in "Soups and Stocks").

❖ ❖ ❖

Egg Salad Sandwiches

Makes: 1 cup / Prep time: 15 minutes / Cook time: 20–25 minutes

- ❖ 4 hard-boiled eggs, peeled
- ❖ ⅓ cup Vegenaise®
- ❖ 1 tsp. regular or Dijon mustard
- ❖ salt and pepper to taste
- ❖ ½ cup cucumber, seeded and diced (optional)
- ❖ 1 stalk celery, chopped
- ❖ 1 Tbsp. minced onion
- ❖ ½ tsp. dried dill (optional)
- ❖ toasted sprouted wheat bread, sprouted wheat tortillas, or salad greens

Mash eggs in a medium bowl with a fork. In a separate medium bowl, blend the mayo and mustard. Season with salt and pepper. Add the optional cucumber, celery, onion, and optional dill. Gently stir in the mashed eggs. Spread on toasted sprouted bread, on sprouted wheat tortillas, or over salad greens.

❖ ❖ ❖

Tuna Salad Sandwich

Makes: 3 servings / Prep time: 8 minutes

- ❖ 6 oz. wild-caught tuna (packed in water), drained
- ❖ ⅓ cup Vegenaise®
- ❖ 1 small celery stalk, finely chopped
- ❖ pinch of onion powder
- ❖ pinch of garlic powder
- ❖ ¼ tsp. dried dill weed
- ❖ pinch of sea salt

In a medium-sized bowl, mix all ingredients together with a fork. Wrap in romaine lettuce leaves or in sprouted wheat tortillas, or spread on sprouted grain bread.

❖   ❖   ❖

Hummus Wraps

Makes: 4 servings / Prep time: 20 minutes

Hummus

- ❖ 1 cup soaked and cooked garbanzo beans, or one 15 oz. can organic garbanzo beans
- ❖ 1 clove garlic, minced
- ❖ 2 Tbsp. onion, chopped
- ❖ 2 Tbsp. extra virgin olive oil
- ❖ 1 tsp. dried parsley flakes
- ❖ sea salt to taste

Toppings

- ❖ a handful of fresh spinach
- ❖ half a bell pepper (green or red), sliced
- ❖ fresh sprouts
- ❖ half a cucumber, sliced

Blend garbanzo beans, garlic, onion, olive oil, parsley, and sea salt in a food processor until it is smooth and has the consistency of refried beans. A little water may be added to achieve desired moistness and consistency. Spread hummus in a sprouted tortilla and fill wrap with spinach, bell pepper, sprouts, cucumbers, and any other desired vegetables.

Tomato Sandwiches

Makes: 2 sandwiches / Prep time: 10 minutes

- ❖ 4 slices sprouted bread
- ❖ 2–3 Tbsps. softened cream cheese, butter, or Vegenaise®
- ❖ 2–4 dark green lettuce leaves
- ❖ 4 large slices of vine-ripened tomatoes, salted
- ❖ thin slices of red onion (optional)
- ❖ 2 thin slices of raw cheese (optional)

Toast bread and spread butter, mayo, or cream cheese on one side of each slice of toast. Top 2 slices of the bread with lettuce, tomato slices, and optional onion and cheese. Close sandwiches with remaining two slices of toast and enjoy!

❖ ❖ ❖

BLT Sandwich

Makes: 2 sandwiches / Prep time: 15 minutes

- ❖ 3 Tbsps. Vegenaise®
- ❖ 1 tsp. mustard
- ❖ 4 slices sprouted grain bread
- ❖ 2 thin slices raw mild cheddar cheese (optional)
- ❖ 1 avocado, peeled, pitted and sliced (optional)
- ❖ 2–3 slices organic, nitrate-free bacon, cooked
- ❖ 2 romaine lettuce leaves
- ❖ 1 medium fresh, ripe tomato, sliced
- ❖ sea salt and pepper to taste

Mix the mayo and mustard together and apply it generously to one side of all 4 bread slices. Layer the cheese, avocado, bacon, lettuce, tomato, salt, and pepper on two slices of the bread. Top with the other two slices of bread. If desired, roll ingredients inside tortillas to make wraps.

❖ ❖ ❖

"Nut" Butter Sandwich

Makes: 2 sandwiches / Prep time: 3 minutes

- ❖ 4 slices sprouted grain bread
- ❖ 4 Tbsps. almond butter or sunflower seed butter
- ❖ 2 romaine lettuce leaves, cut in half

Toast the bread if desired. Spread 2 tablespoons of almond butter or sunflower seed butter on 2 of the slices. Top each one with a leaf or two of lettuce and then the other slice of bread. This light sandwich was inspired by the classic celery and peanut butter snack.

❖ ❖

Soups & Stocks

❖ ❖

Tasty Treasure #11

Making broths and stocks from scratch gives a full, rich flavor to any meal. There is no way those little refined-salt, MSG-enriched, imitation-meat bullion cubes can even come close to comparing in flavor to homemade broths. Plus, there's the added bonus that steamy, natural broths are health promoting—especially during an illness.

❖ ❖

Old-Fashioned Beef Stew

Makes: 6–8 servings / Prep: 20 minutes / Cook: 1 hour

- ❖ 1 lb. hamburger or ground bison
- ❖ 2 Tbsps. butter or extra virgin olive oil
- ❖ 6 cups beef stock
- ❖ 8 oz. tomato sauce
- ❖ 1 onion, chopped
- ❖ 15 oz. tomatoes, blended
- ❖ 1 garlic clove, minced
- ❖ 1 tsp. sea salt
- ❖ 1 tsp. dried oregano
- ❖ 1 tsp. dried thyme
- ❖ ½ tsp. dried and ground rosemary
- ❖ ½ tsp. dried parsley flakes
- ❖ ½ tsp. dried marjoram
- ❖ ¼ tsp. black pepper
- ❖ 1 bay leaf
- ❖ 1 Tbsp. dehydrated cane juice
- ❖ 4–5 red potatoes, scrubbed and chopped (with skins on)
- ❖ 1 cup frozen whole-kernel corn, rinsed under warm water
- ❖ 4–5 medium carrots, sliced

Partially brown meat (it will finish cooking in the soup). Transfer meat to a Crock-Pot or slow cooker and add all of the remaining ingredients. Cook for 5 to 8 hours on medium-high heat. Discard bay leaf before serving.

Nourishing Chicken Noodle Soup

Makes: 6 servings / Prep time: 20 minutes / Cook time: 20 minutes

- ❖ 2 Tbsps. extra virgin olive oil or butter
- ❖ 1 large onion, chopped
- ❖ 3 garlic cloves, minced
- ❖ 2–3 medium carrots, cut into slices
- ❖ 2–3 celery ribs, cut into slices
- ❖ 1½ tsp. dried thyme
- ❖ 1 bay leaf
- ❖ 12 cups homemade chicken stock
- ❖ 8 oz. Tinkyáda® brown rice pasta
- ❖ 1½ cups cooked chicken meat, shredded or chopped
- ❖ 1½ tsps. sea salt
- ❖ 1½ tsp. dried parsley

Place a soup pot over medium heat and coat with oil. Add onion, garlic, carrots, celery, thyme, and bay leaf. Cook and stir for about 6 minutes until the vegetables are softened but not browned. Pour in chicken stock and bring it to a boil. Add the noodles and simmer for 10 minutes or until tender. Add the chicken and salt and continue to simmer for another couple of minutes to heat through.

–or–

Combine everything except the noodles in a large soup pot and bring it to a boil over high heat. Reduce heat and simmer for 5 minutes. Add the noodles and simmer for 10 more minutes.

Note: The noodles in this soup can also be substituted with brown rice or chopped red potatoes.

❖ ❖ ❖

Creamy Ham and Potato Soup

Makes: 6 servings / Prep time: 20 minutes / Cook time: 30 minutes

- ❖ 6 oz. chopped deli ham, nitrate free
- ❖ 2 medium potatoes, diced
- ❖ 2 carrots, sliced
- ❖ ½ cup sliced celery

- ❖ 1 medium onion, chopped
- ❖ 1–2 garlic cloves, minced
- ❖ ¼ cup butter
- ❖ 4 cups chicken stock
- ❖ 2 tsps. sea salt
- ❖ ¼ tsp. freshly ground black pepper
- ❖ 1 cup whole raw milk
- ❖ 2 cups shredded raw cheese

Combine all ingredients except milk and cheese in a soup pot. Cover and bring to a boil. Reduce heat and simmer covered for 25 minutes. Add milk and cheese and heat through for 5 more minutes with lid on.

Cream of Broccoli Soup

Makes: approx. 2 quarts / Prep time: 15 minutes / Cook time: 10 minutes

- ❖ ½ of a large onion, chopped
- ❖ 1 small clove garlic, minced
- ❖ ¼ cup butter
- ❖ 4 cups chicken broth
- ❖ 1 Tbsp. sprouted wheat flour
- ❖ 1 cup milk
- ❖ 1 cup cream
- ❖ 1 tsp. sea salt
- ❖ ¼ tsp. freshly ground black pepper
- ❖ 2 cups shredded cheese
- ❖ 20 oz. frozen broccoli, thawed and chopped

In a soup pot, sauté onion and garlic in the butter for a few minutes. Add 1 cup of the broth and then whisk in the flour. Allow to thicken, and then stir in the remaining broth, milk, cream, salt, and pepper. Allow the mixture to heat through again. Then add the cheese and broccoli. Cover and cook over medium-low heat for about 10 minutes. Serve.

Fiesta Soup

Makes: 4–6 servings / Prep time: 20 minutes / Cook time: approx. 30 minutes

- ❖ 3–4 Tbsps. olive oil or butter
- ❖ 1 cup fresh or frozen corn
- ❖ 1 large red or green bell pepper, seeded and chopped
- ❖ 1 medium yellow onion, chopped
- ❖ 3 cloves garlic, minced
- ❖ 1½ tsps. ground cumin
- ❖ ¼ tsp. black pepper
- ❖ 1 tsp. sea salt
- ❖ 1 tsp. oregano
- ❖ 1 tsp. sage
- ❖ ¼ tsp. marjoram
- ❖ ½ tsp. thyme
- ❖ 3 cups chopped fresh tomatoes or 1 (28-oz.) can diced tomatoes
- ❖ 8 oz. tomato sauce
- ❖ 6 cups chicken stock
- ❖ 1 medium zucchini, diced small

Garnishes:

- ❖ 4 cups corn chips, broken up
- ❖ 2 avocados, diced with a squeeze of lemon and salt and pepper over them
- ❖ ½ cup chopped fresh cilantro
- ❖ 1 cup sour cream
- ❖ 1 cup grated raw cheese

Heat olive oil in a soup pot over medium heat. Add corn, bell peppers, onion, garlic, and all spices. Stir to coat and cook until onions are moderately soft. Add the tomatoes, sauce, chicken stock, and zucchini. Bring soup to a boil and then cover and cook for about 15 to 20 minutes over medium-low heat. Ladle into individual bowls and top with garnishes.

❖ ❖ ❖

Taco Soup

Makes: 6 servings / Prep time: 20 minutes / Cook time: 40 minutes

- ❖ 1 lb. hamburger, browned
- ❖ 1 large onion, chopped
- ❖ 2 Tbsps. olive oil
- ❖ 2 cloves garlic, minced
- ❖ 4 cups beef stock or broth
- ❖ 2½ tsps. sea salt
- ❖ 1 tsp. oregano
- ❖ 4 tsps. chili powder
- ❖ 2 tsps. ground cumin
- ❖ 2 tsps. minced dried onion or onion powder
- ❖ 10 oz. frozen corn, thawed
- ❖ 2 (28-oz.) cans or 6 cups of chunky tomato sauce
- ❖ 4 cups sprouted and cooked pinto and/or kidney beans

Garnishes:
- ❖ raw cheese, grated
- ❖ corn chips, broken up
- ❖ sour cream
- ❖ chives or green onions, sliced

Brown hamburger in a soup pot over medium heat. Add the onions and olive oil. When onions are tender, add garlic, beef stock, and all seasonings. Mix well. Cook for about five minutes, uncovered. Finally, add the corn, chunky tomato sauce, and beans. Mix well. Cover and simmer for 30 minutes. Ladle into individual bowls and top with garnishes.

Vegetarian Taco Soup

Makes: 6 servings / Prep time: 15 minutes / Cook time: 45 minutes

- ❖ 2 cloves garlic, minced
- ❖ ½ onion, chopped
- ❖ 1 bell pepper, chopped
- ❖ 2 (28-oz.) cans chopped organic tomatoes
- ❖ 1 cup fresh or frozen corn *(continued)*

❖ 1 (15-oz.) can pinto beans
❖ 1 Tbsp. chili powder
❖ 1 tsp. cumin powder
❖ ½ tsp. sea salt
❖ 2 medium avocados, chopped
❖ 3–4 sprouted corn tortillas, cut into triangles and baked
until crisp
❖ 3 Tbsps. fresh cilantro, finely chopped
❖ sour cream (optional)
❖ fresh cilantro (optional)

In a large saucepan, sauté garlic, onion, and bell pepper until tender. Add tomatoes, corn, beans, chili powder, cumin, and sea salt. Heat thoroughly, and add avocado, tortilla chips, and cilantro last. Garnish with a dollop of sour cream and fresh cilantro.

❖ ❖ ❖

Indian Lentil Soup

Makes: 4–6 servings / Prep time: 20 minutes / Cook time: 30–35 minutes

❖ 1¼ cups red lentils, rinsed and soaked for about 4–5 hours
❖ 8 cups chicken stock
❖ 2 cups freshly diced tomatoes or 1 (15-oz.) can petite, diced
tomatoes
❖ 2 medium potatoes, scrubbed well and diced with skins left
on (about 2 cups)
❖ 1 medium yellow onion, chopped
❖ 2 tsps. curry powder
❖ 2 garlic cloves, minced
❖ ¼ tsp. black pepper
❖ 1½ tsps. sea salt

Combine all ingredients in a soup pot and bring them to a boil. Reduce heat, cover, and simmer for 20 to 25 minutes. Serve with corn bread.

❖ ❖ ❖

Cream of Tomato Soup

Makes: 4 servings / Prep time: 15 minutes / Cook time: 30 minutes

- ❖ 28 oz. tomato sauce
- ❖ 3 Tbsps. butter
- ❖ 1 medium onion, chopped
- ❖ 1–3 cloves garlic, minced
- ❖ 1 carrot, scrubbed and diced
- ❖ 1 celery stalk, chopped
- ❖ ½ tsp. dried parsley flakes
- ❖ 1¾ tsps. dried basil or 8 fresh basil leaves
- ❖ 2 Tbsps. liquid sweetener
- ❖ ½ tsp. sea salt
- ❖ 3 cups chicken or vegetable stock
- ❖ 1 cup heavy cream

Combine all ingredients except cream in a saucepan. Cook covered for about 30 minutes over medium-low heat. Remove from heat and blend until smooth. Add cream and serve warm with grilled cheese sandwiches.

Cream of Mushroom Soup

Makes: 4 servings / Prep time: 15 minutes / Cook time: 30 minutes

- ❖ 2 cups fresh, organic mushrooms, rinsed and chopped
- ❖ 1 medium onion, chopped
- ❖ 1 clove garlic, minced
- ❖ 2 Tbsps. extra virgin olive oil
- ❖ 2½ cups beef, chicken, or vegetable stock
- ❖ ¾ tsp. sea salt
- ❖ 4 Tbsps. butter
- ❖ ¼ tsp. black pepper
- ❖ ¾ cup raw whole milk
- ❖ 1 cup sour cream

In a soup pot, sauté mushrooms, onion, and garlic in butter or oil over medium heat until tender. Add all remaining ingredients except sour cream and heat to a rolling boil. Add sour cream and stir until thickened. Remove from heat and serve.

Beef Chili

Makes: 8 servings / Prep time: 30 minutes / Cook time: 1 hour

- ❖ 2 lbs. hamburger
- ❖ 3 Tbsps. olive oil or butter
- ❖ 1 large yellow onion, chopped
- ❖ 1–2 cloves garlic, minced
- ❖ 1 large green pepper, seeded and chopped
- ❖ 3 (28-oz.) cans diced tomatoes, pureed
- ❖ 2 cups sprouted and cooked kidney beans
- ❖ 2 cups sprouted and cooked pinto or small red beans
- ❖ 2 cups beef stock
- ❖ 2–3 Tbsps. chili powder
- ❖ 2 tsps. ground cumin
- ❖ 1½ tsps. sea salt
- ❖ ¾ tsp. black pepper

Brown the hamburger in a saucepan with the olive oil or butter. Scramble it finely so that there are no large chunks of meat. Transfer meat to a soup pot and add all the remaining ingredients. Cover and bring to a boil, stirring frequently. Reduce heat and simmer, covered, for about an hour.

–or–

After you have browned the hamburger, transfer the meat to a Crock-Pot and add all of the remaining ingredients. Cook on low all day. Enjoy with cornbread, biscuits, or fresh baked bread or rolls. If desired, top with grated raw cheese and real sour cream.

Chicken and Dumpling Soup

Makes: 6 servings / Prep time: 20 minutes / Cook time: 20 minutes

Dumplings:

- ❖ 2 cups moist sprouted wheat, spelt, or kamut
- ❖ ¼ tsp. sea salt
- ❖ 1 tsp. baking soda
- ❖ 1 Tbsp. butter or coconut oil

Soup:

- ❖ 6 cups chicken broth
- ❖ 2 potatoes, cubed
- ❖ 2 carrots, chopped
- ❖ 2 stalks celery, sliced
- ❖ ¾ cup chopped fresh green beans
- ❖ corn cut from 1 fresh cob
- ❖ ½ onion, chopped
- ❖ 3 cloves garlic, minced
- ❖ 1 tsp. oregano
- ❖ 1 tsp. basil
- ❖ sea salt to taste
- ❖ 1 small piece of chicken, shredded

To make the dumplings, blend the sprouted grain in a food processor until it turns to dough. Add remaining dumpling ingredients and mix well. Form the dough into small balls.

To make the soup, place broth in a large saucepan or stockpot. Add vegetables, herbs, chicken, and dumpling balls. Bring soup to a boil, then reduce the heat and simmer for about 20 minutes, until vegetables are tender and dumplings are cooked through.

Vegetable Chili

Makes: 4 servings / Prep time: 15 minutes / Cook time: 40–60 minutes

- ❖ 2 (28-oz.) cans diced organic tomatoes
- ❖ 2 cups cooked pinto or red beans
- ❖ 1 bell pepper, chopped
- ❖ ½ medium onion, chopped
- ❖ 2 cloves garlic, minced
- ❖ 2½–3 Tbsps. chili powder
- ❖ 2 tsps. cumin
- ❖ sea salt to taste

Place all ingredients in a large saucepan and bring it to a boil. Reduce heat and simmer for 40 minutes to an hour. Serve.

Swiss Chard Soup

Makes: 8 servings / Prep time: 10 minutes / Cook time: 20 minutes

- ❖ 7 medium red potatoes, washed and thinly sliced
- ❖ 1 medium red onion, quartered and sliced
- ❖ 2 cloves garlic, minced
- ❖ 8 cups chicken broth
- ❖ 8 oz. scrambled and browned sausage
- ❖ 2 cups raw milk
- ❖ 1 tsp. sea salt
- ❖ ¼ tsp. black pepper
- ❖ ¾ tsp. basil
- ❖ ¾ tsp. oregano
- ❖ 5 cups chopped or torn Swiss chard

In a large pot, combine all of the ingredients except for the chard. Heat to boiling, then reduce the heat and simmer for about 25 minutes. Add chard and simmer for another 10 minutes. Serve.

Garden Vegetable Soup

Makes: 4 servings / Prep time: 15 minutes / Cook time: 25 minutes

- ❖ 2 cloves garlic
- ❖ ½ cup diced onion
- ❖ ½ cup sliced carrots
- ❖ 3 cups chicken or vegetable broth
- ❖ ½ cup green beans
- ❖ 1½ cups chopped green cabbage
- ❖ 2 Tbsps. tomato puree
- ❖ ¼ tsp. sea salt
- ❖ ¼ tsp. dried oregano
- ❖ ½ tsp. dried basil
- ❖ ½ cup diced zucchini

In a soup pot, sauté garlic, onions, and carrot in a little water or oil. Add broth and all remaining ingredients except zucchini. Bring the mixture to a boil, then reduce the heat and simmer for about 15 minutes, or until nearly tender. Add zucchini and cook for another 5 minutes.

Spicy Vegetable Soup

Makes: 6 servings / Prep time: 15 minutes / Cook time: 30 minutes

- ❖ 2 carrots, chopped
- ❖ 1 red bell pepper, chopped
- ❖ 1 yellow bell pepper, chopped
- ❖ 2 medium red potatoes, cubed
- ❖ 2 stalks celery, sliced on a diagonal
- ❖ ½ onion, chopped
- ❖ 2 cloves garlic, minced
- ❖ 3 Tbsps. olive oil
- ❖ 2 (15-oz.) cans coconut milk
- ❖ 2 Tbsps. butter or coconut oil
- ❖ 1 tsp. sea salt
- ❖ 2 Tbsps. curry
- ❖ 2 cups raw milk or almond milk

Sauté vegetables, onion, and garlic in olive oil for 20 minutes, or until tender. Add coconut milk, butter or oil, salt, and curry, and heat thoroughly. Add raw milk or almond milk and stir. Serve.

Curry Chicken Soup

Makes: 6 servings / Prep time: 15 minutes / Cook time: 30 minutes

- ❖ 2 carrots, chopped
- ❖ 2 celery stalks, chopped
- ❖ 2 red potatoes, chopped
- ❖ 2 bell peppers, chopped
- ❖ ½ onion, chopped
- ❖ 3 cloves garlic, minced
- ❖ 6 cups chicken broth
- ❖ 1 can coconut milk
- ❖ 2 Tbsps. butter
- ❖ ½ tsp. sea salt
- ❖ 1–2 Tbsps. curry
- ❖ 1 cup cooked, shredded chicken

Cook carrots, celery, potatoes, peppers, onion, and garlic in chicken broth for 20 minutes or until tender. Add coconut milk, butter, salt, curry, and chicken. Heat thoroughly and serve.

Mulligatawny Soup

Makes: 6 servings / Prep time: 10 minutes / Cook time: 35 minutes

- ❖ 5 cups chicken stock or broth
- ❖ 2 carrots, chopped
- ❖ 2 stalks celery, chopped
- ❖ 2 cloves garlic, minced
- ❖ ½ an onion, chopped
- ❖ 1 tsp. ginger powder
- ❖ 1 ripe banana, peeled and mashed
- ❖ 3 Tbsps. coconut oil or butter
- ❖ sea salt to taste
- ❖ 15 oz. unsweetened whole coconut milk
- ❖ 1 tsp. curry powder
- ❖ 2 chicken breasts, fully cooked and shredded or chopped
- ❖ 2 cups cooked brown rice

In a soup pot, combine 2 cups of the broth with the carrots, celery, garlic, onion, and ginger. Bring the mixture to a boil, then reduce heat and simmer for about 15 minutes, or until mostly tender. Add the banana and cook an additional 5 minutes. Remove from heat. Blend mixture well with blender or hand mixer, then add the coconut oil, the remaining broth, and the sea salt. In a small bowl, combine the coconut milk and the curry, then stir it into the soup. Add the chicken and rice and heat through. Serve.

❖ ❖

Vegetables & Side Dishes

❖ ❖

Tasty Treasure #12

Cook veggies until they are tender, but still colorful. You can tell if you have overcooked your veggies if there is no color difference between carrots and broccoli.

Tasty Treasure #13

There are a variety of potatoes in nature for a good reason. Russets have a thick, rough brown skin with white insides and store well over the winter in a cold basement or cellar. They are also high in starch and make great mashed potatoes. Red potatoes have a dark pink skin and a white inside. They hold their shape together well in cooking and are therefore preferred over russets for use in soups and potato salad. Yukon Golds have a thin, smooth, light brown skin and yellow insides with a buttery flavor. They are a favorite for taste and diversity and are a good all-purpose choice. They can be used for mashed potatoes, oven baked fries, or soups.

Tasty Treasure #14

For really yummy potatoes, shred them raw and rinse off the starch before cooking. This makes really good hash browns because they don't gum together in a big sticky, black lump like they can if you don't rinse them. Plus, they taste lighter and fluffier.

❖ ❖

Sweet Carrots

Makes: 4 servings / Prep time: 15 minutes / Cook time: 20–25 minutes

- ❖ 6 medium carrots, cut into 4-inch-long strips
- ❖ 3 Tbsps. butter or coconut oil
- ❖ 3 Tbsps. raw honey

Steam carrots until tender, about 20 to 25 minutes. Mix with butter and honey in a bowl until butter is melted. Serve warm.

Baked Beans

Makes: 6 servings / Prep time: 15 minutes / Bake time: 3–4 hours

- ❖ 1 onion, chopped
- ❖ 2 green peppers, chopped
- ❖ 5 cups white beans, pre-cooked "slow and low" or 3 (15-oz.) cans white beans
- ❖ 1 (28-oz.) can tomato puree
- ❖ ¾ cup liquid sweetener
- ❖ ¼ cup unsulphured molasses
- ❖ 3 tsp. Dijon mustard
- ❖ ½ pineapple, chopped (optional)

Mix all ingredients in a large bowl. Then place them in a 9x13 glass pan or a Crock-Pot. Bake for 3 to 4 hours at 325°F, stirring occasionally.

–or–

Quick method: Sauté onion and peppers in a large saucepan until tender, about 15 to 20 minutes. Stir in remaining ingredients and simmer for about 20 minutes or until warmed through.

❖   ❖   ❖

Bread and Butter Pickles

Makes: 1 cup / Prep time: 10 minutes / Marinate: 2 hours

- ❖ 2 Tbsps. raw apple cider vinegar
- ❖ 2 Tbsps. raw honey or maple syrup
- ❖ 1 Tbsp. water
- ❖ ½ tsp. sea salt
- ❖ ½ tsp. mustard seed
- ❖ ½ tsp. celery seed
- ❖ 1 crisp cucumber, sliced

In a small bowl, combine all ingredients except for cucumbers and mix well. Add sliced cucumbers and let marinate for 2 hours. This makes a great garnish for sandwiches.

❖   ❖   ❖

Italian Marinated Vegetables

Makes: 4 servings / Prep time: 20 minutes

- ❖ 1 zucchini, chopped
- ❖ 1 cucumber, chopped
- ❖ 2 tomatoes, diced
- ❖ 2 carrots, diced
- ❖ 1 can olives
- ❖ 1 cup chopped fresh green beans
- ❖ ¼ cup cubed raw cheese (optional)

Sauce:
- ❖ 3 Tbsps. raw apple cider vinegar
- ❖ 3 Tbsps. olive oil
- ❖ ¼ tsp. sea salt
- ❖ 1 tsp. dried oregano
- ❖ ½ tsp. dried basil

Blend ingredients for sauce in a small bowl. Combine vegetables in a medium bowl, then pour sauce over vegetables. Marinate for about 2 hours in the fridge. Serve.

Note: To make a main dish out of this, add ½ cup cubed raw cheese or feta cheese and 1 cup cooked brown rice macaroni noodles.

Marinated Cucumbers

Makes: 2 servings / Prep time: 2 minutes / Marinate Time: 4 hours

- ❖ 1 large cucumber, washed and sliced
- ❖ ¼ cup raw apple cider vinegar
- ❖ 1–1½ cups filtered water
- ❖ ¾ tsp. sea salt
- ❖ ¼ tsp. black pepper

Add all ingredients in a medium bowl. Cover and marinate in the fridge for 3–4 hours. Serve in same bowl, in the marinade.

❖ ❖ ❖

Potato Boats

Makes: 10 halves / Prep time: 1 hour 20 minutes / Bake time: 20 minutes

- ❖ 5 medium potatoes, scrubbed and rinsed well
- ❖ ½ cup plain whole yogurt
- ❖ ½ cup sour cream
- ❖ 4–5 green onions, sliced
- ❖ ½ tsp. seasoned sea salt
- ❖ ½ cup raw cheese, grated

Bake potatoes for 1 hour at 350°F, until a fork comes out easily when inserted. Remove potatoes from oven and cool for a few minutes. When slightly cooler, cut in half lengthwise. With a spoon, scoop out potato flesh, leaving about ¼ inch to support skin. Place flesh in a bowl and mash well. Add yogurt, sour cream, onions, and sea salt. Stir well, then scoop filling back into potato skins and bake for 20 minutes. Top with cheese.

❖ ❖ ❖

Candied Yams

Makes: 4 servings / Prep time: 20 minutes / Cook time: 20 minutes

- ❖ 4 large yams, cut in half or thirds
- ❖ 5 Tbsps. syrup
- ❖ ¼ cup dehydrated cane juice
- ❖ 3 Tbsps. butter or coconut oil
- ❖ 1 tsp. cinnamon
- ❖ ¼ cup fresh, diced pineapple (optional)

Boil yams in salted water. Cook until tender. Pour a little bit of the yam water into the bottom of a 9x13 glass dish. Slice yams crosswise and peel them. Lay one layer in juice. Cover with half the syrup, cane juice, and dabs of the butter. Sprinkle with half of the cinnamon and half of the pineapple pieces. Add another layer of sliced yams. Top with the remaining syrup, cane juice, butter, cinnamon, and pineapple. Bake at 350°F for 1 hour.

❖ ❖ ❖

Mashed Potatoes

Makes: 4 servings / Prep time: 10 minutes / Cook time: 25 minutes

- ❖ enough water to cover potatoes
- ❖ 1 Tbsp. sea salt
- ❖ 6 medium potatoes, scrubbed and cut into thirds
- ❖ ¼ cup milk
- ❖ ¼ cup butter

Bring water and salt to a boil in a large pot. Add potatoes and cook uncovered, boiling, for about 25 minutes, or until potatoes are tender. Drain water and return potatoes to pot. Add milk and butter. Mash with potato masher. Serve warm.

Potatoes Au Gratin

Makes: 6 servings / Prep time: 25 minutes / Bake time: 1 hour

- ❖ 6 medium potatoes, scrubbed and sliced into ¼-inch-thick circles
- ❖ 4 Tbsps. butter
- ❖ 1 small onion, minced
- ❖ 2 gloves garlic, minced
- ❖ ½ green pepper, seeded and finely chopped
- ❖ ½–¾ cup heavy cream
- ❖ 1 Tbsp. sprouted wheat flour
- ❖ 1 tsp. sea salt or seasoned sea salt
- ❖ ¼ tsp. freshly ground black pepper
- ❖ 1 cup shredded raw cheese

Butter a 10-inch casserole dish and arrange the potato slices in dish in overlapping layers. Set aside. Melt half the butter in a skillet and add onion, garlic, and green pepper. Sauté until crisp-tender.

Meanwhile, in a different skillet, melt the remaining butter. When it is bubbly, stir in the cream. When the cream is simmering, whisk in the flour and cook a couple minutes, until thickened, but do not boil the cream! Add the onion mixture, the salt, and the pepper into the thickened cream. Then pour it over the potatoes. Bake at 350°F for about an hour, until potatoes are tender. The last few minutes of baking, spread the shredded cheese on top and remove from oven when melted, about 2 minutes.

Garlic Toast

Makes: 6–8 servings / Prep time: 15 minutes / Bake time: 5–6 minutes

- ❖ 8 slices of sprouted bread
- ❖ 2–3 (or more) cloves garlic, minced
- ❖ ½ tsp. dried parsley flakes
- ❖ ½ cup salted butter
- ❖ 2–3 Tbsps. Parmesan cheese

Partially toast the bread slices. Place a single layer of the slices on a cookie sheet. In a small bowl, stir and mash all remaining ingredients with a fork, except the Parmesan cheese. Blend well. Spread mixture evenly on bread slices and sprinkle with cheese. Bake at 400°F for 5 to 6 minutes.

Green Bean Casserole

Makes: 3 servings / Prep time: 15 minutes / Cook time: 20 minutes

- ❖ 1 small onion, chopped
- ❖ 1 clove garlic, minced
- ❖ 4–5 Tbsps. butter
- ❖ 3 Tbsps. sour cream
- ❖ 20 oz. frozen or fresh green beans
- ❖ 5 slices bacon, cooked and chopped
- ❖ ⅓ cup Traditional Almonds (see "Sprouting Nuts and Seeds" section), chopped small

In a medium frying pan, sauté onions and garlic in butter over medium heat. When onions are softened, add sour cream and drained beans and cook for 1 to 2 minutes. Add the bacon and almond pieces. Serve warm.

–or–

In a medium frying pan, sauté onions and garlic in butter over medium heat. Then mix all ingredients in a casserole dish and heat in the oven at 350°F for 5 to 10 minutes.

❖ ❖ ❖

Oven-Baked French Fries

Makes: 4 servings / Prep time: 15 minutes / Bake time: 40–50 minutes

- ❖ 4 medium potatoes, scrubbed and sliced lengthwise (with skins left on)
- ❖ 3 Tbsps. coconut oil, melted
- ❖ 1 tsp. sea salt or seasoned sea salt
- ❖ ¼ tsp. garlic powder

Slice potatoes and rinse well in a colander (to rinse the starch off). Drain them well and pat dry with a paper towel. Combine potatoes and coconut oil in a medium-sized bowl and toss to coat. Season with salt and garlic powder. Layer them evenly on a slightly greased cookie sheet and bake at 350°F for 40 to 50 minutes or until golden and crisp on the outside. Serve with homemade French Fry Dipping Sauce (see recipe in "Spreads, Sauces, Dips, and Marinades").

Side Potatoes

Makes: 4 servings / Prep time: 8 minutes / Cook time: 15 minutes

- ❖ 3 medium potatoes, scrubbed well with skins left on
- ❖ 3–4 Tbsps. coconut oil
- ❖ 1 tsp. onion powder
- ❖ ¼ tsp. garlic powder
- ❖ ½ tsp. sea salt

Slice potatoes crosswise into ⅛-inch-thick circles. Melt 2 tablespoons of coconut oil in a frying pan over medium heat, adding more as needed in between batches. In a small bowl, combine the salt, onion, and garlic powders. When the pan is hot, add the potatoes in a single layer and sprinkle with some of the seasoning mix. Cook for about 2 minutes and flip with a fork or spatula. Cook the other side for another 1 to 2 minutes. Continue doing this for 3 or 4 batches until all the potatoes are cooked. Serve with homemade French Fry Dipping Sauce (see recipe in "Spreads, Sauces, Dips, and Marinades").

❖ ❖ ❖

Tomato Zucchini Bake

Makes: 4–6 servings / Prep time: 35 minutes / Cook time: 20 minutes

- ❖ 2–3 medium zucchini, washed and sliced on a diagonal
- ❖ 4 medium-to-large tomatoes, washed and sliced
- ❖ 1½ tsps. basil
- ❖ ¼ tsp. sea salt
- ❖ ¾ cup raw cheese, grated

Steam sliced zucchini for about 10 to 15 minutes, or until nearly tender. Pour into a 9x13 glass dish. Top zucchini with tomatoes and basil and bake at 350°F for 20 minutes. When finished, sprinkle with sea salt and grated cheese. Allow the cheese to melt into the tomatoes and zucchini for a couple of minutes, and then serve warm.

Onion Rings

Makes: 5–6 servings / Prep time: 15 minutes / Cook time: 4 minutes per batch

- ❖ ½ cup coconut oil
- ❖ 3 medium yellow onions, peeled
- ❖ ½ cup sprouted wheat flour
- ❖ 1 tsp. sea salt
- ❖ freshly ground black pepper to taste
- ❖ ½ tsp. dried thyme
- ❖ ¼ tsp. oregano
- ❖ ½ tsp. baking powder
- ❖ 1 egg, well beaten
- ❖ ½ cup milk

In a large skillet, melt coconut oil over low heat. Slice and separate the onions into rings. In a medium bowl, whisk the flour, salt, pepper, other spices, and baking powder together. Whisk together the egg and milk. Combine the milk mixture and dry ingredients. Blend well. Dip each onion ring into batter and then drip-drop it into the skillet. Fry until golden, about 2 minutes per side. Flip and cook both sides. Remove with spatula and transfer to paper towels to drain. Add more coconut oil to the skillet as needed. Sprinkle with additional salt, if desired. Serve with homemade French Fry Dipping Sauce (see recipe in "Spreads, Sauces, Dips, and Marinades").

Steamed Vegetables

Makes: 6 servings / Prep time: 15 minutes / Cook time: 20 minutes

- ❖ 1½ cups broccoli, chopped
- ❖ 2 medium carrots, sliced on a diagonal
- ❖ 2 different colored bell peppers, sliced long and thin
- ❖ 1 zucchini, sliced on a diagonal
- ❖ 2 Tbsps. olive oil
- ❖ sea salt to taste

Steam veggies for about 20 minutes, or until tender. Place in a glass bowl and add olive oil and sea salt. Mix well and serve warm.

Twice-Baked Potato Casserole

Makes: 1 (9x13) dish / Prep time: 35 minutes / Bake time: 30 minutes

- ❖ 6 medium Yukon gold potatoes, diced
- ❖ ¾ cup sour cream
- ❖ ½ cup Vegenaise®
- ❖ ½ cup heavy cream
- ❖ ¼ cup butter, softened
- ❖ 1½ tsps. sea salt
- ❖ ½ tsp. freshly ground black pepper
- ❖ 2 garlic cloves, minced
- ❖ 1 cup sliced green onions
- ❖ 3 oz. diced deli ham, nitrate-free
- ❖ 1 cup shredded sharp raw cheese
- ❖ 2 cups organic cornflakes
- ❖ 2 Tbsps. butter, melted
- ❖ ¼ cup grated Parmesan cheese

Cover potatoes with salted water and boil for 15 minutes. Drain and set aside. Meanwhile, in a large bowl, blend the sour cream, Vegenaise®, cream, butter, salt, pepper, garlic, onions, ham, and cheese. Toss the potatoes in the mixture. Grease a 9x13 glass dish and pour the potato mixture into it. Spread evenly. In a separate bowl, crush the cornflakes and mix with 2 tablespoons melted butter. Sprinkle cornflake mixture over potatoes and sprinkle the Parmesan cheese on top. Cover loosely with tin foil. Bake at 350°F for 30 minutes.

Green Beans and Almonds

Makes: 4–6 servings / Prep time: 10 minutes / Cook time: 15–20 minutes

- ❖ 3 cups fresh green beans, washed with ends removed
- ❖ 2 Tbsps. olive oil
- ❖ sea salt to taste
- ❖ ⅓ cup chopped Traditional Almonds (see "Sprouting Nuts and Seeds" section)

Steam green beans for 15 to 20 minutes until tender, but still bright green. Place steamed green beans in a glass bowl and mix in olive oil, sea salt, and almonds. Serve warm.

Stir-fry Potatoes

Makes: 4 servings / Prep time: 10 minutes / Cook time: 35–40 minutes

- ❖ 4–5 medium potatoes, washed well and cut into wedges
- ❖ 3 Tbsps. olive oil
- ❖ 2 tsps. parsley flakes
- ❖ sea salt to taste

Steam potatoes until tender, about 20 to 25 minutes. Place in a fry pan or wok with olive oil and brown over medium heat for 10 to 15 minutes. Add parsley and sea salt and mix. Serve warm.

❖ ❖

Meatless Entrees

❖ ❖

Tasty Treasure #15

Meat isn't an absolute necessity when it comes to getting protein. Grains and beans form a complete protein together, and dairy and eggs are complete proteins on their own. Plus, it's amazing what you can make without meat!

❖ ❖

South of the Border Rice

Makes: 4 servings / Prep time: 15 minutes / Cook time: 1 hour 30 minutes

- ❖ 2 cups cooked brown, wild, or forbidden rice
- ❖ ⅓ cup ground beef (optional)
- ❖ 1 bell pepper, chopped
- ❖ ½ onion, chopped
- ❖ 1 clove garlic, minced
- ❖ ½ cup chopped green chilies
- ❖ ⅔ cup fresh or frozen corn
- ❖ 1 (28-oz.) can organic diced tomatoes, drained
- ❖ 3 Tbsps. chili powder
- ❖ sea salt to taste
- ❖ ½ cup sliced olives

While rice is cooking, brown beef. Then add chopped peppers, onion, garlic, chilies, and corn. Sauté until tender. (If no beef is used, imply sauté the vegetables in a little coconut oil or butter.) Stir in tomatoes, chili powder, and sea salt, and simmer for about 10 minutes. Mix in rice and olives. Can be eaten alone or served in sprouted tortilla shells topped with a little sour cream or yogurt.

❖ ❖ ❖

Seven-Layer Bean Dip

Makes: 6–8 servings / Prep time: 20 minutes

First Layer:
- ❖ 3 cups sprouted and cooked pinto beans, mashed or blended
- ❖ 4 oz. mild green chilies drained (optional)
- ❖ 1 Tbsp. extra virgin olive oil
- ❖ ½ tsp. sea salt
- ❖ 1 tsp. onion powder
- ❖ ¼ tsp. garlic powder

Second Layer:
- ❖ ¼ cup salsa
- ❖ 3 ripe avocados, pitted and mashed well
- ❖ ¼ cup whole plain yogurt
- ❖ ⅛ tsp. garlic powder
- ❖ ¼ tsp. onion powder
- ❖ sea salt, freshly ground black pepper to taste

Third Layer:
- ❖ 16 oz. organic full-fat sour cream or 12 oz. sour cream and ½ cup plain full-fat yogurt
- ❖ 5 Tbsps. homemade Taco Seasoning Mix (see recipe in "Homemade Seasonings and Mixes")
- ❖ ½ tsp. sea salt

Toppings:
- ❖ 5 oz. raw cheese, shredded
- ❖ 15 oz. olives, drained and sliced
- ❖ 2–4 roma tomatoes, seeded, chopped and lightly salted
- ❖ ¼–½ cup sliced green onions or chives

Combine all ingredients for the first layer and mix well. Spread bean mixture in the bottom of a 9x13 pan. Combine all ingredients for the second layer and mix well. Spread the second layer over the first, then mix together the ingredients for the third layer and spread that mixture over the other two. Distribute toppings evenly on top. Serve with salsa and organic tortilla chips.

❖   ❖   ❖

Taco Stacks

Makes: 4 servings / Prep time: 25 minutes

- ❖ 2 (15-oz.) cans organic refried beans
- ❖ 1 recipe homemade guacamole (see recipe in "Spreads, Sauces, Dips, and Marinades")
- ❖ Salsa to taste
- ❖ raw cheese, shredded to taste
- ❖ 2 vine-ripe tomatoes, chopped
- ❖ 1 can olives, sliced
- ❖ sour cream to taste
- ❖ 2 cups chopped green leaf lettuce
- ❖ 1 bag of organic corn chips

For each individual serving, place chips on the bottom of a clean plate, then layer refried beans, guacamole, sour cream, salsa, lettuce, olives, tomatoes, and shredded cheese on top.

❖ ❖ ❖

Spanish Rice

Makes: 3 cups / Prep time: 15 minutes / Cook time: 55 minutes

- ❖ 1 cup brown rice, rinsed
- ❖ 1½ cups chicken or beef stock
- ❖ 15 oz. tomato sauce
- ❖ 1 green bell pepper, seeded and chopped
- ❖ ⅓ cup frozen or fresh corn
- ❖ ½ tsp. sea salt
- ❖ 2 Tbsps. coconut oil or butter
- ❖ 1 tsp. chili powder
- ❖ ¼ tsp. garlic powder or 1 clove garlic, minced
- ❖ 2 tsps. onion powder or 1 small onion, diced
- ❖ ¼ tsp. ground paprika

Place all ingredients in a medium saucepan and bring to a boil. Reduce heat to low and simmer, covered, for about 55 minutes, or until liquid is absorbed. Remove from heat and fluff with fork.

❖ ❖ ❖

Brown and Wild Rice Mix

Makes: 4 cups / Prep time: 5 minutes / Cook time: 1 hour

- ❖ 2 cups brown and wild rice blend, rinsed and drained
- ❖ 4 cups filtered water
- ❖ ¼ tsp. sea salt

Combine rice, water, and sea salt in a saucepan with a lid. Bring to a boil over medium heat, then reduce to low and cover. Simmer for an hour or until all the water is absorbed.

Flavorful Basic Rice

Makes: 9 cups cooked rice / Prep time: 2 minutes / Cook time: 55 minutes

- ❖ 4 cups chicken or beef stock
- ❖ 2 cups long grain brown rice, rinsed well and soaked for 1 hour, then drained
- ❖ ¾ tsp. sea salt
- ❖ 3 Tbsps. coconut oil or butter
- ❖ dash of onion powder
- ❖ dash of garlic powder

Combine all ingredients in a medium saucepan. Bring to a boil over high heat, then cover and reduce to a simmer. Keep covered and simmer for about 55 minutes. Remove from heat, fluff with a fork, and serve.

Bean and Rice Casserole

Makes: 6–8 servings / Prep time: 20 minutes / Rice cook time: 1 hour

- ❖ ⅔ cup olive oil
- ❖ juice from 1 lime
- ❖ 2 cloves garlic, minced
- ❖ ½ tsp. sea salt
- ❖ 1 tsp. parsley
- ❖ 2 tsps. chili powder
- ❖ ½ tsp. cumin

- ❖ 4 cups "slow and low" cooked brown or wild rice
- ❖ 2 cups sprouted "slow and low" cooked black beans or 1 (16-oz.) can organic black beans
- ❖ 2 cups "slow and low" cooked red beans or 1 (16-oz.) can organic red beans
- ❖ ½ medium onion, chopped
- ❖ 1 bell pepper, chopped
- ❖ ½ cup chopped fresh cilantro

In a bowl, mix olive oil, lime juice, garlic, sea salt, parsley, chili powder, and cumin, and set aside. In a large bowl, mix hot rice, beans, onion, and green pepper. Stir in sauce and cilantro. Place in a casserole dish and serve.

Chou Fan

Makes: 4 servings / Prep time: 20 minutes / Cook time: 25–30 minutes

- ❖ 1 crown broccoli, chopped
- ❖ 1 zucchini, sliced on a diagonal
- ❖ 1 carrot, cut on a diagonal
- ❖ 2 stalks celery, cut on a diagonal
- ❖ 1 cup sweet peas with edible pods
- ❖ 1 red bell pepper, sliced long and thin
- ❖ 1 cup sliced fresh mushrooms
- ❖ ½ red onion, thinly sliced
- ❖ 2 cups cooked brown rice
- ❖ 1–2 eggs, slightly beaten (optional)
- ❖ 2 Tbsps. olive oil
- ❖ 1 Tbsp. soy sauce, or soy sauce substitute
- ❖ ½ cup cashews

In a wok, sauté vegetables on medium heat until tender. Add cooked rice and stir. Make a well in the center of the wok and add eggs, if desired. Cook on medium-low until eggs are done, then mix well. Remove from heat and mix in oil, soy sauce, and cashews.

Huevos Rancheros

Makes: 4 servings / Prep time: 10 minutes / Cook time: 35 minutes

- ❖ ½ onion, chopped
- ❖ 2 cloves garlic, minced
- ❖ 1 bell pepper, chopped
- ❖ ½ cup chopped green chilies (5–6 chillies) (optional)
- ❖ 1 (28-oz.) can chopped tomatoes, undrained
- ❖ ½ tsp. sea salt
- ❖ 1 Tbsp. chili powder
- ❖ 8 eggs
- ❖ 1 doz. sprouted corn or wheat tortillas
- ❖ sour cream (optional)
- ❖ shredded lettuce (optional)

Sauté onion, garlic, bell peppers, and chilies in a large skillet until tender. Add tomatoes, salt, and chili powder and heat to a simmer, about 10 minutes. Crack eggs directly into the pan and cover. Let simmer about 5 minutes, or until the whites are hard and the yolks are almost done. Serve over warmed tortillas and top with a little sour cream and lettuce.

Vegetable Alfredo Pizza

Makes: 1 large pizza / Prep time: 50 minutes / Bake time: 14 minutes

Sourdough Crust:

- ❖ ¾ cup water (or enough to make a stiff ball of dough)
- ❖ 1½ tsps. apple cider vinegar, whey, or fresh squeezed lemon juice
- ❖ 2 ½ cups freshly ground, non-sprouted spelt or kamut flour
- ❖ ½ tsp. sea salt
- ❖ 1 tsp. baking soda
- ❖ 1 Tbsp. olive oil
- ❖ cornmeal

Sauce:

- ❖ 4 Tbsps. butter, melted
- ❖ 4 oz. cream cheese
- ❖ 2 Tbsps. milk
- ❖ 2 cloves garlic, minced
- ❖ 2 tsps. parsley

Toppings:

- ❖ 1 (14-oz.) can artichoke hearts, drained and chopped
- ❖ 5–6 medium mushrooms, sliced
- ❖ ⅓ of a red onion, quartered and thinly sliced
- ❖ 1 cup fresh spinach, washed and torn
- ❖ 1 medium zucchini, thinly sliced like pepperoni
- ❖ 1–2 tomatoes, chopped
- ❖ 1 bell pepper, chopped (optional)
- ❖ 1 cup sliced olives
- ❖ 1½–2 cups raw cheese

To make the crust, mix the water with the vinegar, whey, or lemon juice. Mix with flour in a glass bowl until it forms a very stiff ball of dough that picks up all the flour. Cover bowl with a damp cloth and leave in a warm place for 12 to 24 hours. The dough should have bubbles and be about double in size after this time. Add remaining crust ingredients, except cornmeal, and knead them into the dough for about 5 minutes. Roll out on an oiled surface. Dust a pizza pan with cornmeal and transfer the rolled-out dough to the pan, stretching the dough as you go to reach the edges of the pan. Bake for 8 minutes at 425°F before adding toppings.

For the sauce, melt butter and cream cheese in a pan. Mix well. Add milk, garlic, and parsley, and stir with a fork. Spread sauce onto pre-baked pizza crust, then top with prepared vegetables. Bake for 13 minutes at 425°F. Remove from oven and sprinkle the cheese over the top. Return to oven for a minute or two to allow the cheese to melt.

Meatballs

Makes: 25–30 small balls / Prep time: 15 minutes / Cook time: 30 minutes

- ❖ 2 cups freshly sprouted wheat or 1 cup freshly sprouted wheat and 1 cup hamburger
- ❖ 1 egg
- ❖ ¼ cup onion, minced
- ❖ ½ tsp. sea salt *(continued)*

Blend sprouted wheat in a food processor until it forms a ball of dough. Add egg, onion, and sea salt and blend well. With a spoon, form tiny balls, and drop into a buttered skillet. Cook on medium-low heat for about 30 minutes, turning occasionally so the balls get browned on all sides. Add to spaghetti sauce just before serving.

❖ ❖ ❖

Summer Spaghetti Sauce

Makes: 6–8 servings / Prep time: 25 minutes / Cook time: 20 minutes

- ❖ 1 medium onion, chopped
- ❖ 1 small zucchini, diced
- ❖ 2–4 fresh garlic cloves, minced
- ❖ 1 small yellow crook-neck squash, diced
- ❖ a small handful of fresh basil leaves, torn, or 2 Tbsps. dried basil leaves
- ❖ 1 Tbsp. fresh thyme leaves or ½ tsp. dried thyme
- ❖ 2 Tbsps. dehydrated cane juice
- ❖ 2 Tbsps. fresh oregano leaves or 1 tsp. dried oregano
- ❖ ¾ tsp. dried marjoram
- ❖ ½ tsp. freshly ground black pepper
- ❖ 2 tsps. real salt
- ❖ 40 oz. fresh garden-ripened roma tomato puree
- ❖ 6 oz. tomato paste

Chop the onion, zucchini, and garlic. Sauté chopped onion, adding a little fresh tomato puree if needed. When onions are halfway done, add garlic, yellow squash, and sauté until onions are tender. Meanwhile, combine all spices, cane juice, and salt in a small bowl and blend them. In a saucepan, stir the fresh tomato puree and tomato paste together. Add the vegetables and spices to the tomato mixture, stir well, and cover. Bring to a gentle boil over medium heat, reducing to a low simmer for 15 to 20 minutes.

❖ ❖ ❖

Sour Cream and Onion Potatoes

Makes: 6–8 servings / Prep time: 20 minutes / Cook time: 55 minutes

- ❖ 6 medium russet or red potatoes
- ❖ 1 cup sour cream
- ❖ ½ cup plain yogurt
- ❖ 4–6 green onions, chopped
- ❖ 2 tsp. parsley flakes
- ❖ sea salt to taste
- ❖ ½ cup cheese (optional)

Wash potatoes well, shred, and then rinse thoroughly. Steam for twenty minutes, or until tender. In a large bowl, mix sour cream, yogurt, onions, parsley, and sea salt. Add steamed potatoes, and stir together. Pour in a 9x13 glass pan, and bake for 35 minutes at 350°F. Top with cheese if desired.

Summer Stir-fry

Makes: 8 servings / Prep time: 15 minutes / Cook time: 15 minutes

- ❖ 3 Tbsps. olive oil
- ❖ 1 medium onion, chopped
- ❖ 2 carrots, scrubbed and sliced
- ❖ 2 potatoes, scrubbed and diced, skins left on
- ❖ 1 garlic clove, minced
- ❖ 1 tsp. sea salt
- ❖ ¼ tsp. black pepper
- ❖ ½ tsp. oregano
- ❖ ¼ tsp. dried sage
- ❖ ½ tsp. dried parsley flakes
- ❖ 1 medium zucchini, coarsely chopped
- ❖ 1 yellow crookneck squash, coarsely chopped
- ❖ ½ cup fresh or frozen and thawed peas

Combine the olive oil, onion, carrot, potato, garlic, salt, and all the spices in a skillet. Sauté mixture for about 3 to 5 minutes over medium heat, then layer the zucchini and squash on top—don't stir them in yet. Sprinkle the peas on top. Cover and cook over medium heat for 10 minutes, then stir everything together well. Cover and remove from heat. Serve warm.

Potatoes and Asparagus

Makes: 8 servings / Prep time: 10 minutes / Bake time: 28 minutes

- ❖ 3 large red potatoes, scrubbed and diced into bite-sized pieces (with skins left on)
- ❖ 2 Tbsps. olive oil
- ❖ ¾ tsp. sea salt
- ❖ 1 tsp. dried rosemary
- ❖ ¼ tsp. black pepper
- ❖ ½ of a large yellow onion, sliced
- ❖ 2 cloves garlic, minced
- ❖ 10 oz. baby asparagus spears, fresh or frozen and thawed, cut into 2-inch pieces
- ❖ ¼ cup pine nuts or Traditional Almonds (see "Sprouting Nuts and Seeds" section), coarsely chopped
- ❖ ⅓ cup Parmesan cheese (optional)

Combine potatoes, olive oil, salt, rosemary, pepper, onions, and garlic in a bowl. Toss to coat. Spread mixture evenly on a cookie sheet and bake at 450°F for 15 to 18 minutes. Add the asparagus, pine nuts, and Parmesan cheese, if desired. Mix and return to oven for an additional 10 minutes.

Honey Dijon Vegetables Over Rice or Noodles

Makes: 4 servings / Cook time: approx. 45 minutes

- ❖ 1 zucchini, sliced long and thin
- ❖ 1 bell pepper, sliced long and thin
- ❖ 2 carrots, sliced on a diagonal
- ❖ 4 green onions, sliced long and thin
- ❖ ¼ cup raw honey
- ❖ ¼ cup Dijon mustard

Sauté vegetables until tender. Meanwhile, mix honey and mustard thoroughly in a small bowl. Pour over hot vegetables. Serve over rice, noodles, or sprouted and cooked wheat.

Sprouted Grain and Vegetable Casserole

Makes: 4 servings / Prep time: 15 minutes / Cook time: 35–40 minutes

- ❖ 2 carrots, chopped
- ❖ 1 bell pepper, chopped
- ❖ 6–8 medium mushrooms, sliced
- ❖ 1 cup fresh or frozen corn
- ❖ ½ onion, chopped
- ❖ ½ cup barley, soaked for 12 hours, and cooked "slow and low"
- ❖ ⅓ cup sprouted wheat, cooked "slow and low"
- ❖ 1 cup cooked black beans
- ❖ 2 tsps. parsley flakes
- ❖ 1 tsp. oregano
- ❖ ½ tsp. basil
- ❖ 2 cloves garlic, minced
- ❖ ½ tsp. sea salt
- ❖ 3 Tbsps. olive oil
- ❖ ½ cup shredded raw cheese (optional)

Steam veggies for 15 to 20 minutes until tender. Mix with the barley, wheat, beans, herbs, seasonings, garlic, sea salt, and olive oil. Place mixture in a 9x13 glass pan. Bake 20 minutes, or until hot. Top with cheese.

Veggie Tostadas

Makes: 6 servings / Prep time: 15 minutes / Cook time: 10 minutes

- ❖ 6 sprouted corn tortillas
- ❖ 2 cups sprouted pinto beans, pre-cooked
- ❖ ½ tsp. sea salt
- ❖ 2 cloves garlic, minced
- ❖ ¼ tsp. black pepper
- ❖ ½ tsp. chili powder
- ❖ ½ tsp. ground cumin
- ❖ couple dashes organic hot sauce
- ❖ 1 small broccoli crown, diced
- ❖ 1 small zucchini, quartered and sliced
- ❖ 2–3 tomatoes, diced
- ❖ 1 medium yellow crookneck squash, quartered and sliced
- ❖ 1 cup grated raw cheese *(continued)*

Spread tortillas in a single layer on a cookie sheet and bake at 350°F for 5 to 7 minutes, flipping them over halfway through bake time. Warm the beans, salt, garlic, spices, and hot sauce in a saucepan over medium heat. When warm, mash them. Spread this bean mixture on each tostada. Spread mixed veggies on top of bean mixture. Broil for 2 to 3 minutes. Turn oven off and sprinkle a little raw cheese on top of each veggie tostada. Replace in oven until cheese is warm or soft. Serve warm.

Vegetable Lime Fajitas

Makes: 6 servings / Prep time: 15 minutes / Cook time: 20 minutes

- ❖ 2 bell peppers, sliced long and thin
- ❖ ½ red onion, quartered and sliced
- ❖ ¾ cup fresh or frozen white corn
- ❖ 1 cup green chilies
- ❖ ½–1 jalapeño pepper, diced
- ❖ 6 medium mushrooms, sliced
- ❖ juice from 1 lime
- ❖ 1–2 Tbsps. raw vinegar
- ❖ sea salt to taste
- ❖ 3 Tbsps. olive oil

In a large frying pan over medium-low heat, cook all vegetables until tender. Remove from heat and add lime juice, vinegar, sea salt, and olive oil. Toss until coated and serve in sprouted tortillas. This recipe can be made spicier by adding more jalapeño, lime juice, and vinegar. Serve with Tomatillo Salsa (see recipe in "Spreads, Sauces, Dips, and Marinades").

Vegetable Casserole

Makes: 6 servings / Prep time: 20 minutes / Cook time: 1½–2 hours

- ❖ 3 medium potatoes, cut into bite-sized chunks
- ❖ 3 carrots, cut into bite-sized chunks
- ❖ 3 stalks of celery, chopped
- ❖ 1 cup broccoli, chopped
- ❖ 1 cup fresh green beans, halved, with ends removed

- ❖ 1 bell pepper, cut into chunks
- ❖ 1 medium zucchini, cut into chunks
- ❖ ½ cup corn, or fresh corn cut from 1 or 2 cobs
- ❖ ½ of an onion, chopped
- ❖ 3 cloves garlic, minced
- ❖ 1 tsp. parsley flakes
- ❖ ¾ tsp. basil
- ❖ ½ tsp. oregano
- ❖ 2 Tbsps. olive oil
- ❖ ¾ cup chicken broth

Preheat oven to 350°F. Place chopped vegetables, onion, and garlic in a 9x13 pan. Mix parsley flakes, basil, oregano, olive oil, and chicken broth in a bowl. Pour evenly over the vegetables. Cover dish with foil and bake for about 1½ hours, (smaller chunks take less time) or until the vegetables are tender but not overcooked.

Chinese Coleslaw over Rice

Makes: 4 servings / Prep time: 25 minutes

Coleslaw:
- ❖ 6–7 stalks celery with leaves, sliced very thin
- ❖ ½ medium cabbage, sliced very thin
- ❖ 2 large carrots, grated
- ❖ 2 bell peppers, sliced long and thin
- ❖ ½ red onion, or 3–4 green onions, sliced long and thin
- ❖ 1 Tbsp. flax seed
- ❖ 1 Tbsp. sesame seeds

Dressing:
- ❖ 3 Tbsps. raw vinegar
- ❖ 3 Tbsps. extra virgin olive oil
- ❖ 2 Tbsps. maple syrup or honey
- ❖ 1 tsp. sea salt

Slice and chop vegetables in a food processor or by hand and place in a bowl. Mix ingredients for dressing and toss in with salad. Serve over cooked brown, wild, or forbidden rice.

Vegetable Enchiladas

Makes: 6 servings / Prep time: 15 minutes / Cook time: 40 minutes

Sauce:
- ❖ ½ onion, chopped
- ❖ 2 cloves garlic, minced
- ❖ 1 (29-oz.) can tomato puree or crushed tomatoes, undrained
- ❖ ½ tsp. sea salt
- ❖ 1½ tsp. cumin
- ❖ 1 tsp. chili powder

Filling:
- ❖ ½ a red onion, sliced thin and long
- ❖ 1 red bell pepper, seeded and chopped
- ❖ ½ cup fresh mushrooms, sliced
- ❖ 4 tomatillos, peeled, washed, and chopped
- ❖ ½ cup chopped green chilies
- ❖ 1 medium zucchini, chopped

To make the sauce, sauté onion and garlic until tender. Add tomatoes, salt, cumin, and chili powder, and let simmer about 15 minutes.

In a separate pan, sauté chopped vegetables for filling until tender. Wrap vegetables in sprouted tortillas and place in a 9x13 glass pan. Cover with sauce and bake at 350°F for about 25 minutes. Remove from oven and top with a little raw grated cheese, olives, sliced avocado, or lettuce.

Tostada Pizzas

Makes: 3 (12-inch) pizzas / Prep time: 35 minutes / Cook time: 7 minutes

- ❖ 2 cups homemade refried beans or 1 (20-oz.) can of refried beans
- ❖ 6 (12-inch) sprouted grain tortillas
- ❖ ¾ cup yogurt or sour cream
- ❖ 1 recipe homemade guacamole (found in Sauces, Seasonings, and Snacks section)
- ❖ 1 recipe fresh salsa (found in Sauces, Seasonings, and Snacks section)

- ❖ ½ cup olives, sliced
- ❖ 4 tomatoes, chopped
- ❖ 1 cup shredded raw cheese
- ❖ 1 cup lettuce or fresh spinach, finely shredded

Spread refried beans over a tortilla and place another tortilla over the top. Bake until warmed, about 7 minutes. When cooled a bit, top with yogurt or sour cream, guacamole, salsa, olives, tomatoes, raw cheese, and lettuce. Cut into wedges like a pizza and serve.

Homemade Burritos

Makes: 6 servings / Prep time: 25 minutes / Cook time 15 minutes

- ❖ 2 cups cooked pinto beans
- ❖ 3 Tbsps. onion, minced
- ❖ 2 cloves garlic, minced
- ❖ 2 tsps. chili powder
- ❖ ½ tsp. cumin
- ❖ sea salt to taste
- ❖ 6–12 sprouted tortilla shells
- ❖ desired toppings (see directions for suggestions)

Mash beans with a little water to get a refried-bean consistency. Add onion, garlic, spices, and salt and stir well. Transfer to a skillet or saucepan and simmer until onion and garlic are tender. Stir often and add water as needed to keep the consistency.

When done, place a scoop of beans in the center of a warmed tortilla shell and garnish with sour cream or yogurt, salsa, guacamole, chopped tomatoes, sliced olives, shredded raw cheese, and dark leafy greens.

Vegetarian Spaghetti Sauce

Makes: 4–6 servings / Prep time: 10 minutes / Cook time: 30 minutes

- ❖ 2 cloves garlic, minced
- ❖ ½ an onion, chopped
- ❖ 1 bell pepper, chopped
- ❖ 8 fresh mushrooms, sliced
- ❖ 1 (28-oz.) can of tomato puree
- ❖ 2 Tbsps. dehydrated cane juice
- ❖ 2 Tbsps. black strap molasses
- ❖ ½ tsp. sea salt
- ❖ 1 tsp. oregano
- ❖ ½ tsp. basil
- ❖ ½ tsp. anise seed
- ❖ ½ tsp. fennel
- ❖ ¼ tsp. paprika
- ❖ 1 bag of spaghetti noodles (made of brown rice or sprouted wheat), cooked according to directions, or spaghetti squash

In a large saucepan, sauté garlic, onion, pepper, and mushrooms until tender. Add tomato puree, cane juice, molasses, and all herbs and spices. Simmer on low for about 30 minutes to blend flavors. Serve over warm noodles or spaghetti squash.

Cheesy Noodles

Makes: 4 servings / Prep time: 7 minutes / Cook time: 20 minutes

- ❖ 6 oz. Tinkyáda® brown rice pasta (elbow, or penne pasta)
- ❖ 3 Tbsps. butter
- ❖ ¼ cup raw milk
- ❖ 1 tsp. sea salt
- ❖ ½ tsp. onion powder
- ❖ 1 tsp. dried parsley flakes
- ❖ ¼–½ tsp. garlic powder
- ❖ ¼ tsp. freshly ground black pepper
- ❖ 3–4 oz. shredded raw sharp cheddar cheese

Boil pasta in salt water according to package directions, about 14 to 16 minutes. Drain pasta in a colander, rinse under cold water, and set aside. In the same pan used to boil the noodles, melt butter over medium low heat. Add milk and all seasonings and whisk until smooth and thickened. Pour the noodles back into the pan, stir to coat, and then add the shredded cheese, stirring occasionally until melted through. Add more milk if needed. Serve immediately.

❖ ❖ ❖

Avocado Taco Wraps

Makes: 4 servings / Prep time: 15 minutes

- ❖ 8 oz. cream cheese, softened
- ❖ ½ cup sour cream
- ❖ 4 oz. chopped green chilies
- ❖ 2 Tbsps. homemade Taco Seasoning mix (see recipe in "Homemade Seasonings and Mixes")
- ❖ 1 tsp. sea salt
- ❖ 4 (10-inch) sprouted wheat tortillas
- ❖ 2 avocados, peeled and sliced
- ❖ 2 medium tomatoes, thinly sliced
- ❖ 3 green onions, sliced
- ❖ small handful fresh cilantro, chopped
- ❖ 15 oz. olives, drained and sliced

In a small bowl, mix the cream cheese, sour cream, green chilies, taco seasoning, and salt together. Spread about ½ cup of this mixture over each tortilla. Top with avocado, tomatoes, onions, cilantro, and olives and roll up.

❖ ❖

Meaty Main Dishes

❖ ❖

Tasty Treasure #16

We have already mentioned that protein foods should be cooked "slow and low," so we won't bore you with discussing it at length again. But if you prefer not to chew a bite of meat for a full half hour before it's swallow-able, following this simple rule will make your protein foods much more palatable. Crock-Pots are awesome slow, low cookers.

❖ ❖

Chicken, Turkey & Fish

Roasted Chicken

Makes: 8–10 servings / Prep time: 15 minutes / Bake time: 2 hours

- ❖ 5-lb. whole free-range chicken (fresh or frozen and thawed), rinsed with innards removed
- ❖ 4 cups chicken stock
- ❖ 1 medium onion, chopped
- ❖ 6 cloves garlic, peeled
- ❖ 4 Tbsps. melted butter or coconut oil
- ❖ 1 tsp. dried thyme
- ❖ ½ tsp. sea salt
- ❖ ¼ tsp. black pepper

Preheat oven to 375°F. Place chicken belly-up in roasting pan or 9x13 pan. Add all the stock, onions, and garlic to the pan. Mix butter or oil, thyme, sea salt, and pepper in a small bowl. Sprinkle half the mixture over the chicken. Cover with lid or tin foil, sealing the edges. Bake for 1 hour. Remove from oven, remove lid, and flip chicken backside up. Sprinkle with remaining butter mixture. Cover and bake for an additional hour. Remove the lid or foil the last 15 to 20 minutes of baking time.

❖ ❖ ❖

Chicken Gravy

Makes: 3–4 cups / Prep time: 7 minutes

- ❖ all liquid left over from an oven-roasted chicken
- ❖ 3 Tbsps. organic cornstarch
- ❖ sea salt to taste

Pour the roasted chicken drippings through a mesh strainer into a saucepan. Whisk organic cornstarch into ½ cup room temperature water. Pour into drippings. Heat over medium-high heat, whisking constantly, until thickened. Remove from heat and serve with mashed potatoes or rice. Additional chicken stock and/or milk can be added to supplement the drippings, if needed.

Rewarming Cooked Chicken Meat

Heating Time: 3–5 minutes

- ❖ cooked chicken meat
- ❖ a little coconut oil or butter
- ❖ filtered water

Place the cooked chicken, shredded or chopped, in a saucepan with oil and just enough water to cover the bottom of the pan. Cook covered over medium heat until chicken is heated through.

Chicken and Sausage Jambalaya

Makes: 4–6 servings / Prep time: 25 minutes / Cook time: 1 hour 20 minutes

- ❖ 2 cups organic brown or wild rice blend, rinsed and drained
- ❖ 2 tsps. sea salt
- ❖ 4 cups chicken stock
- ❖ 2 bay leaves
- ❖ 1 lb. sausage (nitrate free), cooked and sliced
- ❖ 1 lb. cooked chicken, chopped or shredded
- ❖ 1 green or red bell pepper, seeded and chopped
- ❖ 3 celery ribs, sliced *(continued)*

- ❖ 3–6 garlic cloves, peeled and minced
- ❖ 2 tsps. parsley
- ❖ 1 tsp. oregano
- ❖ 1 tsp. thyme
- ❖ ¼ tsp. black pepper
- ❖ ½ tsp. ground cumin
- ❖ ¼ tsp. cayenne pepper
- ❖ 1 large onion, chopped

Bring rice, salt, chicken broth, and bay leaves to a boil in a large pot. Keep covered and reduce heat to low for 55 minutes. Meanwhile, brown sausage in a saucepan. When thoroughly browned add chicken and heat through. Scrape bottom of the pot with a wooden spoon to loosen browned bits. Set aside until rice is ready. Add rice to the chicken and sausage, then add bell pepper, celery, garlic, remaining spices, and onion. As the vegetables begin to sweat, scrape bottom of the pot again. Add up to 1 cup water if needed. Cover and cook over medium heat for 10 minutes. Do not lift lid until time is up, then remove lid and serve.

❖ ❖ ❖

Mexican-Style Chicken Breasts

Makes: 4 breasts / Prep time: 6–8 hours / Cook time: 12–16 minutes

- ❖ 2 chicken breasts with skin on
- ❖ juice of 1 fresh lime or lemon (about 2 Tbsps.)
- ❖ ½ tsp. dried oregano
- ❖ ½ tsp. chili powder
- ❖ ⅛ tsp. cayenne pepper
- ❖ ¼ tsp. paprika
- ❖ 4 Tbsps. extra virgin olive oil

Marinate the breasts in half the oil and all of the other ingredients for several hours or overnight in the refrigerator. Cook over medium-low heat in the remaining oil, about 6 to 8 minutes each side, until the meat is cooked through and the juices run clear.

❖ ❖ ❖

Chicken Fajitas

Makes: 6 servings / Prep time: 30 minutes / Cook time: 10–15 minutes

- ❖ ¼ cup extra virgin olive oil
- ❖ 1 large fresh lemon, juiced (about ⅓ cup)
- ❖ 1 large onion, chopped or thinly sliced
- ❖ 3 garlic cloves, minced
- ❖ ½ tsp. sea salt
- ❖ 2 tsps. chili powder
- ❖ 1½ tsp. dried oregano
- ❖ 1 tsp. dried thyme
- ❖ 4 cups cooked chicken, shredded
- ❖ 1 red pepper, seeded and cut into strips
- ❖ 1 green pepper, seeded and cut into strips
- ❖ 12 sprouted wheat or corn tortillas

Garnishes:
- ❖ cheese, shredded
- ❖ sour cream
- ❖ guacamole
- ❖ salsa

Mix oil, lemon juice, onion, garlic, salt, and spices together in a saucepan. Cook covered over medium heat until onion is crisp-tender. Add the cooked chicken and replace lid to cook for about 10 to 15 minutes.

Meanwhile, warm tortillas by spreading them on a cookie sheet in a single layer and heating for 2 to 3 minutes in a 250°F oven, until warm and pliable. When chicken is done, add the peppers and lightly toss and sauté until peppers are crisp and tender. Serve in warmed tortillas topped with cheese, sour cream, guacamole and salsa.

Note: You can also make this recipe with uncooked chicken that has been cut into thin strips and marinated in the oil, juice, garlic, onion, sea salt, and spices overnight. Cook strips of chicken and onion together, and add peppers afterward.

❖ ❖ ❖

Enchiladas

Makes: 12 small enchiladas / Prep time: 20 minutes / Bake time: 30 minutes

- ❖ 1½ cups chicken or hamburger, pre cooked and shredded or chopped
- ❖ ½ cup brown rice, precooked
- ❖ 1 cup sprouted and cooked beans
- ❖ 14 oz. chopped tomatoes, drained
- ❖ 1 Tbsp. fresh cilantro, finely chopped
- ❖ 1 tsp. onion powder
- ❖ 1 tsp. ground cumin
- ❖ ½ tsp. garlic powder
- ❖ 1 recipe Red Enchilada Sauce (below)
- ❖ 12 small sprouted corn or wheat tortillas
- ❖ 1 (15-oz.) can black olives, sliced
- ❖ 2 cups raw cheese, grated
- ❖ sour cream

Boil or cook chicken in some oil with a little water and salt and pepper. Shred with a fork or fingers. In a large bowl, combine the meat, rice, beans, tomatoes, cilantro, onion, cumin, garlic powder, and about ⅓ of the enchilada sauce recipe below. Gently toss.

Soften the tortillas by preheating the oven to 300°F and placing the tortillas in a single layer on a cookie sheet. Watch closely and remove from oven when edges begin to curl up (about 2 minutes). Don't over bake! Keep tortillas warm by putting them in a tortilla warmer or wrapping them in a towel.

Spoon a thin layer of enchilada sauce to coat the bottom of a 9x13 glass pan. Fill each tortilla with a small amount of the chicken mixture, roll up, and place them side-by-side in the dish. Bake at 350°F for 30 minutes, then remove and drizzle remaining sauce over the top of them. Sprinkle olive slices evenly on top. Cover top with a sheet of tinfoil and bake for another 20 minutes. Remove from oven again and sprinkle cheese on top. Replace in oven uncovered until cheese is melted (about 3 minutes). Garnish with sour cream.

❖ ❖ ❖

Red Enchilada Sauce

Makes: approx. 2 cups / Prep time: 10 minutes / Cook time: 15 minutes

- ❖ 1 small onion, chopped
- ❖ 2 cloves garlic, minced
- ❖ 2 Tbsps. extra virgin olive oil
- ❖ 14 oz. blended tomatoes or tomato sauce
- ❖ 1 tsp. sea salt
- ❖ ½ tsp. ground cumin
- ❖ ½ tsp. dried oregano
- ❖ ½ cup filtered water
- ❖ 1–3 Tbsps. chili powder (depending on desired heat and flavor)
- ❖ 1½ tsps. dehydrated cane juice
- ❖ ½ tsp. raw apple cider vinegar

Sauté onion and garlic in oil until tender. Add tomatoes, salt, cumin, oregano, water, chili powder, cane juice, and vinegar and let simmer about 15 minutes, uncovered. This may be pureed in a blender or left as is.

Creamy Chicken Enchiladas

Makes: 5 medium enchiladas / Prep time: 20 minutes / Bake time: 30 minutes

- ❖ 4 oz. cream cheese, softened
- ❖ ½ of medium onion, chopped
- ❖ 2 garlic cloves, minced
- ❖ 4 oz. chopped green chilies
- ❖ ½ tsp. chili powder
- ❖ 1 tsp. ground cumin
- ❖ ¾ tsp. sea salt
- ❖ 1 medium tomato, diced
- ❖ 2 cups cooked and chopped chicken
- ❖ 5 (8-inch) sprouted wheat tortillas
- ❖ 1 recipe Cheesy Enchilada Sauce (see recipe below)

In a medium bowl, combine the cream cheese, onion, garlic, green chilies, chili powder, cumin, salt, and tomato. Blend well. Stir in the chicken. Distribute mixture into the sprouted wheat tortillas. Roll up and place in a 9x13 glass baking dish. Top with Cheesy Enchilada Sauce and cover with foil. Bake for 30 minutes in a 350°F oven.

Cheesy Enchilada Sauce

Makes: enough to top Creamy Chicken Enchiladas / Prep time: 15 minutes

- ❖ 4 oz. cream cheese
- ❖ 2 Tbsps. butter
- ❖ ½ cup milk
- ❖ 8 oz. raw cheddar cheese
- ❖ ¼ tsp. garlic powder
- ❖ ⅛ tsp. sea salt
- ❖ 1 (15-oz.) can olives, drained and thinly sliced
- ❖ 1 medium tomato, diced

In a small saucepan over medium low heat, blend the cream cheese with butter, adding in the milk. Stir in the shredded cheese, garlic powder, and sea salt. When mixture is melted through, remove from heat and pour over Creamy Chicken Enchiladas. Top evenly with sliced olives and tomatoes. Bake according to Creamy Chicken Enchilada recipe.

❖   ❖   ❖

Cajun Chicken Melts

Makes: 6 servings / Prep time: 20 minutes / Cook time: 10 minutes

- ❖ 6–8 slices of sprouted wheat bread
- ❖ 10 oz. cooked chicken meat
- ❖ ½ cup minced onion
- ❖ 1 small garlic clove, minced, or ¼ tsp. garlic powder
- ❖ ½ cup sweet green pepper or celery, diced
- ❖ ¼ cup Vegenaise®
- ❖ 1–3 tsps. Cajun Seasoning Mix (see recipe in "Homemade Seasoning and Mixes")
- ❖ 1 cup shredded raw cheese
- ❖ 2 medium tomatoes, sliced

Slightly toast the bread slices and preheat oven to 350°F. In a medium bowl, mix the chicken, onion, garlic, green peppers, mayo, Cajun seasoning, and half of the cheese together. Spread on each slice of bread and top with a slice of tomato and the remaining shredded cheese. Bake for 10 minutes. Remove from oven and serve warm.

Chicken Quesadillas

Makes: 6 servings / Prep time: 20 minutes

- ❖ 12 sprouted wheat or corn tortillas
- ❖ 1½ cups chicken, pre-cooked and shredded or diced
- ❖ raw cheese, grated
- ❖ olives, sliced (optional)
- ❖ green onions, sliced
- ❖ tomatoes, finely chopped (optional)
- ❖ jalapeños, seeded and chopped (optional)
- ❖ sour cream
- ❖ salsa (see recipe in "Spreads, Sauces, Dips, and Marinades")

Warm tortillas in a 250°F oven, until just warm. Spread desired amount of precooked chicken into the center of tortilla, and top with toppings.

Seasoned Trout

Makes: 4 servings / Prep time: 5 minutes / Cook time: 15–20 minutes

- ❖ 2 Tbsps. butter
- ❖ 1–2 tsps. dried thyme
- ❖ ½ tsp. paprika
- ❖ ½ tsp. dried parsley
- ❖ 2 (6-oz.) trout fillets
- ❖ ½ lemon, cut into wedges

Melt half of the butter in a frying pan. Combine all spices in a small bowl. Set trout fillets over melted butter, and sprinkle with half the spice mixture. Cover and cook over medium heat for 7 to 10 minutes. Flip fillets over, adding the remaining butter to the pan and sprinkling trout with the remaining spices. Cover and cook another 7 to 10 minutes, or until fillets are flaky and juices run clear. Serve with lemon wedges.

Halibut with Cream Sauce

Makes: 4 servings / Prep time: 10 minutes / Bake time: 45–50 minutes

- ❖ 2 (6-oz.) halibut steaks
- ❖ 1–2 Tbsps. butter
- ❖ 1 small clove garlic, minced
- ❖ 1–2 tsps. dried parsley
- ❖ sea salt to taste
- ❖ ½ cup heavy cream
- ❖ ½ lemon, cut into wedges

Grease the bottom of a 9x13 pan and place halibut fillets in the bottom. In a saucepan, melt butter. Then add the garlic, parsley, sea salt, and heavy cream. Pour mixture over halibut. Bake for 45 to 50 minutes, or until the flesh flakes and the juices run clear. Serve with lemon wedges.

❖ ❖ ❖

Baked Cajun Fish

Makes: 4 servings / Prep time: 10 minutes / Bake time: 45–50 minutes

- ❖ 2 (6-oz.) salmon, halibut, or trout fillets
- ❖ 2–3 Tbsps. butter
- ❖ 2 tsps. Cajun Seasoning Mix (see recipe in "Homemade Seasoning and Mixes")
- ❖ fresh lemon juice

Grease the bottom of a 9x13 pan and place fish fillets on the bottom. Melt butter in a saucepan, and stir in Cajun Seasoning mix. Sprinkle butter mixture over fillets and bake for 45 to 50 minutes (25 to 30 for trout) at 350°F or until juices turn tender and flesh flakes. Serve with a squeeze of fresh lemon juice, if desired.

❖ ❖ ❖

Seasoned Salmon

Makes: 4 servings / Prep time: 10 minutes / Bake time: 45–50 minutes

- ❖ 2 (6-oz.) salmon steaks
- ❖ 2–3 Tbsps. butter or extra virgin olive oil
- ❖ 2 cloves garlic, minced

- ❖ ¼ red onion, thinly sliced
- ❖ 2 tsps. dried cilantro flakes
- ❖ 2 vine-ripe tomatoes, diced
- ❖ sea salt to taste
- ❖ freshly ground pepper to taste
- ❖ fresh lemon juice

Place salmon steaks into the bottom of a buttered 9x13 baking dish. Pour olive oil over steaks, and sprinkle with garlic, onion, cilantro, tomatoes, sea salt, and pepper. Bake for 45 to 50 minutes at 350°F or until flesh flakes and juices run clear. Serve with a squeeze of fresh lemon juice.

Vegetable Sausage Pizza

Makes: 6–8 servings / Prep time: 25 minutes / Cook time: 15 minutes

- ❖ 1 recipe Yeast-Free Pizza Crust (see recipe in "Traditional Basic Breads")
- ❖ 6 turkey sausage patties
- ❖ 1 small red or yellow onion, chopped
- ❖ 1 recipe pizza sauce (see recipe in "Spreads, Sauces, Dips, and Marinades") or 15 oz. pizza sauce
- ❖ 1 (15-oz.) can black olives, sliced
- ❖ 1 large green pepper, seeded and chopped
- ❖ 3–6 fresh mushrooms, chopped finely (optional)
- ❖ 10 oz. or 3½ cups raw mild cheddar or Monterey Jack cheese, grated
- ❖ 2 roma tomatoes, chopped and lightly peppered and salted

While crust is cooking, cook and scramble sausage patties. Add onion to sausage and cook partially. Place the pizza crusts on a pizza pan or cookie sheet. Spread pizza sauce evenly over the crusts with the back of a spoon. Next, layer the sausage and onion, black olives, green pepper, and mushrooms on top of sauce. Bake at 350°F for 10 minutes. Remove from oven and layer the grated raw cheese and tomatoes on last. Turn oven off and return pizza to oven for 2 to 3 minutes, just until the cheese is barely melted. Remove from oven and cut with pizza cutter before serving.

Hot Italian Sausage Spaghetti Sauce

Makes: 6–8 servings / Prep time: 25 minutes / Cook time: 1 hour 20 minutes

- ❖ ½–1 lb Hot Italian Turkey Sausage (see recipe below) or nitrate-free sausage links
- ❖ 1 large yellow onion, diced
- ❖ 2 cloves garlic, minced
- ❖ 1 large green bell pepper, seeded and chopped
- ❖ 2 cups fresh mushrooms, sliced
- ❖ 28 oz. tomato puree
- ❖ 28 oz. chopped or diced tomatoes, drain and discard juice
- ❖ 2 Tbsps. dehydrated cane juice
- ❖ 2 Tbsps. dried sweet basil
- ❖ ½ tsp. dried oregano
- ❖ ½ tsp. dried marjoram
- ❖ ¼ tsp. dried thyme
- ❖ ¼ tsp. dried whole fennel seeds
- ❖ 1 tsp. sea salt
- ❖ freshly ground black pepper to taste

If you are using Hot Italian Turkey Sausage:

In a large saucepan, brown sausage along with onion, garlic, bell pepper, and mushrooms until sausage is cooked and vegetables are tender. Add tomatoes, dehydrated cane juice, and spices. Simmer for about an hour for flavors to blend. Serve with brown rice spaghetti noodles.

If you are using nitrate-free sausage links:

Thaw links partially and peel the casings off while they are still mostly frozen and discard the casings. Cut the sausage links crosswise into ¼-inch-thick circles. Roll each slice into a little ball. Place them in a single layer in a skillet with a little oil. Cover and cook over medium-low heat, stirring occasionally, to brown evenly, about 10 minutes. Add onion, garlic, bell pepper, and mushrooms and continue cooking until vegetables are tender. Add tomatoes, dehydrated cane juice, and spices. Simmer for about an hour for flavors to blend. Serve with brown rice spaghetti noodles.

❖ ❖ ❖

Pineapple Ham Pizza

Makes: 1 large pizza / Prep time: 45 minutes / Cook time: 15 minutes

Crust:
- ❖ 3 cups moist sprouted spelt or kamut
- ❖ ½ tsp. sea salt
- ❖ 1 tsp. baking soda
- ❖ 1 Tbsp. olive oil

Sauce:
- ❖ 2 cups organic tomato puree
- ❖ ¼ tsp. sea salt
- ❖ 1 Tbsp. plus 1 tsp. dehydrated cane juice
- ❖ 1 tsp. onion powder
- ❖ ½ tsp. garlic powder
- ❖ 1 tsp. dried basil
- ❖ ½ tsp dried oregano

Toppings:
- ❖ ½ fresh pineapple, cored, and cut into small chunks or tidbits
- ❖ 3 oz. deli ham (nitrate free), diced
- ❖ 1½–2 cups raw cheddar or Monterey Jack cheese, shredded

Prepare the crust by blending sprouts in a food processor until they form a ball of dough. Add sea salt, soda, and olive oil, and blend well. Roll out and place on a large, buttered pizza pan. Let rise for 20 minutes, and then bake for 10 minutes at 350°F.

To make the sauce, heat all ingredients in a saucepan over medium heat then reduce heat to medium low and simmer for 10 to 15 minutes to let the flavors blend. When sauce is done, brush the top of the pre-baked pizza crust with a tablespoon of olive oil to prevent juices from toppings saturating the crust, then spread sauce over top.

To prepare the toppings, slice pineapple and place it in a strainer over a bowl to drain excess juices. When drained, place evenly over pizza. Add diced ham, if desired, and bake at 350°F for 12 minutes. Remove from oven and sprinkle with cheese. Return to oven and cook an additional 3 minutes to allow cheese to melt.

Note: This crust and sauce can be used with any number of different pizza toppings. Be creative!

Hot Italian Turkey Sausage

Makes: 2 cups / Prep time: 20 minutes

- ❖ 2 cups ground turkey
- ❖ 1 clove garlic, minced
- ❖ 2 tsps. sea salt
- ❖ 1 Tbsp. whole fennel seeds
- ❖ ½–1 tsp. crushed red pepper flakes
- ❖ ½ tsp. fresh ground black pepper
- ❖ ¼ tsp. paprika

Add garlic and spices to ground turkey in a large glass bowl. Mix well, cover, and refrigerate for 24 hours to allow flavors to blend. Keep in refrigerator uncooked for up to 3 days, or wrap and freeze for longer storage. Use in spaghetti sauce recipe or as a breakfast sausage.

Mexican Chicken Tacos

Makes: 6 servings / Prep time: 15 minutes / Cook time: 6–8 hours

- ❖ 2 chicken breasts
- ❖ ½–1 cup water
- ❖ 2 cups "slow and low" cooked black beans
- ❖ 1 medium yellow onion, chopped
- ❖ 1 bell pepper, chopped
- ❖ 2 cloves garlic, minced
- ❖ 1 cup fresh or frozen corn
- ❖ 1 cup salsa
- ❖ 3 Tbsps. homemade taco seasoning blend (see recipe in "Homemade Seasoning and Mixes")

Place uncooked chicken breasts, cooked beans, onion, pepper, garlic, and corn in a Crock-Pot. Stir in salsa and taco seasoning. Cook on high for 6 hours or on low for about 8. When ready to serve, shred chicken with a fork and stir. Serve with homemade tortillas, lettuce, tomatoes, olives, guacamole, raw cheese, sour cream, and salsa.

Quick-cooking option: cut chicken breasts into 3 to 4 lengthwise pieces. This will shorten Crock-Pot cook time to about 3 hours.

Vegetarian option: Omit chicken breasts and double the amount of beans.

Sausage Las-ghetti

Makes: 6–8 servings / Prep time: 30 minutes / Bake time: 30 minutes

- ❖ ½ lb. sausage, uncooked and sliced
- ❖ 6 Tinkyáda® brown rice lasagna noodles
- ❖ 12 oz. Tinkyáda® brown rice spaghetti noodles
- ❖ ½ medium onion, diced, or 1½ tsps. onion powder
- ❖ 3 Tbsps. olive oil
- ❖ 2 garlic cloves, minced, or ½ tsp. garlic powder
- ❖ 2 (28-oz.) cans of tomato sauce or chunky tomato sauce
- ❖ 2 tsps. dried basil
- ❖ 1 tsp. dried oregano
- ❖ 1 tsp. sea salt
- ❖ ¼ tsp. freshly ground black pepper
- ❖ 2 Tbsps. dehydrated cane juice
- ❖ 8 oz. raw cheese, shredded

While sausages are still partially frozen, remove casings and slice sausage crosswise into circles about ¼ inch thick. Meanwhile, cook lasagna and spaghetti noodles together in salt water, leaving them under cooked by about 5 to 6 minutes. In a large skillet, cook the sausages, onion, oil, and garlic together until onions are tender. Add the tomato sauce, basil, oregano, salt, pepper, and cane juice. Bring to a boil and reduce to simmer, covered, for 5 minutes.

Place all cooked and drained spaghetti noodles in the bottom of a 9x13 or a 9x13 glass dish. Pour all of the sauce mixture over the spaghetti noodles. Place all lasagna noodles in a single layer on top of the sauce. Cover with tin foil and bake at 350°F for 30 minutes. Remove from oven and sprinkle shredded cheese on top. Return to oven, uncovered, for a few minutes until cheese is melted. Remove from oven and let stand for 10 minutes before serving.

❖ ❖ ❖

Marinated Chicken or Turkey Breasts

Makes: 6 breasts / Prep time: 20 minutes / Marinate time: 24–48 hours

- ❖ 6 large chicken or turkey breasts, cut in half
- ❖ ½ cup olive oil
- ❖ ½ cup soy sauce (naturally fermented)
- ❖ ¾ cup sparkling apple cider
- ❖ ¼ cup agave, honey, or maple syrup
- ❖ juice from ½ lemon
- ❖ juice from ½ lime

Mix together olive oil, soy sauce, sparkling apple cider, sweetener, lemon juice, and lime juice. Pour over chicken of turkey breasts and tenderize with a fork. Cover and refrigerate for 24 to 48 hours. Meat can then be barbecued, grilled, baked, or cooked all day in a Crock-Pot.

❖ ❖ ❖

Marinated Turkey Wraps

Makes: 4–6 servings / Prep time: 30 minutes

- ❖ 4–6 homemade tortillas
- ❖ 2 marinated turkey breasts, (see recipe above) cooked, cut up, and chilled.
- ❖ 2 avocados, sliced
- ❖ 2 tomatoes, diced
- ❖ 1 cup chopped lettuce
- ❖ ½ cup sliced olives
- ❖ ½ a medium red onion, thinly sliced
- ❖ homemade dressing of choice (Honey Dijon or Classic Ranch, for example.)

In a tortilla, layer turkey, avocado, tomato, lettuce, olives, and onion. Top with dressing of choice and roll up.

Beef & Lamb

Lamb Chops

Makes: 4 servings /Prep time: 35 minutes / Cook time: 10–20 minutes

- ❖ 4 (3-oz.) lamb chops
- ❖ 2 cloves garlic, minced
- ❖ 3 Tbsps. olive oil
- ❖ 3 Tbsps. broth or water
- ❖ 2 tsps. fresh lemon juice
- ❖ 1 tsp. dried oregano
- ❖ ½ tsp. dried rosemary, ground
- ❖ ½ tsp. dried parsley

Mix together all ingredients but lamb chops. Add chops and marinate for at least 30 minutes. Drain and reserve marinade. Grill chops 5 to 10 minutes (depending on thickness) on each side, basting with marinade while cooking.

Pot Roast

Makes: 6–8 servings / Prep time: 10 minutes / Cook time: 5 hours

- ❖ 1 (3-lb.) pot roast
- ❖ 1 onion, chopped
- ❖ 6 whole cloves garlic, peeled
- ❖ 1½ Tbsps. olive oil
- ❖ 3½ cups filtered water or beef broth
- ❖ 1 tsp. sea salt
- ❖ ¼ tsp. black pepper
- ❖ ¼ tsp. dried rosemary, ground
- ❖ ½ tsp. dried marjoram
- ❖ ¼ tsp. dried thyme

Place roast, onions, garlic cloves, olive oil, and water or beef broth in a 9x13 pan. Combine sea salt, black pepper, dried rosemary, marjoram, and thyme in a small bowl. Sprinkle the seasoning mixture over roast. Cover with aluminum foil and seal the edges well. Bake for 5 hours at 325°F or at 350°F for 3 to 4 hours.

Beef Gravy

Makes: approx. 3–4 cups / Prep time: 7 minutes

- ❖ all drippings left over from baking a beef roast
- ❖ beef stock (if needed)
- ❖ 3 Tbsps. organic cornstarch
- ❖ sea salt to taste

Pour the drippings through a mesh strainer into a saucepan. Add additional beef stock if needed. Whisk cornstarch into ½ cup room temperature water. Pour into drippings. Heat over medium heat, stirring constantly, until thickened. Season with sea salt. Remove from heat and serve with mashed potatoes or rice.

Flank Steak

Makes: 4 servings / Prep time: 10 minutes / Cook time: 5–10 hours in Crock-Pot

- ❖ 1½ lbs. flank steak
- ❖ 1 large onion, chopped or sliced
- ❖ 4 garlic cloves, chopped
- ❖ 1–2 Tbsps. raw agave, dehydrated cane juice, or molasses
- ❖ 2 Tbsps. butter or coconut oil
- ❖ 2 Tbsps. raw apple cider vinegar
- ❖ ¼ cup fresh diced green mild chilies, seeded
- ❖ ½ cup water

Add all ingredients to a Crock-Pot and cook on low for 10 hours or on high for 5 hours.

Tacos

Makes: 4–6 servings / Prep time: 10 minutes / Cook time: 15 minutes

- ❖ 8 sprouted corn tortillas
- ❖ 1 recipe taco filling (see recipe below)
- ❖ shredded cheese
- ❖ sour cream
- ❖ shredded lettuce or fresh snipped cilantro

- ❖ salsa
- ❖ sliced olives
- ❖ chopped tomatoes
- ❖ avocados, thinly sliced

Place tortillas on a cookie sheet in a 350°F oven until edges curl up. Remove from oven and stack them in a tortilla warmer or a glass baking dish with a lid to keep them warm and moist. Fill with taco filling and add desired toppings.

❖   ❖   ❖

Taco Filling

Makes: 8 servings / Prep time: 5 minutes / Cook time: 20 minutes

- ❖ 1 lb. hamburger
- ❖ 3 Tbsps. butter
- ❖ 1 cup water
- ❖ 1½–2 cups sprouted and cooked pinto beans
- ❖ ⅓ cup homemade taco seasoning mix (see recipe in "Homemade Seasonings and Mixes")
- ❖ 1 tsp. sea salt

Brown hamburger in butter. Add water, scraping the bottom of the pan, then add the remaining ingredients and simmer covered for about 7 minutes.

❖   ❖   ❖

Real Hamburgers

Makes: 3–4 servings / Prep time: 10 minutes / Cook time: 15–18 minutes

- ❖ 1 lb. ground hamburger
- ❖ ¼ tsp. garlic powder
- ❖ ½ tsp. onion powder
- ❖ ½ tsp. real salt
- ❖ ¼ tsp. black pepper
- ❖ ¼ tsp. hot red pepper flakes (optional)

Stir all ingredients together well and form into patties. Grill or cook in a pan on the stove. Serve on warm toasted sprouted wheat buns with Vegenaise,® mustard, ketchup, tomatoes, and romaine lettuce.

American Spaghetti Sauce

Makes: 4 servings / Prep time: 15 / Cook time: 20 minutes

- ❖ 1 lb. hamburger (or less meat and use more zucchini)
- ❖ 3–4 fresh garlic cloves, minced
- ❖ 1 medium onion, chopped
- ❖ 1 small zucchini, quartered and chopped, or fresh mushrooms
- ❖ 28 oz. diced tomatoes, blended
- ❖ 15 oz. tomato sauce
- ❖ 1½ cups olives, sliced
- ❖ 2 Tbsps. dehydrated cane juice
- ❖ 1½ tsps. sea salt
- ❖ ¼ tsp. black pepper
- ❖ 1 tsp. dried oregano
- ❖ ½ tsp. dried marjoram
- ❖ 1½ Tbsps. dried sweet basil
- ❖ 1 pkg. brown rice spaghetti pasta

In a large saucepan, brown hamburger, garlic, onion, and zucchini. Pour in tomatoes, tomato sauce, olives, cane juice, herbs, and seasonings. Stir and let simmer for 30 minutes to an hour to blend flavors. Serve over brown rice spaghetti noodles.

Beef Stroganoff

Makes: 4 servings / Prep time: 15 minutes / Cook time: 35–40 minutes

- ❖ 1 lb. beef strips or hamburger, browned and cooked
- ❖ 2 Tbsps. coconut oil
- ❖ 1 medium onion, chopped
- ❖ 2 cloves garlic, minced
- ❖ 4 oz. fresh chopped mushrooms
- ❖ 3 Tbsps. butter
- ❖ ½ tsp. sea salt
- ❖ ½ cup beef stock
- ❖ ½ tsp. Dijon mustard
- ❖ 2 tsp. lemon pepper seasoning
- ❖ ½ tsp. dried parsley flakes
- ❖ 1 cup sour cream
- ❖ 1 pkg. Tinkyáda® organic brown rice pasta, prepared

Brown the beef in the coconut oil. Add onion, garlic, mushrooms, and butter. Add remaining ingredients, except the pasta and sour cream. Keep covered, stirring occasionally, until onions are tender. Stir in the sour cream and serve over the pasta.

❖ ❖ ❖

Loaded Burritos

Makes: 6 burritos / Prep time: 25 minutes / Bake time: 30 minutes

- ❖ 6 large sprouted wheat tortillas
- ❖ 8 oz. hamburger, cooked
- ❖ 1 cup sprouted and cooked beans
- ❖ 1 cup brown rice, precooked
- ❖ ½ cup frozen corn, thawed
- ❖ handful fresh cilantro, minced
- ❖ 1 medium tomato, chopped
- ❖ 1 medium onion, diced
- ❖ 2 cloves garlic, minced
- ❖ 1 Tbsp. chili powder
- ❖ ¾ tsp. sea salt
- ❖ 6 oz. raw shredded cheese

Garnishes:
- ❖ tomatoes, chopped
- ❖ lettuce, thinly sliced
- ❖ sour cream
- ❖ salsa

Spread the tortillas in a single layer on a cookie sheet and warm in a 250°F oven for 2 minutes. Promptly remove from oven, stack the tortillas on top of one another, and wrap them in a towel or place them in a tortilla warmer with a lid until needed. When ready, layer all the remaining ingredients in each tortilla one at a time. Roll them up, then wrap each individual burrito in aluminum foil. They can either be baked at 350°F for 30 minutes and served, or frozen for quick and easy lunches or dinners. If they are frozen, increase the bake time to 55 minutes.

❖ ❖ ❖

American Stir-fry

Makes: 6 servings / Prep time: 1 hour 20 minutes / Cook time: 55 minutes

- ❖ ½ lb. hamburger
- ❖ 2 cloves garlic, minced
- ❖ 2 cups fresh organic mushrooms, chopped or diced broccoli
- ❖ ½ tsp. sea salt
- ❖ 1 tsp. dried thyme
- ❖ 1 tsp. paprika
- ❖ 1½ tsp. lemon pepper
- ❖ ½ of large onion, chopped
- ❖ 4 stalks celery, thinly sliced
- ❖ 1½ cups carrots, sliced
- ❖ ½ cup beef broth
- ❖ 1½ Tbsp. organic cornstarch
- ❖ 1 large green pepper, seeded and chopped
- ❖ ¼ cup sour cream
- ❖ 8 cups brown rice, cooked

Scramble the hamburger and garlic on medium heat until browned. Add mushrooms and all seasonings. Stir well. Add all veggies except green peppers. Let cook until veggies are crisp tender. Pour in beef broth and cornstarch mixed with a little cold water. Heat until thickened. Add the green peppers and stir in the sour cream. Serve over warm, cooked brown rice. This will soon become a family favorite!

❖ ❖

Spreads, Seasonings, & Snacks

Tasty Treasure #17

Historically, healthy societies didn't have a lot of bagged, canned, jarred, and boxed foods in their diets—they most likely had none. But these easy foods have become so commonplace in our world that it's hard to imagine a life before their existence. Though they are convenient and fun, they do come at a cost to health. Fortunately, we have created recipes to bring these things into our homes in a more flavorful and nutritious way, and they're not even stale from sitting on a shelf for months.

Tasty Treasure #18

Any kind of nut tastes way better after being soaked in sea salt water for about 12 hours, then dehydrated. They actually pop in your mouth and don't taste bitter like some nuts do. Plus, because of phytic acid neutralization, they are a lot easier to digest.

Spreads, Sauces, Dips, & Marinades

Homemade Mayonnaise

Makes: approx. 1 cup / Prep time: 12 minutes

- ❖ 1 egg, at room temperature
- ❖ 2 Tbsps. fresh lemon juice
- ❖ 2 tsps. Dijon mustard
- ❖ ¼ tsp. sea salt
- ❖ pinch of garlic powder
- ❖ pinch of onion powder
- ❖ 6 Tbsps. extra virgin olive oil
- ❖ 6 Tbsps. grape seed oil

Separate egg and discard the white. Leave yolk in bowl on counter until room temperature. Beat egg yolk, lemon juice, salt, mustard, garlic and onion powders until smooth. While still beating, add the oils in a thin slow stream until all creamy and thickened. Refrigerate for up to two weeks.

Homemade Ketchup

Makes: 2 cups / Prep time: 10 minutes

- ❖ 2 cups tomato puree
- ❖ ¾ tsp. sea salt
- ❖ 2 Tbsp. agave, raw honey, or maple syrup
- ❖ 1 tsp. raw vinegar
- ❖ 1 clove garlic, minced
- ❖ 1 Tbsp. minced onion

Mix all ingredients in a food processor or blender until smooth and well blended. Keeps for about a week.

❖ ❖ ❖

Yogurt Mayonnaise

Makes: ½ cup / Prep time: 5 minutes

- ❖ ½ cup plain yogurt
- ❖ 1 tsp. Dijon mustard
- ❖ ⅛ tsp. sea salt
- ❖ ½ tsp. raw apple cider vinegar

Mix all ingredients together and store in a glass jar. Keeps for about a week in the fridge. Use as a mayonnaise substitute.

❖ ❖ ❖

Homemade Freezer Jam

Makes: 1½ cups / Cook time: 5 minutes

- ❖ 1 Tbsp. fine tapioca granules
- ❖ ⅓ cup water, or juice from berries
- ❖ 1 (16-oz.) bag frozen berries, or about 2 cups fresh
- ❖ 2 Tbsps. liquid sweetener

In a saucepan, soak tapioca in water or juice for 5 minutes, according to directions. Bring to a boil and stir until thick. Add berries and honey or syrup, and place in a jar in the fridge. Will keep about a week.

❖ ❖ ❖

Creamy Fruit Dip

Makes: approx. 1 cup / Prep time: 4 minutes

- ❖ ½ cup sour cream
- ❖ ½ cup whole plain yogurt
- ❖ ¼ cup 100-percent fruit jam
- ❖ 1 Tbsp. liquid sweetener
- ❖ ¼ tsp. cinnamon (optional)

Blend all ingredients together. Serve with slices of fruit such as apples, grapes, bananas, and pineapple.

Bean Dip

Makes: 2½ cups / Prep time: 15 minutes / Cook time: 10 minutes

- ❖ 2 cups sprouted and cooked pinto beans
- ❖ ½ cup filtered water
- ❖ 2 cloves garlic, minced, or ¼ tsp. garlic powder
- ❖ 3 Tbsps. fresh onion, minced, or 1½ tsps. onion powder
- ❖ 1 Tbsp. chili powder
- ❖ 1 tsp. cumin
- ❖ 1 tsp. pure maple syrup or raw honey
- ❖ ½ tsp. sea salt
- ❖ ⅛ tsp. paprika
- ❖ tiny pinch cayenne
- ❖ ½ cup raw cheese (optional)

In a saucepan, mash beans until smooth, and stir in water. Add garlic, onion, and seasonings. Cover, and simmer for 10 minutes, then blend again with a hand blender. Scoop into a bowl, then sprinkle with cheese. May be used as a dip or as a filling for homemade burritos.

❖ ❖ ❖

French Fry Dipping Sauce

Makes: ½ cup / Prep time: 2 minutes

- ❖ ½ cup Vegenaise®
- ❖ 2–3 Tbsps. organic ketchup

Combine Vegenaise® and ketchup. Mix well and keep refrigerated.

Garlic Spread

Prep time: 5 minutes

- ❖ ½ cup butter
- ❖ 1–3 cloves garlic, minced
- ❖ 1 tsp. dried parsley flakes

Stir butter until smooth. Add garlic and parsley and stir well. Spread over hot French bread.

❖ ❖ ❖

Guacamole

Makes: 2 cups / Prep time: 15 minutes

- ❖ 2 ripe avocados, mashed
- ❖ 1–2 tsps. fresh lemon juice
- ❖ 2 small cloves of garlic, minced or ¼ tsp. garlic powder
- ❖ ¼ red onion, diced or ½ tsp. onion powder
- ❖ 1 Tbsp. fresh cilantro, finely chopped
- ❖ ¼ tsp. sea salt
- ❖ 3–4 Tbsps. plain whole yogurt or sour cream
- ❖ 3–4 Tbsps. fresh or bottled salsa

Peel avocados and place in a bowl. Add the lemon juice and mash or blend well until desired texture is achieved. Mix in the other ingredients. Guacamole should be made just before serving as it will start to darken in an hour or two.

❖ ❖ ❖

Strawberry Ginger Dip

Makes: approx. 1 cup / Prep time: 10 minutes

- ❖ 1 cup fresh or frozen strawberries
- ❖ 1 Tbsp. raw honey or pure maple syrup
- ❖ ½ tsp. fresh grated ginger
- ❖ 2 Tbsps. plain yogurt (optional)

Purée strawberries, honey, ginger, and optional yogurt in a food processor. Serve as a dip for apple slices or other fruit. May also be used as a salad dressing when mixed without yogurt.

Yogurt Veggie Dip

Makes: approx. ¾ cup / Prep time: 10 minutes

- ❖ ¾ cup plain yogurt or sour cream
- ❖ 3 Tbsps. minced onion
- ❖ 1 clove garlic, minced
- ❖ 1 tsp. parsley
- ❖ sea salt to taste

Mix all ingredients together and serve with veggies.

Applesauce

Makes: about 2½ cups / Prep time: 5 minutes / Cook time: 20 minutes

- ❖ 3 medium apples, washed, cored, and chopped
- ❖ ¼ cup water
- ❖ 1 tsp. cinnamon

Place chopped apples in a saucepan with water, and bring to a boil. Simmer for 10 to 15 minutes until tender. Blend apples with a hand blender, or transfer to blender and mix for a couple minutes until the desired consistency is reached. Add cinnamon and serve plain or over pancakes.

Strawberry Applesauce

Makes: approx. 3½ cups / Prep time: 5 minutes / Cook time: 15–20 minutes

- ❖ 2 large apples, washed, cored, and cut into chunks
- ❖ 2 cups frozen or fresh strawberries
- ❖ 3 Tbsps. filtered water

Place apples, strawberries, and filtered water in a saucepan with a lid. Cover and let simmer for 15 to 20 minutes, or until apples are very tender. Mash with a fork or hand blender. This is a great topping for pancakes or French toast.

Baked Spinach Dip

Makes: approx. 4 cups / Prep time: 10 minutes / Bake time: 15 minutes

- ❖ 1 cup grated raw cheese
- ❖ ½ cup sour cream
- ❖ 1 cup Vegenaise®
- ❖ 2 tsps. Dijon mustard
- ❖ 2 cups spinach, chopped
- ❖ ½ cup yellow or red onion, minced

Combine all ingredients in a bowl and mix well. Spread mixture evenly into a 9-inch baking dish. Bake uncovered at 325°F for 10 to 15 minutes, or until heated through. Serve with crackers, chips, or French bread.

Artichoke Spinach Dip

Makes: 6 servings / Prep time: 15 minutes / Bake time: 15 minutes

- ❖ 16 oz. cream cheese
- ❖ 1 (15-oz.) jar artichoke hearts
- ❖ 1½ cups finely chopped fresh spinach
- ❖ 1 cup shredded raw cheese

Mix ingredients together and spread mixture into a 9x13 baking dish. Bake for 15 minutes at 325°F, or until hot. Serve with fresh vegetables, homemade crackers, or sprouted wheat pita bread.

Crab/Salmon Dip

Makes: 2 cups / Prep time: 15 minutes

- ❖ 8 oz. cream cheese
- ❖ ¼ cup salsa
- ❖ ¼ cup, or one small can, sliced olives
- ❖ 2 Tbsps. finely minced red or green onion
- ❖ 1 small clove of garlic, minced
- ❖ 1 (6-oz.) can crab meat or ¾ cup cooked and shredded salmon

Mix cream cheese in a medium bowl, and then stir in remaining ingredients. Serve with crackers or vegetables.

Mushroom Gravy

Makes: 8 servings / Prep time: 3 minutes / Cook time: 5 minutes

- ❖ 1 medium onion
- ❖ 1–2 cloves garlic
- ❖ 8 oz. fresh organic mushrooms, washed and sliced or chopped
- ❖ 6 Tbsps. butter
- ❖ 1 tsp. paprika
- ❖ 1 tsp. dried parsley flakes
- ❖ 3 Tbsps. organic cornstarch
- ❖ 2 cups beef or vegetable broth

Sauté onions with garlic and mushrooms in 2 tablespoons of the butter for about 8 minutes, stirring often. Add paprika and parsley. Set aside. In another pan, melt the remaining 4 tablespoons of butter. Mix the cornstarch with a little cold water and whisk it in to the butter to form a paste. Slowly stir broth into thickened butter mixture. Stir in mushroom mixture. Can be served as is or blended until smooth.

❖ ❖ ❖

Easy Dill Dip

Makes: 1 cup / Prep time: 5 minutes

- ❖ ½ cup sour cream
- ❖ 1 cup Vegenaise®
- ❖ 1 small garlic clove, minced
- ❖ 1 tsp. Dijon mustard
- ❖ ½ tsp. dried dill weed
- ❖ ½ tsp. dried parsley flakes

Blend all ingredients together well. Keep refrigerated.

❖ ❖ ❖

Coconut Cream

Makes: approx. 1¾ cup / Prep time: 5 minutes / Chill time: 1 hour

- ❖ 1 (14-oz.) can whole coconut milk (Use only the cream)
- ❖ 2 Tbsps. liquid sweetener
- ❖ 1 tsp. pure vanilla extract

Mix ingredients together and chill to firm.

BBQ Sauce

Makes: approx. 3 cups / Prep time: 15 minutes

- ❖ 8 oz. tomato sauce
- ❖ 6 oz. tomato paste
- ❖ ¾ cup water
- ❖ 3 Tbsps. dehydrated cane juice
- ❖ ¼ cup raw apple cider vinegar
- ❖ 3 Tbsps. extra virgin olive oil
- ❖ ¼ cup molasses
- ❖ 3 garlic cloves, minced
- ❖ 1 medium onion, chopped
- ❖ 2 tsps. chili powder
- ❖ 1 tsp. sea salt
- ❖ 1½ tsps. dry mustard
- ❖ ½–¾ tsp. black pepper
- ❖ ¼ tsp. ground cumin
- ❖ ⅛–¼ tsp. cayenne powder
- ❖ ⅛–¼ tsp. ground cloves
- ❖ ⅛–¼ tsp. dried oregano

Blend all ingredients together. Store for up to a week in the refrigerator.

Peach-Pineapple Salsa

Makes: 3 cups / Prep time: 20 minutes

- ❖ 2 large, ripe tomatoes
- ❖ 1 ripe peach
- ❖ ½ fresh pineapple
- ❖ ½ red onion, chopped
- ❖ 1 clove garlic, minced
- ❖ 2 Tbsps. raw apple cider vinegar
- ❖ 2 Tbsps. pure maple syrup or raw honey
- ❖ ¼ tsp. sea salt

Chop tomatoes, peach, and pineapple into chunks. Add onion and garlic, and process in a food processor until well blended, with some chunks left. Pour in a glass bowl and add vinegar, sweetener, and salt. Serve with tortilla chips.

Tomatillo Salsa

Makes: 4 cups / Prep time: 30 minutes / Cook time: 15 minutes

- ❖ 12 tomatillos, peeled and washed
- ❖ 1 jalapeño pepper, minced
- ❖ 1 bell pepper, finely chopped
- ❖ 1 clove garlic, minced
- ❖ ½ white onion, chopped
- ❖ ¼ tsp. sea salt
- ❖ 1 Tbsp. raw honey or pure maple syrup
- ❖ juice from 1 lime

Finely chop tomatillos and cook in a frying pan over medium-low heat until tender, about 15 minutes. Place in a bowl and cool for about 10 minutes before adding remaining ingredients. Serve with homemade chips.

❖ ❖ ❖

Honey Butter

Makes: 1½ cups / Prep time: 5 minutes

- ❖ ½ cup butter, room temperature
- ❖ ½–1 cup honey

Blend well and keep in a small jar with a tightly fitting lid in the refrigerator. Use a hand mixer for a fluffier mixture.

❖ ❖ ❖

Cinnamon Honey Butter

Makes: 1 cup / Prep time: 5 minutes

- ❖ ½ cup honey
- ❖ ½ cup butter
- ❖ 1 tsp. cinnamon

Cream butter in a bowl and stir in honey. Mix well until fluffy. Add cinnamon and stir until well blended. To use as a sauce for the top of cinnamon rolls or French Toast Casserole, warm honey slightly in an open container in a pot of hot water on low heat. Make sure it doesn't reach over 118°F; 90°F should be plenty warm. Mix with butter and cinnamon and drizzle as desired.

Creamy Honey Dijon

Makes: 2 servings / Prep time: 5 minutes

- ❖ 1 Tbsp. prepared Dijon mustard
- ❖ 1 Tbsp. raw honey
- ❖ 2 Tbsps. plain yogurt
- ❖ ¼ cup olive oil

Mix all ingredients with a fork in a large jar. Keep refrigerated.

Snacks & Crackers

Graham Crackers

Makes: 16 crackers / Prep time: 20 minutes / Bake time: 20 minutes

- ❖ 2 cups sprouted wheat flour
- ❖ ¼ tsp. sea salt
- ❖ ¼ tsp. baking soda
- ❖ 2 Tbsps. dehydrated cane juice
- ❖ 5 Tbsps. liquid sweetener
- ❖ 5 Tbsps. melted butter or coconut oil
- ❖ 2–3 Tbsps. water (enough to make a non-sticky ball of dough)

Mix dry ingredients in a medium-sized bowl. Stir in wet ingredients. Roll onto a buttered cookie sheet with a rolling pin. Score into about 16 large crackers, prick with a fork, and bake for 20 minutes at 350°F.

Sprouted Wheat Thins

Makes: approx: 50 small crackers / Prep time: 15 minutes / Bake time: 15–20 minutes

- ❖ 1 cup sprouted wheat flour
- ❖ ½ tsp. sea salt
- ❖ 2 Tbsps. coconut oil, melted
- ❖ ¼ cup water

Mix dry ingredients together in a bowl, then add wet. Stir until mixture forms a ball of dough. Roll out onto a well-buttered cookie sheet. Poke dough with a fork and bake for 15 to 20 minutes at 350°F, or until golden. Remove from oven, and score into small cracker sizes immediately. Serve with any kind of dip when cooled.

❖ ❖ ❖

Cranberry Nut Mix

Makes: approx. 3 cups / Prep time: 10 minutes / Dehydration time: 8–12 hours

- ❖ 1 egg white
- ❖ 5–10 drops cinnamon bark essential oil (or to taste)
- ❖ 1 cup Traditional Almonds (see "Sprouting Nuts and Seeds" section)
- ❖ 1 cup soaked and dehydrated pecans
- ❖ 1 cup juice-sweetened dried cranberries
- ❖ ½ cup dehydrated cane juice
- ❖ ½ tsp. ground cinnamon
- ❖ ½ tsp. sea salt

Beat egg white in a bowl until frothy and add cinnamon essential oil. Add nuts and cranberries and stir to coat. In a separate bowl, mix together dehydrated cane juice, cinnamon, and sea salt. Pour in nut mixture and stir to coat evenly with cane juice mixture. Place in a dehydrator set for 145°F and dehydrate for about 8 to 12 hours.

❖ ❖ ❖

Homemade Popcorn

Makes: approx. 10 cups / Prep time: 4–5 minutes to make

- ❖ 1 large bowl of hot, organic air-popped popcorn (½ cup unpopped kernels)
- ❖ ¼ cup butter
- ❖ ¼ cup coconut oil
- ❖ 1½ tsps. sea salt

While corn is popping, melt the butter, coconut oil, and olive oil together. Blend and drizzle over the popped corn. Mix to coat evenly. Sprinkle with salt and mix again.

Trail Mix

Makes: 3 cups / Prep time: 10 minutes

- ❖ 1 cup Traditional Almonds (see "Sprouting Nuts and Seeds" section)
- ❖ ½ cup raisins
- ❖ ½ cup flaked, unsweetened coconut
- ❖ 1 cup homemade dried bananas, apples, or other fruit

Toss ingredients together, and store in an airtight container for a quick snack.

Fruity Coconut Balls

Makes: 20–25 balls / Prep time: 20 minutes

- ❖ 1 cup pitted dates
- ❖ ¾ cup dried cranberries
- ❖ 1½ cups dried coconut flakes or shreds (unsweetened)
- ❖ ½ cup soaked and dehydrated pecans
- ❖ ½ cup Traditional Almonds (see "Sprouting Nuts and Seeds" section)
- ❖ 1 Tbsp. maple syrup
- ❖ 1 Tbsp. fresh orange juice
- ❖ 5–8 drops orange essential oil

In a food processor, blend dates, cranberries, 1 cup of the coconut, and nuts. When well blended, add maple syrup, orange juice, and orange essential oil. Mix until well blended. Form mixture into one-inch balls and roll in the remaining coconut.

Caramel Popcorn or Nuts

Makes: approx. 10 cups / Prep Time: 5 minutes / Cook time: 15 minutes

- ❖ ½ cup dehydrated cane juice
- ❖ ¼ cup butter or coconut oil
- ❖ ¼ cup pure maple syrup
- ❖ ¼ cup agave
- ❖ 10 cups popcorn, nuts, or both

In a saucepan, melt butter or coconut oil and add the cane juice, syrup, and agave. Allow the dehydrated cane juice to dissolve over medium-low heat. When it is fully dissolved, heat may be turned to medium to bring to a boil. Allow to boil for approximately 30 seconds. Remove from heat and cool for about five minutes. Place popcorn in a large bowl and remove all unpopped kernels. Pour caramel over the top and stir with a wooden spoon until evenly distributed. If desired, reserve some caramel for nuts or apples. Allow to cool before serving.

❖ ❖ ❖

Soft and Chewy Caramel Corn

Makes: 6–8 servings / Prep time: 20–25 minutes

- ❖ 2 batches popped popcorn (½ cup popcorn kernels total)
- ❖ ½ cup butter
- ❖ 1¼ cup dehydrated cane juice
- ❖ 1 cup raw blue/amber agave
- ❖ ½ tsp. pure vanilla extract
- ❖ ⅛ tsp. baking soda

Pop the corn and set aside in a large, stainless steel bowl. In a medium saucepan, melt the butter over medium heat. When melted (not boiling) add the cane juice and agave. Blend well. Stir continuously over medium heat until mixture comes to a full boil. Allow it to boil gently for about a minute. Remove from heat and add the vanilla. Stir well. Now add the baking soda. The mixture will foam up somewhat. Using a spoon, drizzle the hot foamy caramel mixture over the popped corn. Keep stirring the popcorn to evenly coat all the popped corn with the caramel. As it continues to cool, come back and stir it every few minutes. This caramel corn will stay soft over the next week—if it lasts that long!

❖ ❖ ❖

Baked Caramel Popcorn

Makes: 4–6 servings / Prep time: 15 minutes / Bake time: 1 hour

- ❖ ½ cup unpopped popcorn
- ❖ ¼ cup honey or pure maple syrup
- ❖ ¼ cup molasses
- ❖ ½ cup butter *(continued)*

- ❖ ½ cup dehydrated cane juice
- ❖ ½ tsp. sea salt
- ❖ ¼ tsp. baking soda
- ❖ ½ tsp. pure vanilla extract

Pop popcorn in an air popper. Set aside in a large bowl. Mix the honey or syrup, molasses, butter, cane juice, and salt together, and bring to a boil. Boil for 5 minutes. Remove from heat and stir in the baking soda and vanilla. Pour over popped popcorn. Spread evenly in a roasting pan and bake at 250°F for about an hour, stirring every 15 minutes.

Carob Mint Almonds

Makes: approx. 1 cup / Prep time: 20 minutes / Cool time: 15 minutes

- ❖ ½ cup semisweet carob chips
- ❖ 1 Tbsp. dehydrated cane juice (optional)
- ❖ 5–8 drops peppermint essential oil
- ❖ 1 cup Traditional Almonds (see "Sprouting Nuts and Seeds" section)

In a small saucepan, melt carob chips. Stir in dehydrated cane juice and peppermint essential oil and mix well. Remove from heat and stir in almonds. Place small spoonfuls of carob covered nuts on a plate and allow to cool.

Carob Orange Pecans

Makes: approx. 1 cup / Prep time: 20 minutes / Cool time: 15 minutes

- ❖ ½ cup semisweet carob chips
- ❖ 1 Tbsp. dehydrated cane juice (optional)
- ❖ 5–8 drops orange essential oil
- ❖ ½ cup sprouted and dehydrated pecans
- ❖ ½ cup dried cranberries

In a small saucepan, melt carob chips. Stir in dehydrated cane juice and orange essential oil and mix well. Remove from heat and stir in pecans and cranberries. Place small spoonfuls of carob-covered mixture on a plate and allow it to cool.

Homemade Seasonings & Mixes

Taco Seasoning

Makes: 3½ cups / Prep time: 7 minutes

- ❖ ⅔ cup dried onion granules or onion powder
- ❖ 1¼ cups chili pepper powder
- ❖ 1¾ Tbsps. garlic powder
- ❖ ⅔ cup ground cumin
- ❖ 3½ Tbsps. paprika
- ❖ 3½ Tbsps. dried oregano
- ❖ 2 Tbsps. dehydrated cane juice or granulated maple sugar

Mix all spices together and store in a labeled airtight container.

❖   ❖   ❖

Cajun Seasoning Mix

Makes: appox. ½ cup / Prep time: 5 minutes

- ❖ ¼ cup garlic powder
- ❖ ¼ cup dried oregano
- ❖ 2½ Tbsps. chili powder
- ❖ 2½ Tbsps. dried thyme
- ❖ 1½ tsps. black pepper
- ❖ 1½ tsps. cayenne pepper

Mix all spices together and store in a labeled airtight container.

❖   ❖   ❖

Italian Seasoning Mix

Makes: 1 cup mix / Prep time: 10 minutes

- ❖ ⅓ cup dried oregano
- ❖ 1 Tbsp. garlic powder
- ❖ 2 tsps. onion powder
- ❖ ⅓ cup dried basil
- ❖ 2 Tbsps. rosemary, ground down to 1 tsp.
- ❖ ¼ cup dried thyme

Mix all spices together and store in a labeled airtight container.

Ranch Dressing Mix

Makes: approx. 1½ cups / Prep time: 10 minutes

- ❖ ⅔ cup dried parsley flakes
- ❖ 3 ½ Tbsps. dried dill weed
- ❖ 5 tsps. garlic powder
- ❖ ⅓ cup onion powder
- ❖ ¼ cup sea salt

Mix well and store in an air-tight container. Scoop 5 teaspoons of dry ranch dressing mix and combine with the following ingredients to make a quick ranch dressing:

- ❖ 1 cup Vegenaise®
- ❖ ¼ cup milk
- ❖ ¼ cup plain whole yogurt
- ❖ 1–2 tsps. agave
- ❖ ½–1 tsp. raw apple cider vinegar

Mix well and refrigerate for at least 30 minutes before serving. Keeps for about 2 to 4 weeks.

❖ ❖

✧ ✧

Sweets & Treats

✧ ✧

Tasty Treasure #19

Even though past healthy societies did have some natural sugars, they were limited. It's best to limit sweets—even natural ones—and eat them only after a good meal with fat and protein to slow the absorption of sugar into the system. But since we live in a world where there is a tremendous amount of peer pressure relating to sweets, and because we happened to come up with some five-star desserts, we really wanted to include them.

Tasty Treasure #20

Liquid sweeteners work well in things like muffins and sweet breads where there is already some liquid. Dehydrated cane juice works well in things like cookies, where using liquid may change the consistency.

Tasty Treasure #21

Some families have the rule, "eat everything on your plate or you don't get dessert." In our families—as long as they eat most of their dinner—there's no problem because the dessert is nourishing too. With healthy, raw egg yolks, raw cream, and natural sweetening, our ice creams and frozen desserts are delicious, nutritionally dense whole foods. From our families to yours, enjoy!

✧ ✧

Frozen Desserts

Quick Ice Cream

Makes: approx. 6 cups / Prep time: 10 minutes / Freeze time: 3 hours

- ❖ 2 cups cream, preferably raw
- ❖ ¾ cup whole milk, preferably raw
- ❖ ¼ cup raw blue/amber agave or pure maple syrup
- ❖ 3 tsps. pure vanilla extract

Blend all ingredients with a mixer until soft peaks form and the mixture is fluffy. Place in a shallow container with a lid and freeze until firm.

Vanilla Ice Cream

Makes: approx. 10 cups / Prep time: 40 minutes / Freeze time: 3 hours

- ❖ 2 egg yolks
- ❖ 2 Tbsp. dehydrated cane juice
- ❖ 2 tsps. pure vanilla extract
- ❖ 2 cups raw cream or high-quality whipping cream, *not* ultra-pasteurized
- ❖ 1 cup raw milk
- ❖ ¼ cup pure maple syrup or raw blue/amber agave

Rinse the egg yolk in cold water to remove all raw egg white. In a large bowl, beat the egg yolks with the cane juice. Add the vanilla and maple syrup or agave to the eggs and cane juice. Let sit for 5 to 10 minutes so the cane juice can dissolve. Gently stir in the cream and milk by hand until well blended and pour the mixture into an ice-cream maker.

Follow the directions on your ice-cream maker. Typically, in a maker that uses salt and ice, you will process the ice cream until the motor struggles to churn the ice cream, about 1 to 2 hours. In an indoor ice-cream maker with a refreezable canister, it takes about 20 to 30 minutes. When the ice cream is done churning, scrape it into a shallow freezer container. Stir well, cover with a tightly fitting lid, and freeze for at least 3 hours before serving. (Preferably, make the day before and allow it to freeze overnight, so it can harden sufficiently). This recipe can be halved or doubled.

❖   ❖   ❖

Coconut Vanilla Ice Cream

Makes: approx. 5 cups / Prep time: 20 minutes / Freeze time: 3 hours

- ❖ 2 egg yolks
- ❖ 2 Tbsps. dehydrated cane juice
- ❖ 2 tsps. pure vanilla extract
- ❖ ¼ cup pure maple syrup or raw blue/amber agave
- ❖ 1 cup heavy cream, preferably raw
- ❖ 14 oz. unsweetened whole coconut milk

Rinse the egg yolks in cold water to remove all raw egg white. In a large bowl, whisk egg yolks with the cane juice. Add vanilla and maple syrup to the eggs and cane juice. Let sit for 5 to 10 minutes so the cane juice can dissolve. Gently stir the cream and coconut milk in by hand. When it is blended well, pour it into the ice-cream maker.

Follow the directions on your ice cream maker. When it is finished churning, scrape the ice cream into a shallow freezer container. Stir well, cover with a tightly fitting lid, and freeze in your freezer for at least 3 hours before serving. (Preferably, make the day before and allow it to freeze overnight, so it can harden sufficiently.)

❖ ❖ ❖

Mint-Chocolate Chip Ice Cream

Makes: approx. 10 cups / Prep time: 40 minutes / Freeze time: 3 hours

- ❖ 2 egg yolks
- ❖ 2 Tbsps. dehydrated cane juice
- ❖ 2 tsps. pure vanilla extract
- ❖ ½ tsp. organic peppermint extract, or 2 drops peppermint essential oil (therapeutic grade)
- ❖ ¼ cup raw blue/amber agave or pure maple syrup
- ❖ 2 cups heavy cream, preferably raw
- ❖ 1 cup raw milk
- ❖ ⅓ cup organic chocolate chips, chopped

Rinse the egg yolks in cold water to remove all raw egg white. In a large bowl, beat egg yolks with the cane juice. Let sit for 5 minutes to dissolve. Add the vanilla extract, the peppermint extract, and the agave or maple syrup to the eggs and cane juice. Gently stir the cream and milk in by hand. When it is blended well, pour it into the ice-cream maker.

Follow the directions on your ice cream maker. When it is finished churning, scrape the ice cream into a shallow freezer container. Add the chopped chocolate pieces, stir well, cover, and place in freezer for at least 3 hours before serving. (Preferably, make the day before needed and allow it to freeze overnight, so it can harden sufficiently).

Cherry-Chocolate Chip Ice Cream

Makes: approx. 14 cups / Prep time: 40 minutes / Freeze time: 3 hours

- ❖ 2 egg yolks
- ❖ 2 Tbsps. dehydrated cane juice
- ❖ 1 Tbsp. pure vanilla extract
- ❖ ¼ cup pure maple syrup or blue/amber agave
- ❖ 2 cups raw cream
- ❖ 1 cups raw whole milk
- ❖ ½ cup organic chocolate chips, chopped
- ❖ ½ cup frozen cherries, partially thawed and blended a bit.

Rinse the egg yolks in cold water to remove all raw egg white. In a large bowl, beat the egg yolks with the cane juice. Let stand for 5 minutes to dissolve. Add the vanilla and maple syrup to the eggs and cane juice. Gently stir the cream and milk in by hand. When it is blended well, pour it into the ice-cream maker.

Follow the directions on your ice-cream maker. Process the ice cream for about 1 to 2 hours, or until the motor struggles to churn the ice cream. Then scrape ice cream into a shallow freezer container and stir in the cherries and chocolate chips. Blend well, cover, and place in freezer for at least 3 hours before serving. (Preferably, make the day before needed and allow it to freeze overnight, so it can harden sufficiently).

Strawberry Ice Cream

Makes: approx. 14 cups / Prep time: 40 minutes / Freeze time: 3 hours

- ❖ 2 egg yolks
- ❖ 2 Tbsps. dehydrated cane juice
- ❖ 1 Tbsp. pure vanilla extract
- ❖ ⅓–½ cup pure maple syrup or raw blue/amber agave
- ❖ 2 cups raw cream
- ❖ 1 cup raw whole milk
- ❖ 10 oz. organic frozen strawberries, thawed and gently blended

Rinse the egg yolks in cold water to remove all raw egg white. In a large bowl, beat the egg yolks with the cane juice. Let stand for 5 minutes to dissolve. Add the vanilla and maple syrup to the eggs and cane juice. Gently stir the cream and milk in by hand. When it is blended well, pour it into the ice-cream maker.

Follow the directions on your ice cream maker. Process the ice cream for about 1 to 2 hours, or until motor struggles to churn the ice cream. Then scrape the ice cream into a shallow freezer container and stir in the mashed strawberries. Blend well, cover, and place in freezer for at least 3 hours before serving. (Preferably, make the day before and allow it to freeze overnight, so it can harden sufficiently).

❖ ❖ ❖

Chocolate Ice Cream

Makes: approx. 14 cups / Prep time: 40 minutes / Freeze time: 3 hours

- ❖ 2 egg yolks
- ❖ ½ cup dehydrated cane juice
- ❖ 1 Tbsp. pure vanilla extract
- ❖ ¼ cup pure maple syrup or raw blue/amber agave
- ❖ 4 cups fresh cream
- ❖ 2 cups whole raw milk
- ❖ 3 Tbsps. organic cocoa powder mixed with 1 Tbsp. liquid sweetener

Rinse the egg yolks in cold water to remove all raw egg white. In a large bowl, beat the egg yolks with the cane juice. Let stand for 5 minutes to dissolve. Add the vanilla, and maple syrup to the eggs and cane juice. Gently stir the cream and milk in by hand. When it is blended well, pour it into the ice-cream maker.

Follow the directions on your ice cream maker. Process the ice cream for about 1 to 2 hours, or until motor struggles to churn the ice cream. Then scrape ice cream into a shallow freezer container and stir in the chocolate mix. Blend well, cover, and place in freezer for at least 3 hours before serving. (Preferably, make the day before and allow it to freeze overnight, so it can harden sufficiently).

❖ ❖ ❖

Banana Splits

Makes: 4 servings / Prep time: 15 minutes

- ❖ 4 ripe bananas, peeled and cut in half lengthwise
- ❖ homemade vanilla, chocolate, or strawberry ice cream
- ❖ chocolate syrup (see following recipe)
- ❖ chopped Traditional Almonds (see "Sprouting Nuts and Seeds" section)

Place each split banana in its own serving bowl. Top each one with ice cream scoops, syrup, and chopped almonds. Serve immediately.

Chocolate Syrup

Makes: 1½ cups / Prep time: 10 minutes

- ❖ 1 cup pure maple syrup or raw blue/amber agave
- ❖ ½ cup organic cocoa powder
- ❖ 2 tsps. pure vanilla extract

Blend well and keep refrigerated in an airtight container. This is the perfect ice cream topping. Or, use a spoonful to make chocolate milk!

Strawberry Frozen Yogurt Pie

Makes: 8 servings / Prep time: 30 minutes / Freeze time: 6–8 hours

Topping:

- ❖ ¼ cup Traditional Almonds (see "Sprouting Nuts and Seeds" section)
- ❖ ¼ cup coconut
- ❖ ¼ cup whole dates, pitted
- ❖ 1 Tbsp. butter, melted

Filling:

- ❖ 12 oz. frozen strawberries, partially thawed and mashed or blended
- ❖ 2 cups whole plain yogurt
- ❖ 1 cup sour cream
- ❖ ½ cup pure maple syrup or honey
- ❖ a tiny pinch of sea salt

Partially thaw the strawberries for the filling in a glass bowl on the countertop or in a warm oven. Combine the ingredients for the topping in a small bowl, mix, and set aside. In a large bowl, blend the yogurt and sour cream until smooth. Add the honey or maple syrup and salt and blend again until smooth. Using a fork, mash thawed strawberries to desired texture. Lightly stir the strawberries into the cream mixture—do not blend them. Scrape mixture into a deep pie dish. Freeze for 2 hours. Remove from freezer and sprinkle the topping generously, in an even layer, over the top and gently pat to press into the yogurt mixture. Return to the freezer and freeze an additional 4 to 6 hours. Serve frozen.

❖ ❖ ❖

Frozen Whipped Cream

Makes: 4 cups / Prep time: 5 minutes / Freeze time: 2 hours

- ❖ 2 cups heavy whipping cream
- ❖ 3 Tbsps. pure maple syrup or raw blue/amber agave
- ❖ 1 tsp. pure vanilla extract

Combine all ingredients. Beat with electric beaters until mixture is fluffy and thickened. Do not over beat. This is great to have on hand for topping off hot chocolate, pie, or whatever you desire.

Caramel Nut Ice Cream Pie

Makes: 1 (9-inch) pie / Prep time: 55 minutes / Bake time: 12 minutes / Freeze time: 4 hours

Crust:
- ❖ ¼ cup butter or coconut oil
- ❖ ¼ cup dehydrated cane juice
- ❖ ¾ cup plus 2 Tbsps. sprouted wheat flour

Melt butter in a saucepan, stir in cane juice, then mix in flour until crumbly. Press mixture into pie tin with a spoon and bake for 12 minutes at 350°F or until golden. Remove from oven and cool completely.
(continued)

Caramel:
- ❖ ¼ cup butter
- ❖ ½ cup dehydrated cane juice
- ❖ ¼ cup pure maple syrup
- ❖ ¼ cup raw blue/amber agave

Mix all ingredients in a saucepan. Bring to a boil over medium-low temperature. Make sure cane juice dissolves completely before bringing to boil. Allow the caramel to cool.

Filling & Topping:
- ❖ 2 cups whipping cream
- ❖ 2 egg yolks (3 tablespoons melted butter may be used instead of raw egg yolks)
- ❖ 3 tsps. pure vanilla extract
- ❖ ⅓ cup pure maple syrup
- ❖ ¾ cup chopped Traditional Almonds (see "Sprouting Nuts and Seeds" section)
- ❖ prepared caramel (see recipe above)

Mix together cream, egg yolks, vanilla, and maple syrup in a blender until cream thickens and starts to form peaks. Stir in a ½ cup of almonds, and then slowly drizzle in about a ½ cup of the caramel. Caramel should be streaked throughout the cream mixture. Pour filling into cooled pie crust, drizzle top with additional caramel, and then sprinkle with the remaining ¼ cup of almonds. Freeze for several hours until frozen through, approximately 4 hours.

Chocolate Mint Ice Cream Pie

Makes: 1 (9-inch) pie / Prep time: 40 minutes / Bake time: 12 minutes / Freeze time: 4 hours

Crust:
- ❖ ¼ cup butter or coconut oil
- ❖ ¼ cup carob powder or cocoa powder
- ❖ ¼ cup dehydrated cane juice
- ❖ ½ cup sprouted wheat flour

Melt butter in saucepan. Stir in carob and cane juice, and then mix in flour until crumbly. Press into pie tin with a spoon and bake for 12 minutes at 350°F. Remove from oven and cool completely.

Filling:

- ❖ 2 cups whipping cream
- ❖ 2 egg yolks (3 Tbsps. melted butter may be used instead of raw egg yolks)
- ❖ 3 tsps. pure vanilla extract
- ❖ ⅓ cup pure maple syrup
- ❖ 2 drops peppermint essential oil
- ❖ 2 oz. organic dark chocolate bar, grated

Whip cream, egg yolks, vanilla, and syrup until cream thickens and begins to form peaks. Stir in essential oil and grated chocolate bar, saving some to sprinkle over the top. Pour into cooled pie crust and sprinkle with remaining chocolate shavings. Freeze for about 4 hours, or until solid.

Frozen Banana-Berry Yogurt Pie

Makes: 1 (8-inch) pie / Prep time: 15 minutes / Freeze time: 30–45 minutes

Crust:

- ❖ ¾ cup Traditional Almonds (see "Sprouting Nuts and Seeds" section)
- ❖ ¾ cup dates or raisins

Process the almonds and dates or raisins in a food processor until a ball is formed. Press mixture into a pie dish and crimp the edges.

Filling:

- ❖ 1 cup frozen or fresh berries
- ❖ 1 cup plain whole yogurt
- ❖ 2 ripe bananas, peeled
- ❖ 2–3 Tbsps. honey or pure maple syrup

Blend all ingredients in a blender and pour mixture into the prepared crust. Freeze until firm, and then garnish with fresh berries.

Cookies and Bars

Chocolate Chip Cookies

Makes: approx. 20 cookies / Prep time: 10 minutes / Bake time: 10 minutes

- ❖ 1¼ cups sprouted white wheat flour
- ❖ ¾ tsp. baking soda
- ❖ ⅛ tsp. sea salt
- ❖ ½ cup butter or coconut oil, softened
- ❖ ¾–1 cup dehydrated cane juice
- ❖ 1 tsp. pure vanilla extract
- ❖ 1 egg, beaten
- ❖ ¾ cup chopped organic chocolate bar, organic chocolate chips, carob chips, or ½ cup raisins and ½ cup chocolate chips

Preheat oven to 350°F. Whisk flour, soda, and salt in a large bowl. Mix butter and cane juice well. Add vanilla and egg to butter and cane juice and mix again. Gently blend the wet into the dry ingredients. Stir in chocolate chips. Scoop cookie dough by the tablespoonful onto an ungreased stainless steel cookie sheet. Bake at 350°F for 9 to 10 minutes. This recipe can be doubled.

❖ ❖ ❖

Mint Chocolate Chip Cookies

Make recipe for Chocolate Chip Cookies and add 1 to 2 drops (therapeutic grade) peppermint essential oil or ¼ tsp. organic peppermint extract to wet mixture before mixing it with the flour mixture. Bake according to the Chocolate Chip Cookie recipe.

❖ ❖ ❖

Double Chocolate Chip Cookies

Make recipe for Chocolate Chip Cookies and add 2 tablespoons organic cocoa or carob powder to the flour mixture and 1 to 2 tablespoons raw blue/amber agave or pure maple syrup to the wet mixture before mixing wet and dry together. Bake according to the Chocolate Chip Cookie recipe.

Quinoa Raisin Cookies

Makes: approx. 25–30 cookies / Prep time: 35 minutes / Cook time: 10 minutes

- ❖ 2 eggs
- ❖ 1 tsp. pure vanilla extract
- ❖ 1½ cup dehydrated cane juice
- ❖ ¾ cup butter or coconut oil, softened
- ❖ 1 tsp. baking powder
- ❖ ½ tsp. baking soda
- ❖ ½ tsp. ground cinnamon
- ❖ ⅛ tsp. ground cloves
- ❖ 1½ cups sprouted wheat flour
- ❖ 1 cup quinoa flakes
- ❖ 1 cup shredded coconut
- ❖ ¾ cup organic raisins or dried cranberries

In a medium bowl, beat eggs, vanilla, and cane juice together. Beat in the softened butter or coconut oil. In a large bowl, combine the baking powder, baking soda, cinnamon, cloves, flour, quinoa flakes, and coconut. Mix well. Add the wet ingredients to the dry and stir just until combined. Stir in raisins. Drop on a cookie sheet and bake at 375°F for 10 minutes.

Quinoa Coconut Cookies

Makes: approx. 40 cookies / Prep time: 10 minutes / Bake time: 9–10 minutes

- ❖ 2 eggs
- ❖ ¾ cup pure maple syrup or raw blue/amber agave
- ❖ ¾ cup coconut oil, softened
- ❖ 1 tsp. pure vanilla extract
- ❖ 1½ cups quinoa flakes
- ❖ 1 cup sprouted wheat flour
- ❖ 1½ cup unsweetened shredded coconut
- ❖ ¾ tsp. sea salt
- ❖ ½ tsp. baking soda

Whisk the eggs in a large bowl. Add the liquid sweetener, softened coconut oil, and vanilla. Blend well. In another bowl, mix the quinoa flakes, flour, coconut, sea salt, and baking soda together. Add the dry to the wet mixture and blend. Drop on a cookie sheet by the spoonful. Bake at 350°F for 9 to 10 minutes.

Pregnant Lady's Cookies

Makes: approx. 40 cookies / Prep time: 10 minutes / Bake time: 8–9 minutes

- ❖ ⅔ cup butter or coconut oil
- ❖ ¾ cup dehydrated cane juice
- ❖ 2 eggs
- ❖ ⅓ cup maple syrup
- ❖ 1 tsp. pure vanilla extract
- ❖ 1½ cups sprouted white wheat flour
- ❖ 1¼ cups quinoa flakes
- ❖ ⅛ tsp. sea salt
- ❖ 1 tsp. baking soda
- ❖ ½ cup raisins, dried cranberries, dried coconut, chocolate chips, or any combination of these

Preheat oven to 350°F. In a large bowl, cream the butter or coconut oil and cane juice together until fluffy. Add eggs and blend well. Add the maple syrup and vanilla and blend again. In a medium bowl, mix together the flour, quinoa flakes, salt, and baking soda. Stir the dry ingredients into the wet ones. Roll into one-inch balls and put about 9 on a cookie sheet. Bake for 8 to 9 minutes. These taste like yummy oatmeal cookies.

Honey Butter Cookies

Makes: approx. 20 cookies / Prep time: 20 minutes / Bake time: 12–15 minutes

- ❖ 1½ cups sprouted wheat flour
- ❖ ½ tsp. real salt
- ❖ 1 tsp. baking soda
- ❖ ½ cup coconut oil
- ❖ 1 cup honey
- ❖ 1 egg
- ❖ ½ cup sunflower seed butter

Mix the flour, salt, and soda in a medium-sized bowl. In another bowl, cream the oil, honey, egg, and sunflower seed butter. Combine both mixtures and mix until blended. Dough will be wet. Drop by spoonfuls on a cookie sheet. Bake at 325°F for 12 to 15 minutes.

Sun Butter Cookies

Makes: approx. 2 doz. cookies / Prep time: 20 minutes / Bake time: 10 minutes

- ❖ ¾ cup sunflower seed butter
- ❖ ½ cup coconut oil or butter
- ❖ ½ cup dehydrated cane juice
- ❖ ½ cup pure maple syrup or raw blue/amber agave
- ❖ 2 tsps. pure vanilla extract
- ❖ 1 egg
- ❖ 2¼ cups sprouted wheat flour
- ❖ ⅛ tsp. sea salt
- ❖ ¾ tsp. baking soda
- ❖ ¼ tsp. baking powder

Heat oven to 350°F. Combine sunflower seed butter, oil or butter, cane juice, syrup, and vanilla in a large mixing bowl. Beat at medium speed with a hand mixer until well blended. Add egg, and beat just until blended. In a separate bowl, combine flour, salt, baking soda, and baking powder. Add to the creamed mixture while mixing at low speed. Mix just until blended. Drop by heaping teaspoonfuls onto an ungreased cookie sheet. Use a fork to press a criss-cross pattern into the top of each cookie. Bake 7 to 8 minutes. Cool two minutes on cookie sheet before removing to wire rack to finish cooling.

❖ ❖ ❖

Coconut Balls

Makes: 8 balls / Prep time: 5 minutes

- ❖ 8 whole dates, pits removed
- ❖ ½ cup unsweetened, shredded coconut
- ❖ 8 raw, Traditional Almonds (see "Sprouting Nuts and Seeds" section)

Place dates and coconut in a food processor and blend until well combined. Form into small balls, and press a raw almond into the center of each.

❖ ❖ ❖

Sun Butter Macaroons

Makes: 2 dozen cookies / Prep time: 10 minutes / Refrigerate: 1 hour

- ❖ 1¼ cup unsweetened coconut flakes
- ❖ ¾ cup sprouted wheat flour
- ❖ ¼ tsp. sea salt
- ❖ ⅔ cup coconut oil, at room temperature
- ❖ ½ cup sunflower seed butter
- ❖ ½ cup pure maple syrup
- ❖ 2 tsps. pure vanilla extract

Mix together the coconut flakes, flour, and sea salt. In a separate bowl, blend the coconut oil, sunflower seed butter, syrup, and vanilla. Combine the dry with the wet ingredients using a fork. Scoop the dough onto a wax-paper-lined cookie sheet with a cookie scoop and place it in the refrigerator for 1 hour, or until set.

No-Bake Carob Nut Cookies

Makes: approx. 20–24 small cookies / Prep time: 20 minutes / Chill time: 25 minutes

- ❖ 4 Tbsps. coconut oil
- ❖ 4 Tbsps. pure maple syrup
- ❖ 2 Tbsps. carob powder
- ❖ 1 tsp. pure vanilla extract
- ❖ 1 cup chopped Traditional Almonds (see "Sprouting Nuts and Seeds" section)
- ❖ 1 cup shredded coconut, unsweetened
- ❖ ½ cup sunflower seed or almond butter
- ❖ ¼ cup sunflower seed flour
- ❖ 1 Tbsp. flax seed

Melt coconut oil in small pan over very low heat. Add maple syrup, carob powder, and vanilla, and stir well. In a large bowl, combine almonds, coconut, sunflower seed butter, sunflower seed flour, and flax seed. Pour carob mixture over nut mixture and stir well. Place spoonfuls of the mixture on a cookie sheet and refrigerate until cool.

No-Bake Cookies

Makes: 2 dozen / Prep time: 20 minutes / Refrigerate Time: 1 hour

- ❖ ¾ cup unsweetened coconut flakes
- ❖ ¾ cup plus 2 Tbsps. quinoa flakes
- ❖ ¾ cup sprouted soft white wheat flour
- ❖ ¼ tsp. sea salt
- ❖ ¼ cup coconut oil, softened
- ❖ ½ cup almond or sunflower seed butter
- ❖ 3 Tbsps. cocoa powder or carob powder
- ❖ ½ cup liquid sweetener
- ❖ 1½ tsps. pure vanilla extract

In a medium bowl, combine coconut flakes, quinoa flakes, flour, and salt, and mix well. In a separate bowl, blend coconut oil, almond or sunflower seed butter, liquid sweetener, cocoa powder, and vanilla. Combine the dry with the wet mixture with a fork. Using a cookie scoop, make 24 cookies. Place on wax paper lined cookie sheet and place in refrigerator for 1 hour.

❖ ❖ ❖

Almond Butter Cookies

Makes: 2 dozen cookies / Prep time: 20 minutes / Bake time: 10 minutes

- ❖ ½ cup butter or coconut oil
- ❖ ½ cup almond butter
- ❖ ¼ cup pure maple syrup or raw honey
- ❖ 1 egg
- ❖ 1 tsp. pure vanilla extract
- ❖ ½ tsp. baking soda
- ❖ ½ tsp. sea salt
- ❖ 1½ cups sprouted wheat flour
- ❖ ⅓ cup whole dates, pitted and finely chopped

In a large bowl, cream butter or coconut oil, almond butter, syrup or honey, egg, and vanilla extract. In a separate bowl, mix the baking soda, sea salt, and flour. Blend both mixtures together. Mix in dates. Place by spoonfuls on a cookie sheet and bake at 350°F for 10 minutes.

Macaroons

Makes: 2 dozen / Prep time: 10 minutes / Refrigerate: 1 hour

- ❖ 1¼ cup unsweetened coconut flakes
- ❖ ¾ cup Traditional Almonds (see "Sprouting Nuts and Seeds" section), ground into flour
- ❖ ¼ tsp. sea salt
- ❖ ⅔ cup coconut oil, at room temperature
- ❖ ½ cup liquid sweetener
- ❖ 2 tsps. pure vanilla extract

In a medium bowl, whisk together the coconut flakes, flour, and salt. In a separate bowl, blend coconut oil, liquid sweetener, and vanilla. Using a fork, combine the dry with the wet ingredients. Using a cookie scoop, make 24 macaroons. Place on wax-paper-lined cookie sheet and refrigerate for 1 hour.

Pumpkin Cookies

Makes: 3 dozen / Prep time: 20 minutes / Bake time: 10–12 minutes

- ❖ ½ cup coconut oil
- ❖ ¼ cup butter
- ❖ 1 cup liquid sweetener
- ❖ 2 eggs
- ❖ 1½ tsp. pure vanilla extract
- ❖ 1¼ cups pure pumpkin puree
- ❖ 2½ cups sprouted wheat flour
- ❖ 1 tsp. baking soda
- ❖ ½ tsp. sea salt
- ❖ ½ tsp. ground nutmeg
- ❖ 1 tsp. ground cinnamon
- ❖ 1 cup raisins, organic chocolate chips, or carob chips

In a large bowl, cream the coconut oil and butter together. Add maple syrup, eggs, vanilla, and pumpkin, and cream again. In a separate bowl, mix the dry ingredients together. Add the dry ingredients to the wet and stir in raisins or carob chips. Scoop dough with a cookie scoop and place on a cookie sheet. Bake at 350°F for 10 to 12 minutes.

Valentine Cookie Cutouts

Makes: 12–14 cookies / Prep time: 1 hour 20 min. / Bake time: 10 min.

- ❖ 3¼ cups sprouted soft white wheat flour
- ❖ 1 tsp. baking powder
- ❖ 1 tsp. cream of tarter
- ❖ ¼ tsp. sea salt
- ❖ 3 Tbsps. butter, softened
- ❖ 2 eggs
- ❖ ½ cup raw blue/amber agave
- ❖ 2 tsps. pure vanilla extract
- ❖ ½ tsp. almond extract

Whisk the first 4 ingredients together in a large bowl. Cut in the butter with a fork until evenly distributed throughout flour mixture. In a different bowl, whisk the eggs, and then add the vanilla, almond extract, and agave. Blend well. Hand stir the wet ingredient mixture into the dry. Dough will be somewhat sticky. Cover and refrigerate for 30 to 60 minutes. When chilled, roll out on a silicone mat to be about ⅓ of an inch thick. Cut out with a heart-shaped cookie cutter. Bake on a cookie sheet for 10 minutes at 350°F. Cool completely and frost with the Pink Party Frosting recipe (see recipe in "Frosting and Toppings").

Brownies

Makes: approx. 45 brownies / Prep time: 25 minutes / Bake time: 15 minutes

- ❖ 1 cup butter or coconut oil
- ❖ ½ cup cocoa powder or 6 oz unsweetened chocolate
- ❖ 4 eggs
- ❖ 2 cups dehydrated cane juice
- ❖ 1½ tsp. pure vanilla extract
- ❖ 1½ cups sprouted white wheat flour
- ❖ ⅛ tsp. sea salt
- ❖ ½ tsp. baking soda

Melt the butter in a small saucepan and whisk in the cocoa powder. Remove from heat and let cool in pan. *(continued)*

In a medium bowl, beat the eggs and stir in the cane juice and vanilla. Let the mixture sit while the cane juice dissolves. Grease a 10x15-inch glass dish. In a large bowl, whisk the flour, salt, and baking soda. By this time the butter and chocolate mixture should be cool enough to mix in with the egg mixture. Then add the wet chocolate mixture into the flour bowl and stir gently to blend. With a silicone spatula, spread the brownie mix evenly into the greased dish. Bake at 350°F for 15 minutes. Cool on a wire rack. Frost with Chocolate Buttercream Frosting (see recipe in "Frosting and Toppings") and cut into squares.

❖   ❖   ❖

Carob-Banana Brownies

Makes: 12 brownies / Prep time: 15 minutes / Cook time: 25 minutes

- ❖   1 cup raw, sprouted, then dehydrated sunflower seeds
- ❖   ¼ tsp. sea salt
- ❖   ½ tsp. baking soda
- ❖   1½ Tbsps. butter
- ❖   1½ Tbsps. coconut oil
- ❖   2 Tbsps. roasted carob powder
- ❖   2 Tbsps. raw honey or pure maple syrup (optional)
- ❖   1 ripe banana, mashed
- ❖   1 tsp. pure vanilla extract
- ❖   1 egg

In a food processor, grind sunflower seeds until they form flour. Stir in salt and baking soda, and set aside. Melt butter and coconut oil in a small saucepan until soft. Add carob and honey or maple syrup, and stir well. Mash banana in a bowl. Add vanilla and egg, then add carob mixture and stir well. Last, stir in sunflower flour and mix well. Pour into a buttered 8-inch cake pan and spread evenly. Bake at 350°F for 25 minutes, or until a toothpick comes out clean. Cool and top with Carob Frosting (see recipe in "Frosting and Toppings"). For a lighter flavor, use 1 recipe coconut cream in place of the frosting.

Note: Recipe can be doubled and baked in a 9x13 pan at the same time and temperature.

❖   ❖   ❖

Sun Butter Bars

Makes: 30 bars / Prep time: 15 minutes / Bake time: 10 minutes

Bars:
- ❖ ¾ cup butter or coconut oil
- ❖ 1 cup dehydrated cane juice
- ❖ ½ cup honey
- ❖ 2 eggs
- ❖ ¾–1 cup sunflower seed butter
- ❖ ½ tsp. baking soda
- ❖ ½ tsp. sea salt
- ❖ 1 tsp. pure vanilla extract
- ❖ 3 cups sprouted wheat flour

Mix wet and dry ingredients together in separate bowls, and then them mix together. Press dough into the bottom of a greased 16x12-inch cookie sheet. Bake at 325°F for 10 minutes. Do not over bake. Cool completely. If desired, top with extra sunflower seed butter (see below) and Carob Frosting (see recipe in "Frosting and Toppings"). When complete, cut into bars and serve.

Sun Butter Layer (Optional):

When the bottom cookie layer is baked and cooled, spread a thin layer of sunflower seed butter on top.

Mars Bars

Makes: 1 (9x13) dish / Prep time: 30 minutes / Cook time: 20 minutes

Crust and Crumble Topping:
- ❖ 2 cups dehydrated cane juice or granulated maple sugar
- ❖ 1 cup butter, softened
- ❖ 2 eggs
- ❖ 1 tsp. pure vanilla extract
- ❖ 2¼ cups sprouted white wheat flour
- ❖ 1 tsp. baking soda
- ❖ 1½ cups quinoa flakes or oats
- ❖ 1½ cups shredded coconut *(continued)*

Chocolate Topping:
- ❖ 10 oz. organic chocolate pieces
- ❖ 3 Tbsps. butter
- ❖ ⅓ cup raw milk or evaporated goat milk
- ❖ ¼ cup dehydrated cane juice or granulated maple sugar
- ❖ 1 tsp. pure vanilla extract

To make the crust and crumble topping, grease a 9x13 baking dish with butter. In a medium-sized mixing bowl, beat the cane juice, butter, eggs, and vanilla. In a large bowl, whisk the flour, soda, quinoa or oats, and coconut together. Add the dry ingredients to the wet ingredients and stir to blend. Press ⅔ of the crust mixture into the bottom of the dish.

Combine the ingredients for the Chocolate Topping in a medium saucepan and melt over medium-low heat, stirring well. Pour the mix on top of the crust. Then crumble the remaining crust mix on top. Bake at 350°F for about 20 minutes.

Pies

Blueberry Cream Cheese Pie

Makes: 1 (9-inch) pie / Prep time: 45 minutes / Bake time: 15–18 minutes / Chill time: 2 hours

Single Crust:
- ❖ 1 cup sprouted soft white wheat flour
- ❖ ¼ tsp. sea salt
- ❖ ⅓ cup coconut oil
- ❖ 4 Tbsps. ice-cold water
- ❖ 1½ tsps. raw apple cider vinegar

In a medium bowl, blend sprouted wheat flour and salt together well. Cut in the cold coconut oil with a pastry blender. Add cold water and vinegar and cut it in until blended. Roll dough onto a silicone mat to 11 inches round. Transfer to a pie dish and pinch edges to decorate. Prick the bottom and sides of the crust with a fork to make venting holes. Bake at 350°F for 15 to 18 minutes. Cool completely.

Cream Filling:

- ❖ 16 oz. cream cheese, softened
- ❖ 3 Tbsps. plain whole yogurt
- ❖ 1½ Tbsps. fresh lemon juice
- ❖ ½ cup raw blue/amber agave
- ❖ 1 tsp. pure vanilla extract

Beat cream cheese until smooth. Add yogurt and beat again. Add the lemon juice, agave, and vanilla and beat until smooth. Pour into cooled pie crust and chill for at least 2 hours.

Topping:

- ❖ 10 oz. frozen blueberries, thawed, or fresh blueberries
- ❖ ⅓ cup berry juice from thawed berries or water
- ❖ 2 Tbsps. tapioca granules
- ❖ ⅓ cup raw blue/amber agave

Drain the blueberries, reserving the juice. Set berries aside. In a small saucepan, mix the water or berry juice, tapioca, and agave together. Bring the mixture to a boil over medium heat. Stir constantly until thick. Remove from heat and cool completely before gently mixing in berries. Once cooled, spread evenly over the cream filling and refrigerate for at least an hour before serving. Keep refrigerated.

Mint Chocolate Pie

Makes: 8 servings / Prep time: 25 minutes / Chill time: 3–4 hours

- ❖ 1 (14-oz.) can organic coconut cream
- ❖ 6 Tbsps. melted butter or coconut oil
- ❖ 6 Tbsps. cocoa powder or roasted carob powder
- ❖ 3 drops peppermint extract or 1 drop peppermint essential oil (therapeutic grade)
- ❖ 6 Tbsps. pure maple syrup
- ❖ 1 recipe Coconut Crust, Chocolate Mint Crust, or pre-baked Perfect Single Crust *(continued)*

In a medium-sized bowl, scoop coconut cream from can and stir. In another bowl, pour in melted coconut oil and stir in carob, peppermint oil, and maple syrup. Pour carob mixture into coconut cream, leaving about ¼ cup of the carob mixture remaining in the bowl. Mix well. Pour into a pre-made Coconut, Chocolate Mint, or Perfect Single Crust pie shell (see recipes later in this section) and chill for 3 to 4 hours, or until set. Garnish with remaining carob mixture by drizzling it over the top.

❖   ❖   ❖

Tropical Fruit Pie

Makes: 1 (8-inch) pie / Prep time: 20 minutes / Chill time: 2 hours

Crust:
- ❖ ¾ cup raisins
- ❖ ⅓ cup Traditional Almonds (see "Sprouting Nuts and Seeds" section)
- ❖ ⅓ cup dried, unsweetened coconut

Blend all ingredients in a food processor until a ball forms. If the mixture is too dry, add more raisins or nuts to get a ball consistency. Press into a pie tin, and crimp the edges.

Filling:
- ❖ the cream from 1 can of coconut milk (Use only the cream that has risen to the top of a brand such as Thai Kitchen.)
- ❖ 1½ Tbsp. pure maple syrup
- ❖ 1 tsp. pure vanilla extract

- ❖ ½ a fresh pineapple, cut into bite-sized pieces
- ❖ 2 ripe mangos, diced
- ❖ 1 banana, peeled and sliced
- ❖ ¼ cup dried, unsweetened coconut flakes
- ❖ ¼ cup pecans, chopped

Mix coconut cream, maple syrup, and vanilla together. Fold the fruit and coconut flakes into the mixture and spoon it into the pie crust. Sprinkle pecans on top. Chill for 2 hours before serving.

❖   ❖   ❖

Yam-Butternut Squash Pie

Makes: 1 (8-inch) pie / Prep time: 35 minutes / Cook time: 20 minutes

Filling:

- ❖ 1 cup cooked and mashed yams
- ❖ 1 cup cooked and mashed butternut squash
- ❖ ½ cup pure maple syrup
- ❖ 1 tsp. ground cinnamon
- ❖ ½ tsp. ground ginger
- ❖ ¼ tsp. ground cloves
- ❖ dash of sea salt
- ❖ 1 Tbsp. butter
- ❖ 2 eggs, well beaten

Mix yams, squash, syrup, spices, and salt in a saucepan. When hot, gradually add beaten eggs while stirring. Continue stirring until thickened. Remove from heat and pour into a pie tin. Sprinkle with precooked Crumble Crust (see recipe below) and chopped Traditional Almonds (see "Sprouting Nuts and Seeds" section). Serve chilled or warm.

Crumble Crust:
Makes: 1 cup / Prep time: 5 minutes / Bake time: 10–12 minutes

- ❖ ½ cup flour made from sprouted and dehydrated grain
- ❖ ½ cup chopped dates
- ❖ 3 Tbsps. butter or coconut oil
- ❖ ground cinnamon (optional)

Blend flour, dates, and oil until crumbly. Add optional cinnamon and mix well. To pre-cook, spread mixture onto a cookie sheet and bake at 350°F for 10 to 12 minutes or until golden brown. Sprinkle over the top of pie.

❖ ❖ ❖

Lavender Berry Cream Pie

Makes: 1 (9-inch) pie / Prep time: 30 minutes / Chill time: about 2 or more hours

Coconut Almond Pie Crust:
- ❖ ¾ cup Traditional Almonds (see "Sprouting Nuts and Seeds" section)
- ❖ ¾ cup dried coconut flakes, unsweetened
- ❖ 1 cup whole dates, pitted or ¼ cup pure maple syrup or honey
- ❖ 1 Tbsp. coconut oil or butter, melted
- ❖ a tiny pinch of sea salt

Process all ingredients in a food processor until all pieces are very tiny and crumbly, or about 2 to 3 minutes. It is important not to over process the almonds or they will turn into almond butter! Press the *crumbly* mixture evenly on the bottom and sides of a 9-inch pie dish. Chill for 15 minutes, or put in the freezer for a few minutes to chill faster.

Lavender Cream Filling:
- ❖ 8 oz. cream cheese, softened
- ❖ ¼ cup plain whole yogurt
- ❖ ¼ cup pure maple syrup or raw blue/amber agave
- ❖ 1 Tbsp. berry juice from thawed berries, or 2 tsps. fresh lemon juice (optional)
- ❖ ½ tsp. pure vanilla extract
- ❖ 2 toothpick ends dipped in lavender essential oil (*less* than a drop)

Beat the softened cream cheese until smooth. Then add the yogurt and blend together until creamy. Drizzle in agave and add berry or lemon juice and vanilla. Roll toothpick ends in lavender essential oil. Then stir the oil into the cream mixture with the toothpick. Blend well. Pour into chilled pie crust. Chill or freeze for 30 minutes to an hour before applying the topping.

Berry Topping:
- ❖ 2 cups (16 oz.) frozen berries (blackberries, blueberries, raspberries, strawberries, dark sweet cherries, or a combination)
- ❖ berry juice (from the thawed berries, approx. ⅓ cup)
- ❖ 2 Tbsps. small pearl tapioca (minute tapioca pearls)
- ❖ 2–3 Tbsps. raw blue/amber agave or pure maple syrup

To thaw frozen berries, keep them in the bag they came in (or put them in a waterproof zip-top bag) and place them in a bowl of hot water. After 20 to 30 minutes, the berries should be thawed but still cold, and there should be a fair amount of berry juice in the bag (about ⅓ cup). Pour the berry juice into a small saucepan, then stir in the small tapioca pearls and soak for at least 5 minutes. Bring to a boil over medium heat, stirring constantly, until the mixture is thick and the pearls have turned clear, about 2 to 3 minutes. Remove from heat and stir in agave or maple syrup. Stir in berries, and then spread the topping over the top of the chilled cream filling. Chill for 1 to 2 hours more before serving. Keep refrigerated or freeze.

Carob or Chocolate Mousse Cheesecake

Makes: 1 (9-inch) pie / Prep time: 45 minutes / Bake: 15 minutes

Crust:

- ❖ ⅓ cup melted butter or coconut oil
- ❖ ⅓ cup carob powder or cocoa powder
- ❖ ⅓ cup dehydrated cane juice
- ❖ ⅔ cup sprouted wheat flour

Melt butter or oil in a large saucepan. Remove from heat and stir in carob or cocoa powder and cane juice. Stir in flour and mix well until mixture becomes dark and crumbly. Press into a 9-inch pie pan and bake for 13 to 15 minutes at 350°F. When done, remove from heat and cool completely. In the meantime, prepare the whipped cream topping.

Topping:

- ❖ 2 cups whipping cream
- ❖ ¼ cup liquid sweetener
- ❖ ½ tsp. pure vanilla extract
- ❖ shavings from an organic dark chocolate bar

Whip the cream until thick. Stir in sweetener and vanilla. Remove 1½ cups for the filling and set it aside. Save the rest for the top. Complete filling instructions below. With the ½ cup of cream, spread a layer of whipped cream along the top of the cheesecake. Fill a cake-decorating bag with the remaining whipped cream and make designs around the outside edges of the cheesecake. Sprinkle the chocolate shavings on top. Keep refrigerated. *(continued)*

Filling:
- ❖ 12 oz. cream cheese
- ❖ ⅔ cup dehydrated cane juice
- ❖ ⅔ cup carob or cocoa powder
- ❖ 1 tsp. pure vanilla extract
- ❖ 1½ cups fluffy, already whipped cream

Blend cream cheese in mixer until smooth, and then add the cane juice. Mix well. Add carob or cocoa powder a little at a time and blend well. Mix in vanilla and then fold in the whipped cream. Blend well and spread evenly into the cooled pie crust.

Note: The unique combination of roasted carob powder mixed with dehydrated cane juice creates a slight mocha flavor.

❖   ❖   ❖

Pumpkin Pie

Makes: 1 (8-inch) pie / Prep time: 15 minutes / Bake time: 50 minutes

- ❖ 1 prepared Perfect Single Crust recipe (see recipe later in this section)
- ❖ 1 Tbsp. coconut flour
- ❖ 2 pastured farm eggs, beaten
- ❖ ¾ cup dehydrated cane juice or granulated maple sugar
- ❖ ¼ tsp. ground nutmeg
- ❖ a tiny pinch of ground cloves
- ❖ ¼ tsp. ground ginger
- ❖ ¾ tsp. ground cinnamon
- ❖ 2 tsps. pure vanilla extract
- ❖ 15 oz. pumpkin puree or 1¾ cup banana squash, cooked and mashed
- ❖ ¾ cup evaporated goat milk
- ❖ 1 Tbsp. organic cornstarch

Sprinkle the prepared crust with coconut flour. Place crust in the refrigerator to chill. In a large bowl, combine all of the remaining ingredients and mix thoroughly. Pour the pumpkin mixture into the crust. Bake at 350°F for 20 minutes. Cover the crust edges with aluminum foil and bake for an additional 30 minutes, until a toothpick inserted in the middle comes out clean. Chill the pie before serving. Serve with whipped cream.

Apple Pie

Makes: 1 (8-inch) pie / Prep: 25 minutes / Cook time: 1 hour

Filling:

- ❖ 3 cups granny smith apples, cored, sliced, and (if desired) peeled (about 7 whole apples)
- ❖ ¾ cup dehydrated cane juice or granulated maple sugar
- ❖ ⅛ tsp. sea salt
- ❖ 1 tsp. ground cinnamon
- ❖ 1½ Tbsps. arrowroot powder or organic cornstarch
- ❖ 1 prepared Perfect Double Crust recipe (see recipe later in this section)
- ❖ 1 Tbsp. coconut flour
- ❖ ⅛ tsp. ground nutmeg
- ❖ 2–3 Tbps. butter

In a big saucepan, cover and cook apples over medium heat, stirring occasionally.

Meanwhile, whisk the cane juice, salt, cinnamon, and arrowroot powder together. Add the mixture to the juice that is at the bottom of the cooking apples. Toss into apples as well. Cook until tender and softened but not too soft! They will cook more in the oven.

Sprinkle the bottom crust (which should already be in a pie plate) with the coconut flour and nutmeg. Pour the apple filling on top. Dab the apples with butter. Place the second crust on top and seal by pinching the edges. Sprinkle a little cinnamon and dehydrated cane juice on top and cut a few vents on top. Bake at 400°F for 20 minutes. Turn oven down to 350°F and bake for an additional 30 to 40 minutes. Serve warm with homemade vanilla ice cream.

❖   ❖   ❖

Summer Berry Pie

Makes: 1 (8-inch) pie / Prep time: 30 minutes / Cook time: 5 minutes

Filling:

- ❖ 12 oz. fresh or frozen and partially thawed berries
- ❖ 12 oz. fresh or frozen and partially thawed dark sweet cherries
- ❖ 3 Tbsps. small pearl tapioca or granulated tapioca
- ❖ 2 Tbsps. liquid sweetener

Coconut Crust with Dates:

- ❖ ¾ cup Traditional Almonds (see "Sprouting Nuts and Seeds" section)
- ❖ ¾ cup dried coconut, unsweetened
- ❖ 1 cup whole dates, pitted and chopped
- ❖ 1 Tbsp. coconut oil, melted

Drain thawed berries, reserving juice. Pour about ½ cup of the berry juice over tapioca balls in a medium saucepan and let them sit for a half hour. Meanwhile, blend almonds, coconut, dates, and coconut oil in a food processor, until the mixture is well blended and sticks when pressed together. Press the mixture into an 8-inch pie tin and crimp the edges. To make the filling, bring the soaked tapioca and berry juice to a boil and stir until thick and clear. Remove from heat and stir in berries and honey or maple syrup. Mix well the filling well and pour it into the pie crust. Chill for an hour before serving.

❖   ❖   ❖

Chocolate Mint Crust

Makes: 1 (8-inch) pie crust / Prep time: 15 minutes

- ❖ 1½ cups sprouted soft white wheat flour or ¾ cup almond flour and ¾ cup sunflower seed flour
- ❖ 3 Tbsps. cocoa powder or roasted carob powder
- ❖ 2 Tbsps. liquid sweetener
- ❖ 1 Tbsps. coconut oil, melted
- ❖ 1 drop peppermint essential oil (therapeutic grade) or 3 drops peppermint extract

Combine dry ingredients in a food processor and mix until well blended. While mixer is still running, pour in liquid sweetener, melted coconut oil, and peppermint extract. Mix until well combined, and then press the mixture into an 8-inch pie plate.

❖   ❖   ❖

Coconut Crust

Makes: 1 (8-inch) pie crust / Prep time: 10 minutes

- ❖ 1½ cups dried, unsweetened coconut
- ❖ ½ cup Traditional Almonds (see "Sprouting Nuts and Seeds" section)
- ❖ 2 Tbsps. pure maple syrup
- ❖ 2 Tbsps. coconut oil, melted
- ❖ 1 tsp. pure vanilla extract

Blend coconut and almonds in a food processor until they have become fine crumbs. While the processor is running, slowly add the maple syrup, melted coconut oil, and vanilla. Press into an 8-inch pie plate.

❖   ❖   ❖

Perfect Double Crust

Makes: 1 (8-inch) double crust / Prep time: 10 minutes

- ❖ 2¼ cups sprouted soft white wheat flour
- ❖ ¾ tsp. sea salt
- ❖ ⅔ cup coconut oil
- ❖ 9 Tbsps. ice cold water
- ❖ 1 Tbsp. raw apple cider vinegar

Blend sprouted wheat flour and salt together well. Cut in cold coconut oil with pastry blender until the mixture forms pea-sized crumbs. Mix together the cold water and vinegar and cut it into the dough until blended. Divide the dough into two balls. Roll each out separately on a silicone mat. Transfer one to a pie dish. Fill with your filling of choice and top with the second crust. Pinch edges together and cut vents in the top. Bake according to directions for the filling recipe.

❖   ❖   ❖

Perfect Single Crust

Makes: 1 (8-inch) single pie crust / Prep time: 10 minutes

- ❖ 1 cup plus 2 Tbsps. sprouted soft white wheat flour
- ❖ ¼ tsp. sea salt
- ❖ ¼–⅓ cup cold coconut oil
- ❖ 5 Tbsps. cold filtered water
- ❖ 1 Tbsp. raw apple cider vinegar

Blend sprouted wheat flour and salt together well. Cut in cold coconut oil with pastry blender until the mixture forms pea-sized crumbs. Combine water and vinegar and add to crumbs. Blend with a fork. Roll the dough out on a silicone mat. Transfer it to a pie dish. Some recipes may require that you chill the dough at this point. When finished, fill the crust with your filling of choice and pinch the edges to decorate. Bake according to directions for the filling recipe.

Cakes

Pumpkin Cake

Makes: 1 (10x15-inch) pan / Prep time: 30 minutes / Bake time: 25–30 minutes

Cake:

- ❖ 2 cups sprouted soft white wheat flour
- ❖ ¾ cup dehydrated cane juice or granulated maple sugar
- ❖ 1½ tsps. baking powder
- ❖ 2 tsps. ground cinnamon
- ❖ 1 tsp. baking soda
- ❖ ¼ tsp. sea salt
- ❖ ¼ tsp. ground cloves
- ❖ 4 eggs
- ❖ ¼ cup water
- ❖ 15 oz. pumpkin puree
- ❖ ¾ cup butter or coconut oil
- ❖ ¼ cup pure maple syrup or honey
- ❖ ½ cup raisins, chopped (optional)

Topping:

- ❖ 12 oz. cream cheese
- ❖ ¾ cup butter
- ❖ 3 tsps. pure vanilla extract
- ❖ ⅔ cup pure maple syrup
- ❖ ⅓ cup Traditional Almonds (see "Sprouting Nuts and Seeds" section), chopped (optional)

To make the cake, mix the wet ingredients in a large bowl. In a separate bowl, mix the dry ingredients. Combine both mixtures and mix well. Pour the batter into an ungreased 15x10-inch glass baking dish and bake for 25 to 30 minutes at 350°F. Cool completely. In the meantime, blend all of the topping ingredients, except the almonds, with a hand mixer. When the cake is cool, frost it and sprinkle the almonds on top. Refrigerate.

Real Chocolate Cake

Makes: 1 (9x13) pan / Prep time: 20 minutes / Bake time: about 20 minutes

- ❖ ¾ cup butter or coconut oil, softened
- ❖ 1 cup liquid sweetener
- ❖ 3 eggs
- ❖ ½ cup water
- ❖ 2 tsps. pure vanilla extract
- ❖ 2 cups sprouted soft white wheat flour
- ❖ ½ cup plus 2 Tbsps. cocoa powder
- ❖ 1 tsp. baking soda
- ❖ ¾ tsps. baking powder

In a medium bowl, cream the butter and liquid sweetener, and then add the eggs, water, and vanilla. In a large bowl, whisk the flour, cocoa, baking soda, and baking powder together. Gently stir the dry into the wet, folding it only a few times. Grease and flour a 9x13 pan and bake at 350°F for 20 minutes. Frost after cake is completely cooled.

German Chocolate Cake

Makes: 1 (9x13) pan / Prep time: 30 minutes / Bake time: 30 minutes

Cake:

- ❖ 3 eggs
- ❖ 1 tsp. pure vanilla extract
- ❖ ½ cup buttermilk or water
- ❖ ½ cup coconut oil or butter
- ❖ ½ cup carob powder or cocoa powder
- ❖ 1½ cups sprouted wheat flour
- ❖ ¾ tsp. baking soda
- ❖ ¼ tsp. sea salt
- ❖ 1 cup dehydrated cane juice

In a large bowl, combine the eggs, vanilla, and buttermilk or water. Melt butter or coconut oil in a small saucepan and stir in carob or cocoa powder. Add the carob mixture to the wet ingredients and mix. In a separate bowl, blend the dry ingredients together. Stir the dry ingredients into the wet. Pour the batter into a buttered 9x13 pan and bake for 30 minutes at 350°F, or until baked all the way through. Allow to cool before frosting.

Frosting:

- ❖ 2 eggs
- ❖ 1 cup coconut milk
- ❖ ¾ cup dehydrated cane juice
- ❖ ¼ cup butter or coconut oil (if using coconut oil, add a dash of sea salt)
- ❖ 1½ cups unsweetened coconut flakes
- ❖ ¾ cup chopped Traditional Almonds (see "Sprouting Nuts and Seeds" section) or cashews

In a medium saucepan, mix together the eggs, coconut milk, dehydrated cane juice, and butter or coconut oil. Stir over medium heat until thick and bubbly. Remove from heat and add coconut flakes and nuts. Spread over cooled cake.

❖ ❖ ❖

Chocolate Birthday Cake

Makes: 1 (9x13) pan / Prep time: 25 minutes / Bake time: 35 minutes

- ❖ 1¾ cups sprouted soft white wheat flour
- ❖ 2 tsps. baking soda
- ❖ ½ cup cocoa powder
- ❖ ¼ tsp. sea salt
- ❖ 3 eggs
- ❖ 2¼ cups dehydrated cane juice
- ❖ ½ cup butter, softened
- ❖ 2 tsps. pure vanilla extract
- ❖ ½ cup plain whole yogurt
- ❖ ¾ cup water

Mix the flour, baking soda, cocoa powder, and salt together in a large bowl. In a medium bowl, whisk the eggs and add the cane juice. Blend well, and then whisk in the soft butter. Add vanilla, yogurt, and water. Blend well. Pour the wet mixture into the large bowl with the flour mixture. Stir well to blend together. Grease a 9x13 pan with coconut oil. Pour the cake batter into the pan. Bake at 350°F for 35 minutes. The sides may bake higher than the center. After the cake has completely cooled, use a butter knife to cut the tops of the sides to be the height of the center, if desired.

Rich Chocolate Cake

Makes: 1 (9x13) dish / Prep time: 20 minutes / Bake time: 30 minutes

Cake:

- ❖ 2 eggs
- ❖ 1 cup liquid sweetener
- ❖ 1 tsp. pure vanilla extract
- ❖ 1 cup dehydrated cane juice or granulated maple sugar
- ❖ 1¾ cup sprouted soft white wheat flour
- ❖ ¾ cup organic cocoa powder or carob powder
- ❖ ½ tsp. sea salt
- ❖ 1½ tsps. baking soda
- ❖ 1½ tsps. baking powder
- ❖ ½ cup butter or coconut oil, slightly melted
- ❖ 1 cup boiling water *(continued)*

Beat eggs lightly and add the liquid sweetener, vanilla, and cane juice. Let the mixture sit for 5 minutes to dissolve cane juice thoroughly. In a separate bowl, whisk the flour, cocoa powder, salt, baking soda, and baking powder. Mix the butter or oil into the cane juice and egg mixture. Add the flour mixture and the boiling water. Gently stir the batter a few times until barely blended. Pour batter into a 9x13 glass dish and bake at 350°F for 30 minutes. Cool cake completely before frosting.

Frosting:
- ❖ 1 cup heavy whipping cream
- ❖ 8 oz. organic chocolate chips or 4 chocolate bars
- ❖ 1 tsp. pure vanilla extract

Combine all ingredients. Melt in a double broiler. Once melted, remove the mixture from heat. Let sit for a couple minutes, then spread it evenly over cake.

❖   ❖   ❖

Carrot Cake

Makes: 1 (9x13) pan / Prep time: 25 minutes / Bake time: 35–40 minutes

- ❖ ⅓ cup butter, softened
- ❖ 2 tsps. pure vanilla extract
- ❖ ¼ cup whole plain or vanilla yogurt
- ❖ ¼ cup unsweetened applesauce
- ❖ 2 pastured eggs, beaten
- ❖ ½ cup, unsweetened coconut flakes or chopped raisins
- ❖ 2 cups liquid sweetener
- ❖ 2 cups carrots, grated
- ❖ 2 cups sprouted soft white wheat flour
- ❖ ¼ tsp. sea salt
- ❖ 1½ tsps. ground cinnamon
- ❖ 1 tsp. baking soda
- ❖ 2 tsps. baking powder

Combine all wet ingredients and grated carrot in a large bowl. Mix well. In a separate bowl, combine all of the dry ingredients and mix well. Combine both mixtures and blend. Spread batter into the bottom of a buttered 9x13 pan and bake for 35 to 40 minutes at 350°F, or until a toothpick inserted into the center comes out clean. Cool completely, and then frost with Cream Cheese Frosting (see recipe in "Frosting and Toppings").

Gingerbread Cake

Makes: 1 (9x13) dish / Prep time: 25 minutes / Bake time: 35–40 minutes

- ❖ 2 cups sprouted wheat flour
- ❖ 1½ tsps. ground cinnamon
- ❖ 1 Tbsp. ground ginger
- ❖ ½ tsp. ground nutmeg
- ❖ ½ tsp. sea salt
- ❖ 1 tsp. baking powder
- ❖ 2 Tbsps. coconut oil or butter, softened
- ❖ 6 oz. cream cheese, softened
- ❖ ¼ cup plain whole yogurt
- ❖ 1 cup pure liquid sweetener
- ❖ ½ cup molasses
- ❖ 2 eggs

In a medium bowl, whisk the flour, spices, salt, and baking powder together. In a large bowl, cream butter or coconut oil, cream cheese, and yogurt until smooth. Add the liquid sweetener, molasses, and eggs, and beat until smooth. Add the dry mixture to the wet and stir with a spoon to blend. Pour batter into a greased 9x13 baking dish. Bake at 350°F for 35 to 40 minutes, or until a toothpick inserted in the middle comes out clean. Cool on a wire rack. Serve cooled with whipped cream on top.

❖ ❖ ❖

No-Flour Carrot Cake

Makes: one 9x13 pan / Prep time: 20 minutes / Bake time: 35–40 minutes

- ❖ 2 cups freshly sprouted soft white wheat, processed to form a ball
- ❖ ¾ cup dehydrated cane juice or granulated maple sugar
- ❖ 1 tsp. baking soda
- ❖ ½ tsp. sea salt
- ❖ 1 tsp. ground cinnamon
- ❖ 3 cups carrots, shredded
- ❖ 3 Tbsps. butter or coconut oil, melted
- ❖ 4 eggs
- ❖ ½ cup Traditional Almonds (see "Sprouting Nuts and Seeds" section) or pecans, chopped *(continued)*

Mix all of the ingredients together in a food processor or mixer, and pour them into a buttered 9x13 pan. Bake at 350°F for 35 to 40 minutes. Top with Cream Cheese Frosting (see recipe in "Frosting and Toppings").

❖ ❖ ❖

Oatmeal Soda Cake

Makes: 1 (9x13) pan / Prep time: 25 minutes / Bake time: 30–40 minutes

- ❖ 1 cup rolled oats
- ❖ ½ cup butter
- ❖ 1½ cups boiling water
- ❖ 1¾ cups sprouted soft white wheat flour
- ❖ ¾ tsp. sea salt
- ❖ 2 tsps. baking soda
- ❖ ½ tsp. baking powder
- ❖ 1 tsp. ground cinnamon
- ❖ ¼ tsp. ground nutmeg
- ❖ 2 eggs
- ❖ 1¼ cups dehydrated cane juice
- ❖ 2 tsps. pure vanilla extract

Combine the oats, butter, and water in a large bowl and let stand for 25 minutes. Meanwhile, in another bowl, whisk the flour, salt, baking soda, baking powder, and spices together. In a third bowl, beat the eggs until light and foamy. Add the cane juice to the eggs, beating well. Then add the vanilla. Pour the egg mixture into the oat mixture and stir. Add the dry ingredients and mix well. Pour the batter into a greased and floured 9x13 pan and bake at 350°F for 30 to 40 minutes. Cool cake completely and frost with honey butter (see recipe in "Spreads, Sauces, Dips, and Marinades").

❖ ❖ ❖

Cheesecake

Makes: 1 (9-inch) cake / Prep time: 30 minutes / Bake time: 45–50 minutes

Crust:
- ❖ 1½ cups sprouted wheat flour
- ❖ ½ cup Traditional Almonds (see "Sprouting Nuts and Seeds" section), ground in blender or food processor
- ❖ 1 tsp. ground cinnamon (optional)
- ❖ 2 Tbsps. butter, melted
- ❖ ¼ cup coconut oil, melted
- ❖ 2½ Tbsps. liquid sweetener

Mix flour, almonds, and cinnamon together. Add the melted butter, coconut oil, and liquid sweetener. Stir well and spread onto the bottom and sides of a cheesecake pan.

Filling:
- ❖ 24 oz. cream cheese
- ❖ 3 eggs
- ❖ ½ cup liquid sweetener
- ❖ 1 tsp. pure vanilla extract

Blend cream cheese until smooth and add one egg at a time. Blend well while scraping the sides of the bowl. Add the liquid sweetener and vanilla and blend until well mixed. Pour into crust. Bake in a preheated oven set at 350°F for 45 to 50 minutes, or until golden and firm set. Cool on wire rack. After 20 minutes, remove the side of the cheesecake pan.

Optional Topping:
- ❖ 100 percent fruit jam
- ❖ 1 Tbsp. liquid sweetener
- ❖ ½–1 cup fresh or frozen and thawed strawberries (sliced), blueberries, cherries or raspberries

Stir jam and liquid sweetener together. Spoon the jam mixture onto the thoroughly cooled cheesecake and top with fresh berries. Chill at least 4 hours before serving.

Note: You can also top this basic cheesecake recipe with caramel and pecans for another variation.

Other Sweets

Creamy Tapioca Pudding

Makes: 4–6 servings / Prep time: 30–35 minutes

- ❖ 6 egg yolks
- ❖ 1 cup liquid sweetener
- ❖ ⅓ cup dehydrated cane juice
- ❖ 10 cups whole raw milk
- ❖ ¾ cup organic tapioca granules
- ❖ 1½ Tbsps. pure vanilla extract

In a medium saucepan, whisk the egg yolks well. Add the liquid sweetener and cane juice and blend well. Add the milk, and then stir in the tapioca granules. Let soak for 10 minutes before heating. After 10 minutes, warm over medium heat, stirring constantly, until the mixture comes to a boil. Remove the mixture from the heat and stir in the vanilla. Pudding will thicken as it cools. For quicker cooling, pour hot pudding mixture into individual bowls and set them in the fridge or freezer for a few minutes. Enjoy warm or chilled. Refrigerate any leftovers.

Carrot Pudding

Makes: 12 servings / Prep time: 25 minutes / Cook time: 2 hours

- ❖ ½ cup butter
- ❖ ½ cup coconut oil
- ❖ ¾ cup dehydrated cane juice
- ❖ 2 eggs
- ❖ 1 tsp pure vanilla extract
- ❖ ¼ tsp finely grated orange peel
- ❖ ¼ cup pure maple syrup
- ❖ 2 cups grated carrot
- ❖ 2½ cups sprouted wheat flour
- ❖ 2 tsps. baking soda
- ❖ ½ tsp. sea salt
- ❖ 1 tsp. ground cinnamon
- ❖ ½ tsp. ground nutmeg

- ❖ 2 cups raisins (or 1 cup raisins and 1 cup chopped dates)
- ❖ 1 cup chopped Traditional Almonds (see "Sprouting Nuts and Seeds" section) or pecans

In a mixer, cream together the butter, coconut oil, and dehydrated cane juice until fluffy. Add the eggs, vanilla, orange peel, maple syrup, and carrots. In a separate bowl, mix together the flour, baking soda, sea salt, cinnamon, and nutmeg. Pour the dry ingredients into the wet ingredients a little at a time while the mixer is running. Add raisins and nuts last. Distribute the batter evenly between 3 wide-mouth quart jars. Place the lidded jars in a large kettle filled halfway with water. Steam for two hours and serve hot with Lemon Sauce (see recipe in "Spreads, Sauces, Dips, and Marinades").

Apple Crisp

Makes: 1 (9x13) dish / Prep time: 25 minutes / Cook time: 50 minutes

- ❖ 1½ tsps. ground cinnamon
- ❖ 1 Tbsp. organic cornstarch
- ❖ 1⅓ cup dehydrated cane juice
- ❖ 7–8 large apples, cored, sliced, and (if desired) peeled
- ❖ ⅓–½ cup blue/amber agave
- ❖ 2 cups sprouted soft white wheat flour
- ❖ ⅛ tsp. sea salt
- ❖ ⅓ cup unsweetened shredded coconut or quinoa flakes
- ❖ ¾ cup cold butter or chilled coconut oil

In a large bowl, blend the cinnamon, cornstarch, and ⅓ cup cane juice. Toss the apple slices in the mixture until coated. Layer evenly in a buttered 9x13 glass dish and drizzle with agave.

In another bowl, blend the flour, salt, coconut or quinoa flakes, and the remaining cup of cane juice. Cut in the butter or coconut oil until the mixture is crumbly. Crumble on top of apples. Bake uncovered at 350°F for 50 minutes, or until juices are thickened. Serve warm with homemade vanilla ice cream.

Coconut Rounds

Makes: 8 servings / Prep time: 5 minutes

- ❖ 8 whole dates, pitted
- ❖ ½ cup unsweetened, dried coconut flakes

Place dates and coconut in a food processor and blend until well combined. Form into small balls and keep in an airtight container in the refrigerator.

Frosting and Toppings

Chocolate Buttercream Frosting

Makes: approx. 3 cups / Prep time: 15 minutes

- ❖ 1 cup (8 oz.) cream cheese
- ❖ ½ cup butter
- ❖ 6 Tbsps. cocoa powder
- ❖ 1 tsp. pure vanilla extract
- ❖ ½ cup pure maple syrup
- ❖ ½ cup dehydrated cane juice

Blend cream cheese and butter together until smooth. Add cocoa powder, vanilla, maple syrup, and dehydrated cane juice. Mix well.

Best Chocolate Frosting

Makes: enough to frost a 9x13-inch cake / Prep time: 20 minutes

- ❖ ½ cup butter, softened
- ❖ 2 cups dehydrated cane juice
- ❖ 2 tsps. pure vanilla extract
- ❖ ⅓ cup raw milk
- ❖ ½ cup cocoa powder

Beat butter until smooth. Add cane juice and beat again until well blended. Add vanilla and milk. Beat on high until fluffy. Add cocoa powder and blend well. Frost the cake of your choice. The cane juice will dissolve and be smooth in an hour or two. This recipe can be doubled.

Cream Cheese Frosting

Makes: approx. 1 cup / Prep time: 5 minutes

- ❖ 2 (8-oz.) pkgs. cream cheese
- ❖ 3 Tbsps. pure maple syrup
- ❖ ½ tsp. pure vanilla extract

In a mixing bowl, whip cream cheese until smooth. Add maple syrup and vanilla and blend well.

❖ ❖ ❖

Pink Party Frosting

Makes: approx. 2 cups frosting / Prep time: 10 minutes

- ❖ ½ cup raw blue/amber agave
- ❖ ½ tsp. beetroot powder
- ❖ 1 Tbsp. pure vanilla extract
- ❖ 8 oz. cream cheese, softened
- ❖ ½ cup butter, softened

In a small bowl, whisk the agave, beetroot powder, and vanilla together and set aside for 10 minutes. In a medium sized bowl, beat the cream cheese until smooth. Add the butter and cream again until smooth. Add the vanilla, agave, and beetroot powder mixture and blend well. This frosting is colored with beetroot powder, which has no detectable flavor, and it doesn't look like the fluorescent pinks that are commercially made. Instead, it's a beautiful, perfect pink color.

❖ ❖ ❖

Chocolate Syrup

Makes: 1½ cups / Prep time: 10 minutes

- ❖ 1 cup liquid sweetener
- ❖ ½ cup organic cocoa powder
- ❖ a tiny pinch of sea salt
- ❖ 2 tsps. pure vanilla extract (optional)

Combine all ingredients. Blend well and keep refrigerated in an airtight container. This makes the perfect ice cream topping, or you can use a spoonful to make quick chocolate milk.

Yogurt Topping

Makes: 4 servings / Prep time: 3 minutes

- ❖ ⅓ cup plain yogurt
- ❖ 1 tsp. liquid sweetener
- ❖ 1 tsp. ground cinnamon

Mix yogurt, honey, and cinnamon together, and either stir into apples, or serve over the top.

Whipped Cream

Makes: approx. 4 cups / Prep time: 20–25 minutes

- ❖ 2 cups cream
- ❖ a tiny pinch of sea salt
- ❖ 1 tsp. pure vanilla extract
- ❖ 4 Tbsps. pure maple syrup

Beat cream and salt until soft peaks form. Add vanilla and syrup and blend. Use immediately or cover and keep in the refrigerator for up to two days.

Chocolate Layer-Cake Frosting

Makes: enough to frost top and sides of 2 (9-inch) cake layers / Prep time: 30 minutes / Chill time: 8 hours

- ❖ 1¾ cups heavy cream
- ❖ 2 tsps. pure vanilla extract
- ❖ 3 cups organic milk chocolate pieces

Bring cream to a boil over medium heat. Remove from heat. Add the chocolate pieces and vanilla and do not stir for 5 minutes, then stir until smooth. Transfer to a large mixing bowl. Cover and chill for about 8 hours, or overnight. Beat on medium speed for about 40 seconds, or until a fluffy and spreading consistency.

Chocolate Drizzle Icing

Makes: enough for a 9x13-inch cake / Prep time: 27 minutes

- ❖ 1 cup cream
- ❖ 1½ cups organic chocolate or carob chips

Bring cream to a boil over medium heat. Remove from heat and add the chocolate pieces. Let sit without stirring for 5 minutes, and then stir until smooth. Cool for 15 minutes, then spoon and spread evenly over the top of a 9x13-inch cake.

❖ ❖ ❖

Whipped Sour Cream

Makes: approx. 2½ cups / Prep time: 10 minutes

- ❖ 2 cups sour cream or coconut cream
- ❖ a tiny pinch sea salt
- ❖ 1 tsp. pure vanilla extract
- ❖ 4–6 Tbsps. pure maple syrup

Combine all ingredients and beat well to blend.

❖ ❖ ❖

Chocolate Frosting

Makes: approx. 1½ cups / Prep time: 15 minutes

- ❖ ⅔ cup dehydrated cane juice powder
- ❖ 5 Tbsps. raw milk
- ❖ ½ cup butter
- ❖ 1 tsp. pure vanilla extract
- ❖ 1 Tbsps. coconut oil
- ❖ 2 Tbsps. cocoa powder

Combine the cane juice and milk in a small bowl. Let it sit for a few minutes so the cane juice can dissolve. Then beat in the remaining ingredients. Keep refrigerated.

❖ ❖ ❖

Carob Frosting

Makes: ½ cup / Prep time: 5 minutes

- ❖ 2 Tbsps. butter
- ❖ 2 Tbsps. coconut oil
- ❖ 4 Tbsps. honey
- ❖ 2 Tbsps. carob powder

In a bowl or blender, blend butter and coconut oil until it is mixed well. Add honey and mix well again. Add carob powder and stir until blended.

Buttercream Frosting

Makes: enough to frost a 9x13-inch cake / Prep time: 6 minutes

- ❖ 16 oz. cream cheese, softened
- ❖ ½ cup butter, softened
- ❖ ½ cup liquid sweetener
- ❖ 1 Tbsp. pure vanilla extract

Beat cream cheese until smooth. Then add butter and beat again. Add the liquid sweetener and vanilla. Blend well. Keep cake refrigerated after frosting.

Lemon Sauce

Makes: ¾ cup / Cook time: 10 minutes

- ❖ 4 Tbsps. melted butter or coconut oil
- ❖ the juice of 2 lemons
- ❖ the rind of 2 lemons, finely grated
- ❖ 2 tsps. pure vanilla extract
- ❖ ½ tsp. ground nutmeg
- ❖ ¼ tsp. sea salt
- ❖ ½ cup pure maple syrup
- ❖ ½ cup liquid sweetener

Melt the butter or coconut oil in a small saucepan and add the rest of the ingredients. Stir well and heat. Serve over Carrot Pudding (see recipe in "Other Sweets").

Coconut Cream Topping

Makes: approx. 1¾ cup / Prep time: 5 minutes / Chill time: 1 hour

- ❖ 14 oz. coconut cream
- ❖ 2 Tbsps. pure maple syrup
- ❖ 1 tsp. pure vanilla extract

Mix ingredients together and chill for about an hour, or until firm.

❖ ❖

Section 5

Last But Not Least

❖ ❖ ❖ ❖ ❖ ❖ ❖ ❖ ❖ ❖ ❖ ❖ ❖ ❖ ❖

Weight & Measurement Equivalents

- ❖ 3 teaspoons. = 1 tablespoon = ½ fluid ounce
- ❖ 6 teaspoons = 2 tablespoons = 1 fluid ounce
- ❖ 4 tablespoons = ¼ cup = 2 fluid ounces
- ❖ 5 tablespoons plus 1 teaspoon = ⅓ cup
- ❖ 8 tablespoons = ½ cup = ¼ pint = 4 fluid ounces = 1 stick of butter
- ❖ 12 tablespoons = ¾ cup = 6 fluid ounces
- ❖ 16 tablespoons = 1 cup = ½ pint = 8 fluid ounces = ½ pound
- ❖ 2 cups = 1 pint = 16 fluid ounces = 1 pound
- ❖ 4 cups = 2 pints = 32 fluid ounces = 1 quart = 2 pounds = ¼ gallon
- ❖ 6 cups = 3 pints = 48 fluid ounces = 1½ quarts = 3 pounds
- ❖ 8 cups = 4 pints = 64 fluid ounces = 2 quarts = ½ gallon = 4 pounds
- ❖ 12 cups = 6 pints = 96 fluid ounces = 3 quarts = 6 pounds
- ❖ 16 cups = 8 pints = 128 fluid ounces = 4 quarts = 1 gallon = 8 pounds
- ❖ 3 gallons = 384 fluid ounces = 12 quarts = 24 pints = 48 cups = 24 pounds
- ❖ 3 ½ gallons = 1 barrel
- ❖ 5 gallons = 640 fluid ounces = 20 quarts = 40 pints = 80 cups = 40 pounds
- ❖ 4 pecks = 1 bushel = 32 quarts

Recommended Products, Equipment, & Books

Recommended Products

Dagoba Organic Chocolate®

Premium chocolate chips, chocolate bars, and cocoa powder
1105 Benson Way, Ashland, OR 97520
800-393-6075 / www.dagobachocolate.com

Sunspire Natural Chocolates

Organic semi-sweet, grain sweetened chocolate chips
c/o WorldPantry.com, Inc.
1192 Illinois Street, San Francisco, CA 9410707
510-346-3860 / www.sunspire.com

Fage USA Dairy Industry Inc.

Creamy, plain, and whole Greek-style yogurt
1 Opportunity Drive, Johnstown Industrial Park, Johnston, NY 12095
866-962-5912 / www.fageusa.com

Straus Family Creamery

Plain whole yogurt with cream on top, pastured butter
P.O. Box 768, Marshall, CA 94940
www.StrausFamilyCreamery.com

Stonyfield Farm

Plain, whole yogurt with cream on top
10 Burton Drive, Londonderry, NH 03053
800-pro-cows / www.stoneyfield.com

Brown Cow Farm™

Plain, whole yogurt with cream on top
3810 Delta Fair Blvd., Antioch, CA 94509
888-hay-lily / www.browncowfarm.com

Tropical Traditions

Excellent high quality virgin Coconut oils, coconut cream, coconut soap, and lotions
P.O. Box 333, Springville, CA 93265
866-311-2626 / www.tropicaltraditions.com

Seeds of Change™

Organic and heirloom seeds
P.O. Box 15700, Santa Fe, NM 87592
888-762-7333 / www.seedsofchange.com

High Mowing Seeds

Organic and heirloom seeds
76 Quarry Rd., Wolcott, VT 05680
802-472-6174 / www.highmowingseeds.com

Real Foods Market

Traditional foods, certified grass-fed, pastured raw dairy products and meats
420 West 800 North, Orem, UT 84057
866-284-REAL or 801-224-0585 /www.real-foodsmarket.com

Food Directions, Inc. (Tinkyáda®)

Excellent organic brown rice pastas
120 Melford Drive, Unit 8, Scarborough, Ontario M1B 2X5 Canada
888-323-2388 / www.tinkyada.com or www.ricepasta.com

Mt. Capra

Powdered Goat-milk whey—alkalinizing and natural mineral source
279 SW 9th St., Chehalis, WA 98532
360-748-4224 / www.mtcapra.com

Mott's® LLP

Unsweetened organic applesauce without preservatives
900 King Street, Rye Brook, NY 10573 USA
800-426-4891 / cosumercare@motts.com

Santa Barbara Olive Co., Inc.

Canned olives without preservatives
12477 Calle Real, Santa Barbara, CA 93117
800-624-4896 / www.sbolive.com

Small Planet Foods® (Muir Glen)

Organic tomato sauce, paste, canned tomatoes, pizza sauce, pasta sauce, ketchup
P.O. Box 9452, Minneapolis, MN 55440
800-832-6345/ www.muirglen.com

Woodstock Farms®

Organic frozen vegetables and fruits
P.O. Box 999, Dayville, CT 06241 USA
http://www.woodstock-farms.com

Nature's Path Foods, Inc.

Organic fruit-juice, sweetened cornflakes
250 H Street, #275, Blaine, WA 98230 USA
www.naturespath.com

Food For Life Baking Co., Inc.

Organic and sprouted cereals, sprouted 7-grain bread, English muffins, and sprouted corn tortillas
P.O. Box 1434, Corona, CA 92878-1434
800-797-5090 / www.foodforlife.com

Cascade Fresh Inc.

Pastured, natural sour cream and Mediterranean yogurt
P.O. Box 33576, Seattle, WA 98133-9998
800-511-0057 / www.cascadefresh.com

Organic Valley®

Heavy whipping cream, pastured and grass-fed butter
1 Organic Way, La Farge, WI 54639
888-444-6455 / www.organicvalley.com

Petaluma Poultry®

Organic free-range chicken
2700 Lakeview Hwy., Petaluma, CA 94955
800-556-6789 / www.petalumapoultry.com

Shelton's Premium Poultry

Free-range ground turkey and turkey sausage
204 N Loranne, Pomona, CA 91767
800-541-1833 / www.sheltons.com

Baird Honey

Really yummy raw honey
Spanish Fork, Utah 84665
801-798-0915

Follow Your Heart®

Mayonnaise made with grape seed oil and without eggs (Vegenaise®)
Chatsworth, CA 91311
www.followyourheart.com

Wholesome Sweeteners

Organic unsulfered molasses, dehydrated cane juice (Sucanat), raw blue/amber agave
Sugar Land, TX 77478
www.organicsyrups.biz

Maple Syrup Producer's Cooperative (Shady Maple Farms)

Organic pure maple syrup
Plessisville, Quebec G6L2Y8 Canada
www.citadelle-camp.coop

Amy's Kitchen, Inc.

Organic bottled salsa and pasta sauces
P.O. Box 449, Petaluma, CA 94953
www.Amys.com

Sungold Foods, Inc.
Excellent organic sunflower seed butter
501 42nd St. NW Box 3022, Fargo, ND 58108
800-437-5539 / www.sunbutter.com

The Hain Celestial Group, Inc. (Imagine)
Organic free-range beef and chicken broths
Melville, NY 11747 USA
800-434-4246/ www.imaginefoods.com

Summer's Sprouted Flour Co.
Organic sprouted flours and cereal
PO Box 337 Torreon, NM 87061
505-384-0337 / www.creatingheaven.net

Organic Pastures
Grass-fed, pastured and raw dairy products
www.organicpastures.com

Radiant Life
Grass-fed raw butter, ingredients for homemade baby formula
888-593-8333 / www.radiantlifecatalog.com

Alta Dena Dairy
Dye-free cheeses made with raw milk
City of Industry, California 91744

Garden of Life, Inc.
Excellent probiotics and cod-liver oil
West Palm Beach, FL 33407
www.gardenoflife.com

Organic Brands, LLC (Rapunzel)
Organic unrefined whole cane sugar, cornstarch, cocoa powder, baking yeast
New York, NY 10011
www.rapunzel.com

J.R. Carlson Laboratories, Inc.
Norwegian cod-liver oil
Arlington Hts., IL 60004-1985
888-234-5656/ 847-255-1600

Bob's Red Mill Natural Foods
Non-aluminum baking powder, baking soda
5209 S.E. International Way, Milwaukee, OR 97222
www.bobsredmill.com

Seelect Herb Tea Co.
100% natural food colorings
1229 W. Shelly Court, Orange, CA 92868
714-771-3317 / www.seelecttea.com

Frontier Natural Products Co-Op (Simply Organic)
High quality organic spices, organic extracts
Norway, IA 52318
800-669-3275 / www.frontiercoop.com

NOW Foods
Lactose powder for homemade formula, acerola powder
Bloomingdale, IL 60108
www.nowfoods.com

Redmond Trading Company, L.C.
Real Sea Salt, organic seasoned salts, natural powdered clay for medicine (Redmond clay)
475 West 910 South, Heber City, UT 84032
800-367-7258 / www.redmondclay.com/www.realsalt.com

Young Living Essential Oils
High-quality, therapeutic-grade essential oils
Lehi, UT 84043
www.younglivingoils.com

American Botanical Pharmacy
High-quality organic whole-food supplements (Superfood Plus) and potent herbal medicines
Santa Monica, CA
800-herb-doc / www.herbdoc.com

Real Purity

Natural shampoo and cosmetics
P.O. Box 2858, Crossville, TN 38557
800-253-1694 / www.realpurity.com

Aubrey Organics, Inc.

Pure aloe vera, unscented lotion, facial products, hair products
Tampa, FL
813-877-4186 / www.aubrey-organics.com

Dr. Bronner's and Sun Dog's Magic

Organic lotions, lip balm, soap bars, liquid hand soaps
PO Box 28, Escondido, CA 92033
760-743-2211 / www.drbronnersundog.com

Terressentials

Organic liquid hand soaps, hair products, facial products, deodorants
Middletown, MD 21769
www.terressentials.com

Burt's Bees, Inc.

Natural beeswax lip balm and diaper ointment
P.O. Box 13489, Durham, NC 27709
www.burtsbees.com

EcoNatural Solutions, Inc.

St. Claire's Organic premium mints
Boulder, CO
www.econaturalsolutions.com

Seventh Generation, Inc.

Liquid dish soap, dishwasher soap, laundry soap and much more
60 Lake Street, Burlington, VT 05401-5218
800-456-1191 / www.seventhgeneration.com

Recommended Equipment

Excalibur Products

Excellent Food Dehydrator
6083 Power Inn Road, Sacramento, CA 95824
916-381-4254 / www.excaliburdehydrator.com

William-Sonoma

Food processors and ice-cream makers
Box 7456, San Francisco, CA 94120-7456
800-541-2233 / www.williamsonoma.com

Blend Tec

Excellent blender. It will blend anything
www.blendtec.com

L'Equip NutriMill

Grain Mill

Bamix

Electric Hand blender
www.bamix-usa.com

Hamilton Beach

A good heavy duty food processor. Get one between 400 and 500 watts.
www.hamiltonbeach.com

Zerorez

Excellent carpet cleaning without any scents or chemicals
4123 South 420 West, Murray, UT 84123
866-ZEROREZ / www.myzerorez.com

Recommended Books

All of these books are directed at improving the health, nourishment, and well-being of the body, mind, and spirit—all of which affect your overall health.

Nutrition and Physical Degeneration
By: Weston A. Price, D.D.S.
An eye-opening, historical, and detailed book on how diet affects our minds and bodies that includes over 150 pictures and documentations of what the author found traveling the world.

Know Your Fats: The Complete Primer for Understanding the Nutrition of Fats, Oils, and Cholesterol
By: Mary G. Enig, PhD

The Maker's Diet
By: Jordan S. Rubin, NMD, PhD

Nourishing Traditions: The Cookbook that Challenges Politically Correct Nutrition and the Diet Dictocrats
By: Sally Fallon, with Mary G. Enig, PhD
A recipe book with valuable information on traditional foods and preparation methods.

Eat Fat, Lose Fat: The Healthy Alternative to Trans Fats
By: Dr. Mary Enig and Sally Fallon
A must read for those who want to understand what fats to eat or want to find coconut oil recipes.

Real Food: What to Eat and Why
By: Nina Plank
A great easy-to-read book without too much detail that provides information on a variety of real foods.

Healthy Nutrition: Your Easy to Follow Guide for a Healthy Diet
By: Sharon B. Combs

The Untold Story of Milk: Green Pastures, Contented Cows and Raw Dairy Foods
By: Ron Schmid, ND

The Word of Wisdom: A Modern Interpretation
By: John A. Widtsoe and Leah D. Widtsoe

Essential Eating: A Cookbook
By: Janie Quinn

Essential Eating: The Digestible Diet
By: Janie Quinn

Traditional Foods Are Your Best Medicine: Improving Health and Longevity with Native Nutrition
By: Ronald F. Schmid, ND

The Fourfold Path to Healing: Working with the Laws of Nutrition, Therapeutics, Movement and Meditation in the Art of Medicine
By: Thomas S. Cowan, MD, with Sally Fallon and Jaimen McMillan

Virgin Coconut Oil: How It Has Changed People's Lives, and How It Can Change Yours!
By: Brian and Marianita Jader Shilhavy
Answers all of the questions you might have about coconut oil and has recipes too.

Whole Foods Companion: A Guide for Adventurous Cooks, Curious Shoppers, & Lovers of Natural Foods
By: Dianne Onstad
This book has a description and nutritional table on each grain, vegetable, and so forth.

Taking Charge of your Fertility: The Definitive Guide to Natural Birth Control, Pregnancy Achievement, and Reproductive Health
By: Toni Weschler, MPH

The Truth About Children's Health: The Comprehensive Guide to Understanding, Preventing, and Reversing Disease
By: Robert Bernardini, M.S.

How To Raise A Healthy Child in Spite Of Your Doctor
By: Robert S. Mendelsohn, MD

You Can Heal Your Life
By: Louise L. Hay
An important resource for acquiring positive thoughts and good, old authentic self love.

Remembering Wholeness
By: Carol Tuttle, RET
An awesome book on transforming yourself and your thoughts.

Feelings Buried Alive Never Die
By: Karol K. Truman

When the Body Says No:
Understanding the Stress-Disease
Connection
By: Gabor Maté, MD

The Cholesterol Myths
By: Uffe Ravnskov, MD, PhD

A Life Unburdened: Getting Over
Weight and Getting On with My Life
By: Richard Morris

The Milk Book
By: William Campbell Douglass, MD

Milk, Money, and Madness
By: Naomi Baumslag, MD, MPH, and Dia L.
Michels

The No-Grain Diet
By: Dr. Joseph Mercola
Discusses the importance of eliminating white
flour and white sugar.

Nutrition in Biblical Times
By: Ruth F. Rosevear

Recipes for Life
By: Becky Mauldin

The Schwarzbein Principle
By: Diana Schwarzbein, MD and Nancy Deville

The Wheel of Health
By: G. T. Wrench

Pottenger's Cats: A Study In
Nutrition
By: Francis M. Pottenger, Jr., MD

Notes

1. Sally Fallon with Mary G. Enig, PhD, *Nourishing Traditions: The Cookbook that Challenges Politically Correct Nutrition and the Diet Dictocrats*, revised 2nd ed. (Washington, DC: New Trends Publishing, Inc., 2001), 453.

2. Francis M. Pottenger, Jr., MD, *Pottenger's Cats: A Study in Nutrition*, 2nd ed. (La Mesa: Price-Pottenger Nutrition Foundation, Inc., 2005), 1–2.

3. Ibid., 6, 9–13, 15, 22, 25, 39, 41; Wikipidia.org, "Francis M. Pottenger, Jr." http://en.wikipedia.org/wiki/Francis. Accessed January 23, 2010.

4. John A. Widtsoe and Leah D. Widtsoe, *The Word of Wisdom: A Modern Interpretation* (Salt Lake City: Deseret News Press, 1950), 194–195, referencing, J. I. Rodale, *The Healthy Hunzas* (Emmaus: Rodale Press, 1949), 158.

5. Fallon and Enig, *Nourishing Traditions: The Cookbook that Challenges Politically Correct Nutrition and the Diet Dictocrats*, 534.

6. Martha M. Grout, MD, MD(H), "Aspartame–History of Getting FDA Approval," http://www.arizonaadvancedmedicine.com/articles/aspartame.html. Arizona Center For Advanced Medicine. Accessed February 6, 2009.

7. Dorway.com, "Department of Health and Human Services: Symptoms attributed to Aspartame in complaints submitted to the FDA," April 20, 1995. http://www.dorway.com/92_symptoms.gif. Accessed February 6, 2009.

8. Fallon and Enig, *Nourishing Traditions: The Cookbook that Challenges Politically Correct Nutrition and the Diet Dictocrats*, 48–49.

9. Widtsoe and Widtsoe, *The Word of Wisdom A Modern Interpretation*, 129.

10. Fallon and Enig, *Nourishing Traditions: The Cookbook that Challenges Politically Correct Nutrition and the Diet Dictocrats*, 13–15.

11. John R., Christopher, MH, *Just What is the Word of Wisdom?*, revised edition, (Springville: Christopher Publications, 1941, revised 2005), 10–12.

12. Jim Meyers, Newsmax.com, "Soft Drinks Reportedly Linked to Health Problems," December 8, 2005. http://archive.newsmax.com/archives/articles /2005/12/8/142651.shtml. Accessed March 27, 2009; *Renal Business Today*, "Sugary Soft Drinks Linked to Kidney Disease," December 3, 2008, http://www. renalbusiness.com/hotnews/sugary-soft-drinks-linked-to-kidney-disease.html. Accessed March 27, 2009; Donna Miller, *Citizen News*, "Slow poisoning by diet

soft drinks," March 25, 2004, http://www.thecitizen.biz/cms/index.php?id=574. Accessed March 27, 2009.

13. Jeff Donn, Martha Mendoza, Justin Pritchard, Associated Press, "AP: Drugs found in drinking water," March 10, 2008, http://www.usatoday.com/news/nation/2008-03-10-drugs-tap-water_N.htm. Accessed January 7, 2009.

14. Widtsoe and Widtsoe, *The Word of Wisdom A Modern Interpretation*, 116; Weston A., Price, DDS, *Nutrition and Physical Degeneration*, 6th edition (La Mesa: The Price-Pottenger Nutritional Foundation, Inc., 1945, revised 2004).

15. Len McGrane, "Is Mineral Water Healthy? Just Try Living Without It!," June 10, 2008, *EzineArticles.com*, http://ezinearticles.com/?Is-Mineral-Water-Healthy?-Just-Try-Living-Without-It!&id=1239812. Accessed March 27, 2009.

16. G. T. Wrench, *The Wheel of Health: The Source of Long Life and Health Among the Hunza* (Mineola: Dover Publications, Inc., 2006), 117.

17. Ibid.

18. Christopher Doering, "Bill would ban non medical drug use in U.S. livestock," March 17, 2009, http://www.reuters.com/article/healthNews/idUSTRE52G5UL20090317?feedType=RSS&feedName-healthNews. Accessed March 27, 2009.

19. Price, *Nutrition and Physical Degeneration*, 384–385.

20. The Doctrine and Covenants (Salt Lake City: The Church of Jesus Christ of Latter Day Saints, 1989), Section 89:17.

21. Sally Fallon with Mary G. Enig, Ph. D., *Nourishing Traditions: The Cookbook that Challenges Politically Correct Nutrition and the Diet Dictocrats*, revised second edition (Washington, DC: New Trends Publishing, Inc., 2001), 436.

22. Ibid.,12.

23. Ibid., 12–13.

24. Wrench, *The Wheel of Health, The Source of Long Life and Health Among the Hunza*, 90; Price, *Nutrition and Physical Degeneration*, 259–262; Fallon and Enig, *Nourishing Traditions: The Cookbook that Challenges Politically Correct Nutrition and the Diet Dictocrats*, 436.

25. Fallon and Enig, *Nourishing Traditions: The Cookbook that Challenges Politically Correct Nutrition and the Diet Dictocrats*, 28.

26. Rose Lee Calabro, *Living in the Raw: Recipes for a Healthy Lifestyle* (Santa Cruz: Rose Publishing, 1998), 1.

27. Marie A. Boyle, and Eleanor Noss Whitney, *Personal Nutrition* (St. Paul: West Publishing Company, 1989), 63–64.

28. Fallon and Enig, *Nourishing Traditions: The Cookbook that Challenges Politically Correct Nutrition and the Diet Dictocrats*, 366–367.

29. Old and New Testaments, Authorized King James Version (Salt Lake City: The Church of Jesus Christ of Latter-day Saints, 1989), Mathew 15:36;

Genesis 19:3; Genesis 18:8; Deuteronomy 26:9; Numbers 11:5; Genesis 9:3; Luke 14:34; 2 Kings 4:2.

30. Wrench, *The Wheel of Health: The Source of Long Life and Health Among the Hunza*, 10–11, 27.

31. Ibid., 90.

32. Price, *Nutrition and Physical Degeneration*, 259–262.

33. Ibid.

34. Ibid., 302–306, 309.

35. Wrench, *The Wheel of Health: The Source of Long Life and Health Among the Hunza*, 17.

36. Fallon and Enig, *Nourishing Traditions: The Cookbook that Challenges Politically Correct Nutrition and the Diet Dictocrats*, 452.

37. Wrench, *The Wheel of Health: The Source of Long Life and Health Among the Hunza*, 99.

38. Fallon and Enig, *Nourishing Traditions: The Cookbook that Challenges Politically Correct Nutrition and the Diet Dictocrats*, 116.

39. Ibid., 149, citing Valerie MacBean, *Coconut Cookery*, 244; Wrench, *The Wheel of Health: The Source of Long Life and Health Among the Hunza*, 90, 96; Price, *Nutrition and Physical Degeneration*, 259–264.

40. Wrench, *The Wheel of Health: The Source of Long Life and Health Among the Hunza*, 99, 117.

41. Ibid., 90.

42. Ibid., 96.

43. Ibid., 27.

44. Doctrine and Covenants 89:14,16–17.

45. Ibid., 89:10–11.

46. Ibid., 89:12–13, 15.

47. Ibid., 89:5, 7–9.

48. Fallon and Enig, *Nourishing Traditions: The Cookbook that Challenges Politically Correct Nutrition and the Diet Dictocrats*, 112, 115, citing Dr. Edward Howell, MD, *Food Enzymes for Health and Longevity*.

49. Ibid., 453.

50. Ibid., 452.

51. Ibid., 452.

52. Ibid., 112.

53. Natural Therapy Pages, " Benefits of Sprouted Grains," http://www.naturaltherapypages.com.au/article/Benefits_Sprouted_Grains. Accessed September 14, 2009.

54. Essentialeating.com, "Essential Eating Sprouted Foods," 2008, http://www.essentialeating.com/ResourcesSprouted.asp. Accessed January 14, 2009.

55. Carrie L'Esperance, "Acid and Alkaline Balance," http://www.innerself.com/Health/lesperance03273.htm. Accessed January 14, 2009.

56. Wrench, *The Wheel of Health: The Source of Long Life and Health Among the Hunza*, 99.

57. Fallon and Enig, *Nourishing Traditions: The Cookbook that Challenges Politically Correct Nutrition and the Diet Dictocrats*, 512.

58. The Cornucopia Institute, "The Authentic Almond Project," http://www.cornucopia.org/almonds/. Accessed January 9, 2009.

59. CDC, "Smoking: Attributable Mortality, Years of Potential Life Lost, and Productivity Losses—United States, 2000–2004," http://www.cdc.gov/mmwr/preview/mmwrhtml/mm5745a3.htm. Accessed January 21, 2010; Press Release, "Morbidity and Mortality Related to Tobacco Use," http://www.cdc.gov/tobacco/data_statistics/fact_sheets/fast_facts/. Accessed September 14, 2009.

60. Rosemary Fifield, "Almonds Get a Raw Deal," February 6, 2008, http://www.coopfoodstore.com/content/almonds-get-raw-deal. Accessed January 9, 2009.

61. Fallon and Enig, *Nourishing Traditions: The Cookbook that Challenges Politically Correct Nutrition and the Diet Dictocrats*, 80.

62. Ibid., 80–81.

63. Price, *Nutrition and Physical Degeneration*, 427–428.

64. Ibid., 427.

65. Wrench, *The Wheel of Health: The Source of Long Life and Health Among the Hunza*, 96.

66. Ibid., 90.

67. New York Times Archives, "Bad Milk," April 30, 1874, http://query.nytimes.com/gst/abstract.html?res=990DE6DC1139EF34BC4850DFB26683 8F66FDE&scp=1&sq=bad+milk+April+30%2C+1874&st=p. Accessed January 23, 2010.

68. Raw-Milk-Facts.com, "A Brief History of Raw Milk's Long Journey . . ." http://www.raw-milk-facts.com/milk_history.html. Accessed January 23, 2010.

69. Fallon and Enig, *Nourishing Traditions: The Cookbook that Challenges Politically Correct Nutrition and the Diet Dictocrats*, 15, referencing Zikasis, et al, *Journal of Dairy Science*, 1977, 60:533; K. Oster, *American Journal of Clinical Research*, Apr 1971, Vol II(I).

70. Mary Shannon, "Do Soy Foods Negatively Affect Your Thyroid? A Look at the Downsides of Soy," updated January 9, 2009, http://www.thyroid-info.com/articles/soydangers.htm. Accessed January 9, 2009; Fallon and Enig, *Nourishing Traditions: The Cookbook that Challenges Politically Correct Nutrition and the Diet Dictocrats*, 477.

71. Nikki Moustaki, *Parakeets* (Neptune City: T.F.H. Publications, 2006), 78.

72. Breathing.com, "Never Use a Microwave," 1997–2008, http://www.breathing.com/articles/microwaves.htm. Accessed January 14, 2009.

73. Ibid.

74. George J. Georgiou, PhD. "The Hidden Hazards of Microwave Cooking," April 2006, http://www.aaimedicine.com/jaaim/apr06/hazards.php. Accessed January 14, 2009.

75. Ibid.

76. Ibid.

77. Ibid.

78. Breathing.com, "Never Use a Microwave." Accessed January 14, 2009.

79. Fallon and Enig, *Nourishing Traditions: The Cookbook that Challenges Politically Correct Nutrition and the Diet Dictocrats*, 476.

80. Thefreelibrary.com: "Curb Cravings with Quinoa," December 18, 2007, http://www.thefreelibrary.com/Curb+Cravings+with+Quinoa-a01073846255. Accessed January 14, 2009.

81. International Specialty Supply, "Sprouts for Optimum Nutrition," http://www.sproutnet.com/Press/sprouts_for_optimum_nutrition.htm. Accessed January 23, 2010; David Niven Miller, "Sprouting," *Grow Youthful: A Practical Guide to Slowing Your Aging.* http://www.growyouthful.com/tips/recipes/sprouts.php. 2003. Accessed March 28, 2009.

82. Miller, "Sprouting," Accessed March 28, 2009.

83. Jordan S. Rubin, NMD, PhD, *The Maker's Diet* (Lake Mary: Siloam A Strang Company, 2004), 148–149.

84. Fallon and Enig, *Nourishing Traditions: The Cookbook that Challenges Politically Correct Nutrition and the Diet Dictocrats*, 116.

85. Anne B. Bond, "Care2 Directory of Natural Sweeteners," September 8, 1999, http://www.care2.com/greenliving/directory-of-natural-sweeteners.html. Accessed January 13, 2009.

86. Reallyrawhoney.com, "Health Benefits of Eating Really Raw Honey," http://www.reallyrawhoney.com/healthfacts.php. Accessed January 13, 2009.

87. Debra Lynn Dadd, "Agave Nectar," 2005, http://www.sweetsavvy.com/sweeteners/summary.php?id=Agave%20Nectar. Accessed January 13, 2009; Global Healing Center, "Is Agave Nectar Safe?", November 9, 2009, http://www.globalhealingcenter.com/natural-health/is-agave-nectar-safe. Accessed January 23, 2010.

Recipe Index

❖ ❖ ❖ ❖ ❖ ❖ ❖ ❖ ❖ ❖ ❖ ❖ ❖ ❖ ❖ ❖

About the Authors

Jɪʟʟᴀʏɴᴇ Cʟᴇᴍᴇɴᴛs enjoys teaching classes on whole food cooking in the community as well as at the Young Family Living Farm. She has appeared on the cooking segments of *Good Things Utah* and *Studio 5* with her dessert creations, has catered for conventions, and regularly makes and sells her desserts.

Jillayne also loves writing, whether it's fiction or non-fiction, and performing manuscript makeovers. She enjoys vegetable gardening, reading to and spending time with her children, and dating her husband. You can visit her website at www.jillayneclements. com or view her blogs at, www.jillayneclements.blogspot.com and www.cedarfortauthors.blogspot.com.

MICHELLE STEWART was born and raised in Utah. She has enjoyed cooking since she was a little girl. Michelle turned her health around years ago by making food her medicine. She decided that modifying other cookbook recipes to be healthy was less than fun and began compiling her own recipes. She has a gift for making nutritious, delicious foods that still taste like familiar American foods. Michelle has a passion for true health. She has had a decade of education in the fields of holistic health, nutrition, food, modern and traditional diets, and energy medicine. She has also drawn from her experiences and from history to find the source of health. She is an experienced real-food educator, talented whole-food chef, and author. You can visit her website at www.getrealwithfood.com or view her blog at www.gettingrealwithfood.blogspot.com

❖ ❖ ❖ ❖ ❖ ❖ ❖ ❖ ❖ ❖ ❖ ❖ ❖ ❖ ❖ ❖

❖ ❖

Contact Us

We love to hear from our readers and get feedback on our recipes. Please contact us with any questions or comments. Log on to www. getrealwithfood.com for tips on how to sprout, additional recipes, visual how-to videos for making some of our recipes, and much more information. You can also email Jillayne at writeme@jillayneclements. com or Michelle at treasuredcooking@gmail.com.

❖ ❖